D0235343

Weather Watch

Weather Watch

DICK FILE

FOURTH ESTATE · *London*

First published in Great Britain by
Fourth Estate Limited
289 Westbourne Grove
London W11 2QA

Copyright © 1990 by Guardian News Service Ltd
and R. F. File

The right of Dick File to be identified as author of this
work has been asserted by him in accordance with
Copyright, Designs and Patents Act 1988.

British Library Cataloguing in Publication Data
File, Dick
Weather watch.
1. Weather
1. Title
551.5

ISBN 1-872180-12-4

All rights reserved. No part of this publication may be
reproduced, transmitted or stored in a retrieval system, in
any form or by any means, without permission in writing
from Fourth Estate Limited.

Typeset in Ehrhardt by Yorkhouse Typographic,
Hanwell, London W7.
Printed and bound by Biddles Ltd, Guildford, Surrey.

CONTENTS

History versus the future 5; The birth of the atmosphere 5; Gaia theory 5; Early ice ages 6; Continental drift 6; Extinction of the dinosaurs 7; Future work on fossils 7; Human evolution 8; Ice cores 8; Polar ice caps 9; Evidence from oceans and lakes 10; Beetles, pollen and tree remains 10; Carbon dating 11; Tree rings 12; Cave paintings and early migration 12; Sea levels and lake levels 13; Raised beaches and isostatic adjustment 14; Burial mounds and stone circles 15; Weather in the ice age 16; Weather at the peak of warmth 16; Early civilisations 17; Ancient Egypt 18; The Ancient Greeks 19; The Romans 20; Weather in the Bible 20; The Vikings and early medieval times 21; The Little Ice Age 21; Diarists, chroniclers and artists 22; Frost fairs 23; Alpine glaciers 24; The year without a summer 24; Dustbowl America 24; Another minor peak 25; Ice age threat 25; Record decade 26

Constituents of the air 27; Vertical structure 28; The boundary layer 29; Troposphere and tropopause 31; The stratosphere 32; The energy cycle 33; Pressure patterns 35; The rotating Earth 36; Geostrophic wind and surface wind 37; Weather on the other planets 38; Vertical motion 39; Unstable conditions and lapse rates 40; Inversions 41; Is the airmass stable? 42; Day and night variations 43; Inside a cloud 44; An introduction to airmasses 45; Tropical Maritime 47; Tropical Continental 49; Polar Continental 50; Polar Maritime 51; Arctic Maritime 52; Returning Polar Maritime 52; Warm fronts 53; Cold fronts 54; The warm conveyor belt 56; Cold front waves and warm front waves 56; Occluded fronts 58; Polar lows and comma clouds 59; Life cycle of a depression 60; Families of depressions 62; Anticyclones 63; The polar front jet stream 64; Rossby waves 65; Blocking patterns 66; Warm and cold advection 67; Convergence and divergence 68; Vorticity 70; Oceanography 71

sation trails and changes in cloudiness 247; El Niño events 248; Cloud seeding 249; Major schemes 251; Inland seas and lakes 251; The water cycle and the rain-forests 252; Rain-forest destruction 253; CFCs and the ozone hole 253; City pollution 255; Acid rain 256; Principle of the greenhouse effect 259; Carbon dioxide sources 260; Where in the world. . .? 261; Carbon dioxide 'sinks' 262; Greenhouse feedback mechanisms 263; Biosphere 2 263; Other greenhouse gases 264; The observed warming 265; Land and sea temperatures 266; Is the warming caused by human activity? 267; Global climate models 268; The future 269; An optimistic view 269; A pessimistic view 269; Some middle-of-the-road forecasts 271; Changes in the polar regions 272; Changes in the temperate latitudes 272; Changes in the tropics 273; The predicted rise in sea level 273; Other sources of power 274; Wind, wave and tidal power 274; Solar power 275; Insulation 276; Incentives for reducing emissions 276

ACKNOWLEDGEMENTS

I should like to thank all those who have contributed towards the production of this book including Ken Ingamells for his work with the photographs and James Peet for the diagrams, but notably my wife, Heather, for her typing, help and advice. I am also grateful to those who nurtured my enthusiasm for weather, starting with my parents, then later Tim Thornton (at Cranbrook School in Kent) and more recently Peter Wickham (as Chief Instructor of the Met Office College). One of the pleasant aspects of working in meteorology is the sense of a shared interest, so I must also express my gratitude to my colleagues and friends, both within the Met Office and outside.

FOREWORD

NOW THAT we've all turned an interesting shade of green, there comes a pressing need for a bit of solid background to our understanding of the atmosphere – this fragile apple-skin thick layer of air in which we live, and to which we do nasty things.

Solid background, I said, not indigestible, and heaven forfend, please not another textbook on atmospheric physics. My colleague and friend Dick File has come to the rescue with this splendid, authoritative reader.

British children are fortunate that the national curriculum will expose them to meteorology from 5 to 16 years old. Children will delight in a delve or three into this volume, but we grown-ups need it most. Bombarded on all sides by half-digested reports in the Press, sound bites of science on the radio and the contrived controversy of the environmental heavies on TV, how *can* we have any opinions of even tap-room quality? Read this book. Not all at once, keep it by the bed.

In my time, I confess, I have read many meteorological papers which have induced sleep faster than a glass of port, but not here. The author has produced a fascinating series of bite-sized chunks which can, in many cases, be read on their own, and in any order. The chunks themselves cover simply everything in weather and the climate from the birth of the atmosphere through to the greenhouse effect. Quite apart from the 'good read' aspect, there is a wealth of useful statistics and helpful diagrams, but with a wrist-slapping lack of jargon. The book is so up-to-date that it even includes the new temperature record set at Cheltenham recently.

Now for a spot of naked prejudice. Most books about the weather are written either by general science writers (often American) or by remote academics, and very few by sharp-end, hands-on weather forecasters – mainly because we have this demanding evening job locked in hand-to-hand combat with the elements, and haven't the time. Dick File is one of this breed, and British, and it shows.

This book will neither waste your time nor insult your intelligence. Most important of all, a working weather man can communicate a little of the sheer excitement of the best job in the world. The author shares this lifetime love with us in a most engaging and readable way, and reminds me of why I joined.

Ian McCaskill
30 August 1990

INTRODUCTION

IT IS said of the British that, when two people meet, their opening exchange is about the weather. This can be interpreted as the result of our changeable climate. After all, it would be meaningless for two Egyptians meeting in July to say 'Another sunny day then', while in Britain it is at least reasonable to express some surprise. (Such opening remarks may also reflect a certain reserve or even politeness since they allow either party to depart after a sentence or two if they are in a hurry.)

However, the climate in Norway or Vancouver is just as changeable, and Britain is not the most difficult place on Earth for which to forecast. Southern Chile, the Falklands, Tasmania and New Zealand are all tricky, as are the tropical rain-forests. Islands tend to be difficult as there are few upwind observations, and there is less information available in the southern hemisphere than in the northern.

This book is mainly about weather, but it also deals with climate. Weather is the state of the atmosphere at any one time, or over a short period of time (a day or a week), whereas climate is a summary of weather over perhaps 30 years. Climate is sometimes defined as 'the average of the weather' but a straightforward average hides important facts. A hurricane may be the most memorable weather event during a year, but it can be lost in that year's average statistics of wind speed.

One hurricane per decade may not seem too significant for a Caribbean island, but it will be enough to influence building design and the location of harbours, and may even deter potential tourists.

The book starts with a run through the history of climate, including the extinction of the dinosaurs, the ice ages and the climate extant during the building of Stonehenge; thus we progress via the 'Little Ice Age' to the present day. Some science creeps in here as we consider haloes, hurricanes and heat-waves. Professional meteorology is a science rather than an art; on the other hand, forecasting a few hours ahead for one's own benefit relies on skill and experience, and thus smacks of art. I have tried to analyse and explain the efforts of amateur and professional forecasting.

Weather forecasting is a broad subject ranging from computer predictions to old-fashioned sayings. Weather lore can vary from the useful and interesting to the amusing and ridiculous. The reason for its continuing fascination is that weather has such an overwhelming influence on our landscapes and our lives. Britain and the Sahara are different because of their differing climates (and to a lesser extent because of their geological make-up, but climate has ultimately determined the soil structure too). Humans have, throughout evolution, always been influenced by the weather. We have even, quite literally, been shaped by the climate. People who are short and well-covered in fat are better able to withstand the cold than tall, thin people. Hairy people are also better insulated than those with hairless skins, but the process of evolutionary selection has been complicated by the wearing of clothes. Perhaps the best-known example of adaption is the protection from sunburn afforded by the presence of melanin in people with dark skin. Since we appear to have originated in Africa, this example should perhaps be turned around so that it is expressed as the development of pale skins by those living well away from the Equator. Blonde hair and fair skins are certainly far more common north of latitude 50°N in Europe, and such colouring renders us more prone to skin cancer if we emigrate to countries in lower latitudes, such as Australia. Despite having evolved in the tropics, there are few places on Earth where humans cannot survive without outside help. The Polar ice caps, high mountains and deserts are the problem areas.

The most hostile frozen wastes are the Arctic (where beyond latitude 80°N there is little land and even Eskimos find it hard) and the Antarctic (where scientific communities rely on outside help). Reykjavik, the capital of Iceland, is at latitude 64°N. Coal-mining takes humans even further poleward to 78°N in Svalbard (Spitsbergen).

Mountains higher than 18,000 ft (5500 m) are almost impossible to endure for long periods. At this altitude the pressure is about 500 mbar (millibars), roughly half that at sea level. So unless one can breathe more deeply each breath only delivers half as much oxygen. In the Andes of South America, indigenous Indians have somewhat barrel-shaped chests as an adaptation to the high altitudes.

If a desert has no vegetation whatsoever then it is virtually impossible for it to support life, for the animals at the bottom of the food chain must have something to eat. It is conceivable that given an underground water supply, humans could exist on a diet of migrating birds and animals; in practice, however, even the Tuareg of the Sahara inhabit areas with sporadic rainfall and engage in trade to obtain some of their essentials.

It is noticeable that within the British Isles land values are higher in the climatically favoured areas where agriculture is more productive and life more comfortable.

The main attraction of retiring to Spain, Cyprus or even Australia seems to be the prospect of a sunny climate; and warmth and sunshine are certainly part of the allure of most holidays. (Some guidance on holiday weather is given in Chapter 9.)

Regional variations in culture stem both from history and from climate. For example, Scots who emigrate to Australia will almost certainly fall in with the idea of outdoor barbecues, a custom rather rarer in Scotland. And it is not just leisure; our houses, our food and most of our jobs are all influenced to a greater or lesser degree by climate, sometimes through a series of small but cumulative decisions.

And so we return to an earlier theme of the relationship between climate and weather. When we generalise we talk about climate; when we plan a specific event, be it a barbecue or football game, then it is the weather on the day that counts. We watch the forecast on television or listen to the radio; we study the newspaper weather map. We look through the list of city reports to see how the weather is going in Rome or Sydney.

British weather is perhaps the main subject of this book, but world features such as tropical rain, droughts, cyclones and monsoons are not neglected. At home the effect of weather on commerce and lifestyles is given a fresh look. Imagine going home on a warm and sunny April afternoon; because the weather is pleasant we may walk half a mile rather than catching a bus, then we spend time in the garden rather than watching television, perhaps we drink fruit juice, beer or wine rather than a cup of tea. There are obvious implications for public transport and sales of beer, but also hidden commercial impacts. The television ratings drop and the consumption of electricity for heating, lighting and television is depressed.

The modern world has reduced the importance of the weather from the almost life-or-death power it once held to a subtle background factor, but it is still there, every day of our lives. Even those working underground cannot totally avoid its effects.

Chapter 1 describes some of the history of our climate and sets the scene for the final chapter, which deals with the future. Is the climate changing? That is one of the key questions facing scientists. The quick answer is 'yes' and some of the more general predictions for the future are gradually becoming crystallised. The mechanisms and some forecasts are given in Chapter 11.

Meteorology is an earth science, but one with few absolutes. One can rarely say 'never' in the weather business. The temperature usually decreases upwards (but not when an inversion is present); a June day is usually warmer than an October day (but not if you are on the east coast of Britain with a northeast wind); a pall of smoke in the atmosphere is usually industrial pollution (unless a stroke of lightning has set off a bush fire). Exceptions and uncertainties are usually indicated in the text.

Most of the temperatures, speeds and so on are expressed in round terms and are not meant to be taken as precise values, nor are the conversions from miles to kilometres, etc., intended to be exact. Meteorological units are a nightmare mixture of different systems and I have tended to follow those in common use, though generally avoiding the knot (the nautical mile per hour). Conversion tables are included in the Appendices, along with climate data. A glossary is included to help with technical terms.

Whilst I may have drawn upon many academic works, to whose authors I owe a debt, the opinions given here are my own.

Chapter 1

EVIDENCE OF PAST CLIMATES

HISTORY VERSUS THE FUTURE

THIS CHAPTER takes a gallop through history, looking at past climates and some of the methods used to find out about them. History not only helps us to understand the present and to view it in its true context, but it is also a key which allows us a glimpse into the future. If we want to know what a warmer world would be like then one way to find out is to study the warm climate of 3000 BC.

By and large, it is a chronological account without much in the way of explanation. The reasons for changes, unfortunately far from complete, are given in the final chapter of the book. As we think about past climates, the spectre of future changes keeps rearing its head.

THE BIRTH OF THE ATMOSPHERE

Our knowledge of the history of the atmosphere is patchy. The Universe is around 15 billion (15,000,000,000) years old and our solar system about 4.5 billion years in age. From this time onwards it appears that the Earth and the major planets have all been located in virtually their present orbits around the Sun. When the Earth initially compacted into its spherical shape (technically an oblate spheroid, since it is very slightly flattened near the Poles), the atmospheric constituents would have been very different, including much hydrogen and helium. Through early geological time the atmosphere changed as huge volcanic eruptions pushed out a new mixture of gases and as water vapour condensed into water.

GAIA THEORY

Just as volcanoes change the atmosphere, so plants and animal life can alter the mixture of gases under which they originally evolved. Therefore the constituents which we have today are neither those with which the Earth started, nor those under which life was born. The 'Gaia' theory

theory looks on the complete planet as a living organism of which the soil, plants, animals, oceans and atmosphere are all parts. These parts, according to the theory, are all interrelated and changes to one part will set off a complex series of reactions which will cause changes to the other parts. The Earth has remained hospitable to life for over 3 billion years which is unlikely to have happened by chance according to the innovative scientific thinker Jim Lovelock who proposed the theory. Therefore the plant and animal life must collectively react to maintain suitable conditions for life in general (which may or may not include humans). Even without totally accepting the Gaia theory, its underlying 'whole planet philosophy' should lead us to take better care of our atmosphere and our planet. After all, if we think of ourselves as part of a huge body, then we cannot afford to let one part grow sick. An intelligent person tries to look after his liver and heart. Even without the Gaia theory, it is self-evident that we only have one atmosphere.

EARLY ICE AGES

Our knowledge of our evolution is at present based on little more than scraps of evidence. It used to be thought that there had only been four or five ice ages, and all within the last one or two million years. Now it is now clear that ice ages occurred much earlier in the Carboniferous period (between 345 and 280 million years ago) and the Permian period (between 280 and 250 million million years ago), and that there were many of them, interspersed with warmer interglacials. The heyday of the dinosaurs and of the flying reptiles was about 150 million years ago, and warmer climates seem to have been the norm then, although no doubt there were fluctuations. Evidence from fossils of a tiny sea creature, *Globigerina pachyderma* shows that the waters were colder in some periods than in others. This species has the bizarre trait of coiling itself to the left when growing in cold water and to the right in warmer water. Fossilised corals are another source of information because they can show an annual growth ring somewhat akin to that of trees.

CONTINENTAL DRIFT

We can find evidence of past climates by looking at the geology of an area; for instance, red loam soils are indicative of a savannah-type climate with a limited wet season. Unfortunately, because of continental drift we cannot make direct deductions from such sources. Even if we know when it was hot, we still need to know where. Coal can be found in the Antarctic but this does not necessarily mean that the climate there was warm enough for abundant plant life 200 million years ago, since the continent actually drifted into its present position.

On a shorter time-scale such movements of the great 'plates' of the Earth's crust are too slow to be significant. Continental drift and other earth movements have been less relevant from the point of view of charting climatic history over the last couple of million years, except where they have an important local effect such as opening up a narrow sea strait and allowing the flow of water. The Mediterranean has at various times in its history been dry – a salt-encrusted basin with a searingly hot climate. The water of the Nile evaporated somewhere in the east of this great depression. Earth movements, as well as rising sea levels, finally allowed the sea water back in through the Straits of Gibraltar.

EXTINCTION OF THE DINOSAURS

The great majority of dinosaurs seem to have died out, probably quite suddenly, at the end of the Cretaceous era about 65 million years ago. Speculation about their demise includes the strong possibility that the climate abruptly altered, becoming much colder. If rapid enough, this change could have stopped the growth of plant-life and deprived the herbivorous species of dinosaur of their basic food supply. Carnivores would also have starved as their prey dwindled. But what could have caused the climate change? It is easier to provide theories of more gradual warming or cooling (as covered in Chapter 11) than of abrupt shifts, but there are two obvious mechanisms that would bring about abrupt cooling. The first possibility is that a huge meteorite hurtling in from space could explode on the Earth's surface throwing dust and meteoritic particles into the atmosphere in sufficient quantities for the Sun's heat to be much diminished for a period of several years. By this time the climate would have been 'kicked' into a cooler phase. As the snow-cover increased then more of the Sun's energy would be reflected back into space, and thus the cooling would continue. Alternatively, a series of massive volcanic erup-tions could produce a similar amount of dust with the same result. A combined mechanism is also possible whereby a huge meteorite is the trigger for volcanic eruptions.

FUTURE WORK ON FOSSILS

During the twenty-first century geologists, perhaps aided by astronomers, botanists, climatologists and others, will surely bring us the answers to many of these questions about the Earth's earlier climates and the evolution of life. After all, the geological evidence locked up in sedimentary rocks is abundant, the problem lies in the piecing together of evidence from a variety of sources to make a coherent and reasoned history. We may eventually end up with a detailed chronology which lists scores of ice ages.

HUMAN EVOLUTION

During the past million years or so there has been a further series of ice ages, typically perhaps 50 to 100 thousand years in length and separated by warm interglacials which may, on average, have been rather shorter. The past one to three million years has also been the period during which the human race has been evolving from its ape-like ancestors. One may speculate that forced migrations occurred which accelerated our evolution.

The average world-wide temperature during the ice ages was about 5C (9F) lower than at present. The equatorial climate was perhaps only slightly cooler than today, while over the ice sheets and near their edges it was probably 10 to 15C (18 to 27F) cooler than now. During one advance the ice sheets reached as far as the Thames and covered much of the present day Soviet Union, most of Canada and even parts of the USA, including the Great Lakes. The ice caps on the Alps, Rockies and other mountain ranges were much more extensive than today. During the last ice age, which ended only 15 thousand years ago, Britain was again covered with ice many metres thick as far south as Yorkshire. Our climate then was similar to that of Baffin Island, the Canadian Arctic or Central Iceland today. The geological evidence for recent ice ages is overwhelming. Glacial U-shaped valleys, north-facing corries high in the mountains, moraines of glacial debris and scores of other features are abundant in Scotland, Wales, parts of Ireland and in the English Lake District. At Glen Roy near Fort William there are terraces known as the 'parallel roads' high on the side of the valley where a lake, created by a huge dam of ice, had its successive shorelines. The ice in the main valley near Spean Bridge must have been hundreds of metres thick, even in this melting phase of a waning ice age. When people ask if our climate has warmed up, then one answer is 'yes, by several degrees over the last 15,000 years'.

ICE CORES

One way of learning about the weather of the past millennia, is to study ice cores – deep sections through the ice caps of Greenland or the Antarctic, and analyse their oxygen content. There are two sorts of oxygen, the common oxygen 16 and the less common oxygen 18 (heavy oxygen): when water evaporates, condenses, freezes or melts the proportions change. During warm periods there is more heavy oxygen. On the surface of an ice cap there is an annual cycle of snow accumulation and thawing, and the end result is a series of layers which can be used to work out the climate history. In Greenland, for example, there are thousands of years repre- sented in the huge ice cap. As each winter adds new snow, the layers below are compressed and spread outwards, with icebergs shed annually from the coasts.

Even at a depth of 1000 m (3300 ft) in a core sample from Northern Greenland, layers could be seen which enabled the age to be established as 8300 years. The deepest cores, sometimes going down to deep bedrock, are very compressed but still allow a good deal of analysis, and those from Camp Century in Northern Greenland cover 150,000 years. They illustrate the cold phase from about 100,000 to 15,000 years ago, which was the last ice age, but even then the weather was not without its fluctuations. This is a happy hunting ground for those looking for regular cycles to try to prove scientific theories. It would be exciting to uncover an eleven-year rhythm which would link snowfall or temperature to the cycle of sunspots, but the real evidence does not support this. (But perhaps there is some sort of eleven-year cycle which just does not show up in snowfall?) Scientists have also searched for many other longer cycles like 10,000 years, etc, and have had some success, which supports the Milankovitch theory (see Chapter 11), but also many irregular changes.

One very important discovery from the ice cores is that, as the climate warmed up around 10,000 years ago, the carbon dioxide in the atmos- phere increased and methyl sulphonic acid (a product of plankton) decreased. This provides strong evidence that plankton in the ocean played a part in controlling the natural greenhouse effect. Less plankton seems to mean more carbon dioxide.

POLAR ICE CAPS

At the present time we have ice caps at each Pole but this has not always been so. The Antarctic continent lies fairly symmetrically about the South Pole, so this is land-based ice, in places thousands of metres thick. In some other areas the ice is thin and mountains (known as 'nunataks') poke up through it. Round the edges are sections of 'ice shelf' from which portions occasionally break away as huge tabular icebergs. (In the north- ern hemisphere the ice processes on Greenland are not dissimilar.)

The Arctic is mainly ocean but is surrounded by an almost complete ring of land, comprising the Soviet Union's northern coasts, Alaska, Canada, Greenland, Iceland and Scandinavia. Within the Arctic region, the area of sea ice shrinks somewhat during the summer and expands again during the late autumn and winter. The same patterns can be seen on Mars which has two 'ice caps' which shrink and expand with the Martian seasons. Mars is entirely land and the 'ice' is a thin covering of solid carbon dioxide, but the principle is similar.

However, we must not fall into the trap of imagining that two polar ice caps on Earth are inevitable. The Antarctic continent was once joined to India and has drifted to its present position. The ring of continents and islands almost surrounding the Arctic Ocean is, in terms of geological time, a temporary arrangement which prevents ocean currents from reaching the North Polar region. So at the present geological time we have a rare occurrence of not just one but two polar ice caps. This was not true a hundred million years ago and will not be true a hundred million years hence. It is certainly part of the cause of the current series of ice ages, but it cannot be the whole cause. There was little difference in the position of the continents 20,000 years ago from those shown on our maps today and in that time the ice age has retreated.

EVIDENCE FROM OCEANS AND LAKES

One of the places where evidence can accumulate in undisturbed layers is upon the ocean floor. Dead marine organisms, if not dissolved or eaten on the way down, will build up century by century to give a record that the marine biologist can assess. A million years or more of indirect evidence of climate is available by studying these ocean-floor layers for warm- and cold-water species. Abrupt changes in the Earth's magnetic field help researchers to date the sedimentary layers.

On land, near the edges of ice sheets, lakes receive an annual influx of fine silt brought in by the meltwater from the nearby glaciers and ice sheets. With a rapid melt the rock grains will be coarser and the layer thicker. Thus a study of lake 'varves', as they are known, can yield a history of the last 10,000 years. Sweden has good sites, probably Canada too, and the mud layers from Lake Saki in the Crimea have provided a complete record from 2200 BC onwards.

BEETLES, POLLEN AND TREE REMAINS

Certain beetles are characteristic of specific temperature regimes. When they die the soft parts are soon destroyed but the hard shell-like parts remain among particles of silts and sands. Using a microscope, some kind of climate chronology can be established back to the last ice age and beyond. The pollen of each species of tree or plant can be identified under a microscope. Though pollen may be wind-blown, the distances involved are usually small. Many grains of pollen are preserved in peat bogs. The pollen of warmth-loving trees such as ash and lime may alternate with the hardier willow, birch and alder. Expertise and great patience are called for to achieve a reliable sequence from such studies. Sometimes rather more substantial plant remains are found in post-glacial bogs and lakes, including tree roots. Again the tree species itself will be of interest. Holly, for example, normally grows only where the coldest month is above minus 1 Celsius (30F).

CARBON DATING

If we find a series of tree remains, such as those on the upland moorlands of Scotland above the present tree-line, then carbon dating will tell us their approximate age. The method can only be used for plant and animal remains.

Most of the carbon in the world is carbon 12 but the reaction of cosmic rays with the atmosphere means that the air contains a proportion of radioactive carbon 14. This carbon 14 is absorbed along with carbon 12 by all living organisms, whether they are plants as they grow or animals as they eat, drink and breathe. When they die the intake of the radioactive carbon 14 ceases and the amount in the dead plant or animal starts to decrease. This is because carbon 14 gradually 'decays' or changes into carbon 12. The half-life of the radioactive isotope (i.e. the time taken for half of the isotope to change) is 5700 years. Using all this information it is therefore possible to calculate the age of dead organic matter from the proportion of carbon 14 remaining.

This radioactive dating method is quite good for determining the age of wood, bone and other remains up to about 30,000 years old but errors are always present. A calibration system has been developed, partially by analysing items of known age from ancient Egypt. Dates are often quoted as 'corrected' meaning that the results of the straightforward scientific tests have been adjusted to try to eliminate systematic errors. Even so, there are still problems. For example the nuclear testing of the 1950s and early 1960s led to a carbon 14 maximum around 1963. The environment in which the specimen lived, or in which it has lain since death, will also have an effect. Incredibly, the flesh of a freshly dead seal from Antarctica was analysed as 500 years old due to environmental complications! This was perhaps because ice and trapped air which had been locked up in the interior of the continent had distorted the result, or possibly it was due to upwelling of ancient deep Antarctic water which had been out of contact with surface conditions. The bones of the same seal indicated an age of 150 years.

Despite such problems, radiocarbon dating is invaluable when there is no alternative.

TREE RINGS

It is well known that we can work out the age of a tree by counting the rings. Some rings are thicker than others, but what do the thick rings signify?

In the colder parts of the World, including Northern Europe, a warm year will be a good growing year and will produce a thicker ring. This will be especially true for trees on elevated sites nearing their altitude limit. In other warmer climates it is the availability of moisture which is the key factor. In Spain, for example, a thick annual growth ring might indicate a wet year.

The oldest trees in the world are Bristlecone Pines in western USA which can live to 5000 years. Dead trees can extend the sequence back further but we need to tie together the records of the live and dead specimens by finding a run of years which exactly match. It is possible to get some sort of complete history for up to 10,000 years or more. If we are not too fussy about precise years, then radiocarbon dating can be used to check the antiquity.

As the individual tree gets older the rings become narrower, since each tiny addition means a significant increase in the cross-sectional area of the tree trunk.

Yet another difficulty arises from the individual nature of trees. One growing near a stream may have no problems with water shortage and will be affected by temperature alone, or the death of surrounding trees may provide more light and therefore encourage a growth spurt for a remaining specimen. The scientist's problems are manifold, but by using numerous samples ('replication') and by cross-referencing different sites, the history gradually emerges.

CAVE PAINTINGS AND EARLY MIGRATION

The earliest humans left little in the way of records though they did sometimes provide evidence in the form of animal bones and shellfish where they camped and ate. However, cave paintings, the earliest of which date back 30,000 years or more, show clearly the animals which they were hunting. When the ice age was covering northern Europe, humans were living in France and Spain and painting the walls of caves at Lascaux and Altamira with bison and other wild cattle, rhinoceros and deer. The weather would have been cooler by a few degrees but not unendurable. In the Soviet Union (areas of which were not covered in ice due to lack of snowfall, but which were bitterly cold), it was mammoths that humans pursued. At the time of the ice age, lower sea levels meant that the Bering Strait did not exist and people could find their way across from eastern Siberia into North America. This seems to have been the origin of the North American Indians though there were at least two waves of such migrations. Whether they subsequently found their way down the coast or through an ice-free corridor between the Rockies ice cap and the North Canadian ice sheet is not known. The sea-crossing from Southeast Asia to Australia was shorter than now but considerable when humans arrived there perhaps 40,000 years ago.

The most surprising of the paintings and drawings are those from southern Algeria in the central Sahara, dating from 5000 to 3000 BC (i.e. at least 5000 years after the very end of the ice age) which show elephant, antelope, rhinoceros, giraffe and apparently cattle-herding. There are even paintings of boats, though it is possible that these depicted scenes which the artist had experienced elsewhere. Nevertheless the inescapable conclusion is that the Sahara was much wetter than it is now. The presence of certain trees could perhaps be put down to underground water sources left over from the wetter periods of the previous ice age, but grass- and bush-eating animals must point to higher rainfall. We also know that Lake Chad was far larger at this time.

Annual migration has probably occurred among some species of birds, mammals and insects for millions of years, but the ending of the ice age would once again have quite literally opened up new landscapes to migratory species. Birds which had already become used to migrating would only have to overshoot by a few miles to establish new territory. They had the ability to extend their range just as soon as the northward-moving plants and insects allowed them to do so.

SEA LEVELS AND LAKE LEVELS

When the climate warms, the sea level rises for two reasons. Most obvious is the melting of the ice locked up in the ice caps of Antarctica and Greenland. Less obvious, but now thought to be slightly more important, is the expansion of the ocean waters as they warm. Neither process happens immediately and there may be a lag of tens or hundreds of years before there is full adjustment to the new, warmer, ice-free regime. Floating ice makes no difference when it melts, since ice displaces its own weight of water. An iceberg therefore just fills up the 'gap' in the ocean which it has itself occupied. Scientific evidence suggests that when the most recent series of ice ages commenced (perhaps about 0.8 million years ago) the sea level fell by around 100 m (300 ft). Since the last ice age finished 15,000 years ago the resulting rise in sea level has also been about 100 m (300 ft). Britain was joined to the Continent until around 8000 years ago, i.e. 6000 BC, before which the Thames flowed northwards to a mouth somewhere in what is now the southern North Sea, near the present Dogger Bank. The English Channel and Straits of Dover simply did not exist. Ireland was already cut off from the land bridge with Europe by the time the Straits of Dover were created. This meant that snakes and some other species did not make it to Ireland when the climate warmed after the last ice age. By the time snakes had reached Britain, the Irish Sea already blocked their pathway westward.

Around much of the world there are signs that lakes were considerably larger during the warm phase of 6000 to 2000 BC than their remnants are today. Fish remains and old shorelines provide the evidence. Lake Chad on the southern fringe of the Sahara is a notable example, and the Caspian Sea was also immense. In North America, the Great Salt Lake in Utah is just a remnant of the former Lake Bonneville, and many Californian lakes were larger then than they are now. Whether their larger size was due to higher rainfall or to ground water left over from the previous phase of climate is difficult to judge.

The sea level maximum would have occurred near the end of the warm phase, perhaps around 2000 BC, when the World's oceans were probably just a metre or two (3 to 6 ft) higher than today.

When the sea levels were rising most rapidly during the phase between 8000 and 5000 BC, the rate of rise was perhaps 1 to 2 m (3 to 6 ft) per century. This might be thought harmless to humans, but the inroads into the land would have happened in great storms and thus, as far as the people were concerned, quite suddenly. It is probable, as the climate researcher Hubert Lamb has suggested, that communities in coastal areas were occasionally overwhelmed, maybe at night, and thereby drowned.

RAISED BEACHES AND ISOSTATIC ADJUSTMENT

Evidence of sea levels comes partially from land features such as raised beaches. These are small terraces where waves have created a shoreline which is now inland or above the present beach. The work of correlating one section of raised beach with another or of dating any of them is difficult because of land movements.

As the huge ice caps melted, the plates of the Earth's crust were no longer compressed into the Earth by the immense weight. Scandinavia was like a dinner plate floating in a bowl of thick soup but slightly weighed down by a block of ice. When the weight of ice was removed the plate gradually came upwards. In the case of Scandinavia, and to a lesser extent Scotland, the rising of the land due to the melting of the great ice sheets continues today. It is as if the mini-continent of Scandinavia is breathing a sigh of relief as it lifts itself back up. Some parts of Sweden are even now rising at about one metre per century. Broadly speaking, northern Britain is also still rising, with the result that the southern coasts of England and Ireland are being slightly tilted downwards into the sea. If the sea level now starts to rise it will be accentuated in the sinking regions.

One can imagine the difficulties of trying to assess ice-age sea levels from Scandinavian beaches or where there is volcanic or earthquake activity or large movements of the Earth's crust, but the tropics provide extra evidence. Corals grow only where the water temperature exceeds 18 C (64 F) and only in shallow water, so they have a great, and as yet largely untapped, future in climatic detective work.

BURIAL MOUNDS AND STONE CIRCLES

In Britain, long barrows were starting to be used for burials around 3000 BC. Over the following 1500 years Stonehenge was built and altered several times. Avebury (Wiltshire) and many other stone circles were erected. Numerous round barrows were also constructed. Whilst there is no doubt that many of the stone circles and barrows are aligned with the Sun and probably also with the Moon and stars, it is arguable whether they were exclusively astronomical observatories or settings for religious rituals – probably astronomy and religion were inextricably mingled and people were trying to make sense of day and night, varying seasons and varying weather. What is certain, though, is that all this activity went on in a climate which was warmer than that today, probably by almost 2 C (say 3 or 4 F). This may not sound much but is the equivalent of moving a couple of hundred miles further south, e.g. from Wiltshire to Western France. When one thinks of the stone circles at Castlerigg on a Cumbrian hill near Keswick, at Callanish in Lewis or the Ring of Brodgar in Orkney, then the mellower climate of that time seems an important factor. It has been suggested that it must necessarily have been less cloudy in prehistoric times to make stone circle sites a viable proposition for astronomical purposes, but that notion does not ring true.

The marvellous remains of later villages like Skara Brae in Orkney seem less bleak in the light of a warmer climate. The warmest period over much of the Earth was from 5000 to 3000 BC but in higher northern latitudes where the ice caps were still melting the optimum may have been reached as late as 2000 BC.

WEATHER IN THE ICE AGE

The last ice age has been outlined as the period from about 100,000 to 15,000 BP (before present). During that time (and almost certainly during the previous ice ages) the tropics would still have been warm, but presumably a degree or so cooler than now. The tropical rains which created the equatorial rain-forests would still have occurred and, as now, they would have moved north and south with the seasons. Scotland, Wales and Northern England were covered in a huge depth of ice and it can be imagined that conditions were similar to those in Greenland today. Winter temperatures would have been almost continuously sub-zero with gale-force winds sometimes blowing across the ice surface. In summer melting snow and ice would have been a dominant theme and rain, drizzle and snow would all have occurred, much as they do in Greenland's summer today. Depressions would have come and gone as they do today, but mainly on a more southerly track towards France or Spain. Calm days would have been quite pleasant if anyone had been there to enjoy them. Sunshine totals for the year might well have been higher than at present on the high ground of what was then ice plateau. Even southern parts of Britain would have been almost uninhabitable, though perhaps a hunting party would have made the odd foray northwards from France. The landscape near the edge of the ice sheet would have included gravels and sand – the outwash debris of glaciation. Judging by the weather in Iceland and Labrador today there would have been some days with warm winds blowing the dust around. Tornadoes might have been more common with the warm sunshine and colder air aloft. By contrast, northerly winds would at times have brought appalling cold. Temperature variations from day to day and from month to month would have been greater than now.

WEATHER AT THE PEAK OF WARMTH

The main transition from cold to warm took place between 20,000 BP and perhaps 8000 BP (6000 BC). If we take 6000 to 2000 BC as the peak of the present interglacial and imagine the weather in that period, then we would correctly expect the whole world to be warmer. In the tropics, with

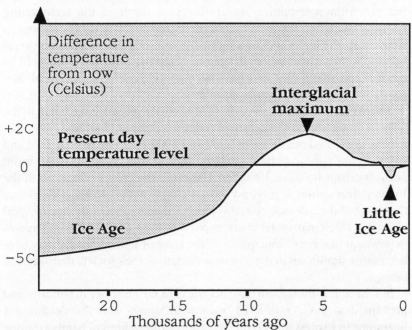

A schematic graph of temperature variations over the past 25000 years. During the Ice Age the Earth was about 5 degrees Celsius cooler than now. (This is an average figure for the entire globe. The British Isles, for example, was over 10 degrees Celsius cooler.) The increase in detail shown over the past 1000 years is due simply to better information. Minor fluctuations have no doubt always occurred.

higher land, sea and air temperatures, tropical cyclones (hurricanes) would have been more vigorous, fuelled by all that warm moist air. Tropical rains would perhaps have been even heavier and more extensive than now, at least in the early part of the interglacial.

In Britain, once the ice had melted, trees flourished even on the hills of the north. The stumps of ancient forests on the Scottish uplands are part of the evidence. In England warmth-loving plants and animals were widespread and pond turtles lived as far north as East Anglia. Winters would still have included cold snaps with frost and short-lived snowfalls, but overall the weather would have been like central or southwestern France at the present time. Settled communities developed and flourished, notably in Wiltshire.

EARLY CIVILISATIONS

There is no doubt that the period from 10,000 to 3000 BC saw tremendous climatic changes, mainly the initial change towards a warmer Earth, but not without temporary reversals. As a result of the temperature patterns changing, warm and cold air would meet in different regions from today, the highs and lows formed in different places and some areas became wetter whilst others dried out. From the evidence discovered so far, it seems that it may first have become wetter as it warmed and then drier, but this is a huge generalisation.

The African tropical rains extended northwards past Lake Chad to the Tibesti mountains in the centre of today's Sahara until around 6000 BC, but the area dried out between 6000 and 3000 BC. The Middle East and India do not appear to have become drier at this time, but when it did occur (perhaps between 1900 and 1000 BC) the great civilisations of the Indus valleys suffered. It is easy to look simply to the changing climate as the cause of their demise, but this kind of theory ignores the sociological elements which may be far more important, even down to the individuals in power at that time. The quirks of the ruler or military leader may have been more significant in determining the fate of their society than climatic change.

In China, it is thought to have been 2 C (3.6 F) warmer in summer and perhaps 3 to 5 C (5 to 9 F) warmer in winter with the decline not beginning in earnest until 1100 BC. The northern limit of bamboo (along the January 0 C (32 F) isotherm) was 200 miles further north in 3000 BC.

Australia too seems to have been wetter at the time of the last maximum of post-glacial warmth.

ANCIENT EGYPT

Cave paintings have already been mentioned as a human source of climate information but written records are even better and Egypt was the first major source. Many societies have a traditional flood story like that of Noah in the Bible, but since there is usually not even an attempt at a date, the story on its own is of little value.

The advantage of Ancient Egyptian history is that it was nearly always linked to the pharaoh ruling at the time, whose dates we know. Also, it was usually recorded at the time that it happened or at least within 20 years or so, at the death of the pharaoh. Many of the tomb walls were covered with pictorial histories of the events of his reign even before his death, as the tomb was prepared long in advance. For rulers like Tutankhamun who died suddenly at an early age, then it was more of a rush job, but the chronology would have been all the more precise. There are stories of famine, of plagues of locusts and also of abundant water when the annual flood of the Nile was even greater than usual.

Ancient Egypt was quite naturally obsessed with the Nile, virtually its only source of water. Every year, summer rains fall in central Africa around Lake Victoria, in Ethiopia and Sudan and swell the Blue and White Niles. They join at Khartoum and the water flows northwards through Egypt. There the river level rises through September and falls gradually through October, November and December. Historically, when the Nile rose, the water flooded the land on either side of the river, carrying nutrient-rich silt with it. The diversion of the water through major channels and then tiny water-courses was controlled by humans. The river levels were recorded, for example at the Nilometer at Cairo, so there are some written records since about 3000 BC and especially since AD 600. We know that the area was becoming drier around 3000 BC when the first pyramids were built. At this time the level of Lake Rudolph in East Africa dropped, giraffes and rhinoceros disappeared from Egypt and the Nile levels became lower. However, we should not read too much into the disappearance of animals: in the rock-cut tomb at Saqqara about 4 million mummified Ibis have been found, preserved in pots – an eloquent testimony to our ability, even in the time of the later pharaohs, to deplete other species. Since the Aswan Dam was built, creating Lake Nasser, the flow has been regulated below that point. Even today Egypt, with its population of 50 million (similar to the UK), is almost completely dependent upon the Nile for water, and so is at the mercy of the weather elsewhere in Africa, just as in the times of the pharaohs.

THE ANCIENT GREEKS

Whilst the Ancient Greeks have not provided us with much in the way of climatic history, they can be said to have started the science of meteorology. They correctly related climate to latitude bands, and the day-to-day weather with different wind directions and therefore different air masses.

Aristotle (384 to 322 BC) wrote his treaty *Meteorologica* and his pupil Theophrastus (380 to 285 BC) produced a collection of forecasting rules and weather lore entitled *On Weather Signs*, which can be regarded as an early version of a forecaster's reference book. Alexander the Great was at this time travelling widely with his army into central Asia and India, broadening the knowledge of the world, and Aristarchus was on the point of a scientific breakthrough in estimating the size of the Earth (which he considered round) and the distance to the Sun.

One interesting instance of day-to-day weather from Greek times is worth quoting. At the sea battle of Salamis in 480 BC between the Athenians and the Persians led by Xerxes, the local winds proved a decisive factor. The Greeks knew that the onset of the sea-breeze occurred mid-morning and were able to make use of it in their smaller and more manoeuvrable boats to overcome the Persian fleet.

THE ROMANS

The Roman Empire extended all around the Mediterranean. Great cities like Leptis Magna in Libya remind us that North Africa was said to be the Granary of Rome, but we should be wary of concluding that rainfall was much more than today, for wheat is still grown to the south of the Mediterranean. The elephants still remaining in the region of Algeria and Tunisia at the time of Hannibal in 220 BC were probably a relic population, cut off from those south of the Sahara.

In Britain, the northern outpost of the Roman Empire, Hadrian's Wall (constructed AD 122 to 128) was for a time the northern boundary, though this was briefly superseded by the Antonine Wall across Central Scotland. Whether it was the ferocity of the people to the north, or the Romans' dislike of the colder climate, they never did control all of Scotland. Surprisingly, however, they built many roads and camps in upland England including a road almost along the summit of the mountain High Street, 2718 ft (828 m) high in Cumbria. Even assuming that the climate was still a fraction warmer, the weather for road-users must sometimes have been appalling in the winter months. The recall of the Roman forces from Britain in AD 409 had more to do with the decline of their empire than the climate, but it is thought to have been hastened by the freezing of the River Rhine in a very cold winter. This had allowed the 'Barbarian' tribes including the Vandals to cross the river on the last day of December AD 406 on their way to sack the City of Rome.

WEATHER IN THE BIBLE

In studying the weather-related comments in the Bible, we must bear in mind that they were written of the Middle East, yet, even so, many of them can be translated to Europe and still make sense. 'Out of the South cometh the whirlwind' (Job 37:9), and also 'An east wind shall come, the wind of the Lord shall come up from the wilderness, and his spring shall become dry and his fountain shall be dried up' (Hosea 13:15). In addition to drought, the east wind in winter brings cold weather both in the Levant and in Europe. 'Shall it not utterly wither, when the east wind toucheth it' ask Ezekiel (17:10).

St Luke seems to have been something of an amateur meteorologist for he wrote 'When ye see a cloud rise out of the west, straightway ye say,

There cometh a shower; and so it is', and also 'When ye see the South wind blow, ye say, There will be heat; and it cometh to pass' (St Luke 12: 54, 55).

THE VIKINGS AND EARLY MEDIEVAL TIMES

The expansion of the Vikings into Britain, Russia, Iceland and finally Greenland came during a period (AD 700 to 1000) when the climate was slightly warmer than now, perhaps by rather less than 1 C (1.8 F). It seems to have reached a minor peak around AD 1000 to 1300 which has not been equalled since (despite the warmth of the 1900s). (Our climate now is therefore the warmest for 700 years.)

Around AD 1200 the Viking sailings to Iceland and Greenland began to be affected more by ice. By AD 1342 the traditional short sea route from Iceland to Greenland along the 65th parallel of latitude had been abandoned in favour of a more Southerly route. For the Norse colony in Greenland life must have become desperately hard. Ships stopped calling and finally the colony died out around AD 1450.

The period of warmth in Norman times and just after allowed vineyards to flourish in Britain, often tended by monks.

The period AD 1284 to 1311 seems to have been particularly favourable. Records now not only include individual events, such as storms which destroyed or changed the old coastlines, but also harvest dates and prices of crops, which reflect the weather during the whole growing season. Many of the upheavals of the Middles Ages were political, or the result of events in which climate probably played little or no part, such as the arrival of the Black Death or bubonic plague in Europe in AD 1348 to 1350.

THE LITTLE ICE AGE

This dramatic name has been given to the coolest period in the middle of the current millennium.

At its widest definition it lasted from AD 1420 to 1850. A narrower definition would be AD 1600 to 1720. The time chosen depends partially on whether we take a British, European or northern hemisphere view.

During this period the temperatures in northern Europe were generally about 1 C (almost 2 F) lower than in the current century. Springs were particularly cold and late, with March averaging as much as 2 C (4 F) below the current values in central Europe. Seas around Iceland may have been 5 C (9 F) cooler; this would have increased the temperature contrast between Europe and the Arctic, thus encouraging deeper, more violent depressions. Temperatures in the tropics were probably very similar to the present day. It is likely that there was permanent snow-cover on the Cairngorms and Ben Nevis at this time, rather than the odd patch or two of snow which survive through our current summers. Glaciers advanced in the Alps, traditional crops failed more often, but by no means every year, and some hard decisions had to be taken – for example whether to abandon a vineyard. Thermometer readings from Europe since AD 1650 provide, for the first time, instrumental evidence for this cooler period, even allowing for the different exposure of the instruments at that time. What little evidence there is from the southern hemisphere suggests that it was cooler there too, but perhaps not in the Antarctic. If this was a worldwide cooling, then variations in the output of heat from the Sun are a possible cause. The relative scarcity of sunspots reported in this period suggest a solar link. (There is further information on sunspots in Chapter 11.)

DIARISTS, CHRONICLERS AND ARTISTS

The weather information which can be gleaned from the diarists of the seventeenth and eighteenth centuries is patchy and subjective. Pepys and Evelyn certainly lived during a cold era but there is a tendency to repeatedly use phrases like 'the coldest within living memory'. One might suspect that their acquaintances were indulging in exaggeration or suffering from amnesia, though it is true that this period was in the Little Ice Age.

Samuel Pepys visited a vineyard in summer 1661 at Hatfield House, but was unimpressed, commenting on the coldness of the day. This was one of the few vineyards that kept going through this adverse time. Nevertheless, there were hot summers in 1665 and again in 1666, preceding the Great Fire of London, which broke out in September when the buildings had become tinder-dry.

John Evelyn also wrote diaries and travelled a good deal. He described blowing sand (which he likened to that in Libya) around Thetford in September 1677. Later it was the great frost fair of 1683-84 which caught his attention. On 23 December 1683 he wrote, 'the smallpox very prevalent and mortal; the Thames frozen'. On 24 January 1684 he recorded:

'. . . the trees not only splitting as if lightning-struck but men and cattle perishing in divers places, and the very seas locked up with ice that no vessels could stir out or come in. The fowls, fish and birds and all our exotic plants and greens universally perishing. Many packs of deer destroyed, and all sorts of fuel so dear that there were contributions to preserve the poor alive. Nor was this severe weather much less intense in most parts of Europe, even as far as Spain and the most southern tracts. London, by reason of the excessive coldness of the air hindering the ascent of the smoke, was so filled with this fuliginous steam of sea-coal that hardly could one see across the streets; and this filling the lungs with its gross particles exceedingly obstructed the breath, so as no one could scarcely breathe. There was no water to be had from the pipes and engines; nor could the brewers and divers other tradesmen work; and every moment was full of disastrous accidents.'

Storminess seems to have been more common between 1550 and 1750 than now. The northwesterly winds which had delayed Julius Caesar's expeditions to Britain in 55 and 54 BC, and also the Norman invasion in AD 1066, had been quite normal, but that was not true of the storm which destroyed the Armada in June 1588, and the one described by Daniel Defoe in November 1703 was really extreme and is rightly known as the 'Great Storm of 1703'. Altogether 8000 people are thought to have died in northwest Europe, most of them sailors in the English Channel and North Sea.

By the nineteenth century, evidence from artists such as Turner between 1830 and 1840 makes us realise that cities were becoming places of smoke pollution, but his rich sunsets may also owe something to the dust in the stratosphere from volcanic eruptions.

FROST FAIRS

The roll-call of years when the River Thames froze over in London during past centuries makes an impressive list, including 1663, 1666, 1677, 1684, 1695, 1709, 1716, 1740, 1776, 1795 and 1814.

However, we cannot make direct comparison with the absence of ice in today's London. Then, the river was almost dammed by London Bridge and the stagnant, less tidal flow above the bridge would have made the river more prone to freezing. In recent times there has been much effluent of warm water from drains, factories and even power stations into the river. Even so, the ice fairs of the past were certainly made possible by severe spells of at least a week or two, and the people took advantage of the excuse for fairs by selling chestnuts, skating and generally enjoying themselves.

ALPINE GLACIERS

Farmers in the Alps have had good reason to watch the glaciers advance and retreat. Generally they reached their maximum extent around 1820 to 1850, perhaps as a result of the Little Ice Age but delayed by a century or so due to the time taken for the full cycle of snow accumulation, compression into ice and subsequent glacier movement. During the past hundred years the glaciers have been retreating, as is clearly proved from old etchings and photographs compared with modern ice-free valleys. The bodies of climbers who fell to their deaths from Alpine peaks during the last century have been recovered in recent years due to the melting of ice.

THE YEAR WITHOUT A SUMMER

The Little Ice Age was perhaps coming to an end when a series of volcanic eruptions played a part in delaying the recovery to 'normal' conditions. Volcanoes erupted in Iceland in 1783, in the West Indies in 1812 and in the Philippines in 1814, but it was the violent explosive eruption of Tambora at latitude 8°S in the East Indies during 1815 that really did the damage. The dust veil must have covered a significant proportion of the Earth, for in the northern hemisphere 1816 was notably cold and became known as 'the year without a summer'.

DUSTBOWL AMERICA

During the 1930s a series of hot dry summers in the central states of the USA led to the 'dustbowl' era. Once again the causes were not solely meteorological. Over-intense agriculture with a high reliance on a restricted range of crops was also to blame. One mighty say that ploughing or cultivating the land during very dry weather is always a risk. If rain falls and the crops grow, then the soil will be held together by the plants; however, if the drought persists and strong winds follow, then the topsoil will start to blow. During the 1930s the dust from the broad flat lands in the Mississippi drainage area was born aloft and reached the northeastern states. Farmers saw their crops fail and hardship ensued. A poignant evocation of the consequences of this disaster can be found in John Steinbeck's novel *The Grapes of Wrath*. People blamed, amongst other things, radio waves for changing the climate, just as some blamed nuclear tests for any poor weather in the 1960s. Perhaps it was just bad luck that caused the run of dry summers. Like the tossing of a coin, one sometimes gets several tails in a row.

In 1988 there was something of a repeat and the Mississippi River was so low that barges could not operate. People blamed the greenhouse effect this time – and finally they had at least hit upon a plausible culprit. There is a connection between the amount of carbon dioxide in the atmosphere and the climate, but whether it was the true cause of the 1988 US summer is very doubtful.

An alternative way of looking at this event is to appreciate that we get hot and cold days, hot summers and cold summers, because the weather will never settle into a single mode. This has always been true, even when people planted the first crops several thousand years ago. To look for a single simple cause is futile. It is like asking for a one-word summary of world history.

ANOTHER MINOR PEAK

For most of this century the climate has been thought of as stable, even fixed. The period from 1900 to 1960 was reasonably warm over most of the globe. For a long time 1940 was quoted as a recent minor peak of warmth, at least in the northern hemisphere. It has also been suggested that this period tended to lack extreme weather, but statistically it is difficult to prove this type of hypothesis. Journalists love records, some of which are more meaningful than others. For instance, does the coldest April Tuesday in Cardiff for seven years qualify as a record? Certainly some of the media interest, at times bordering on amazement, in flood and droughts elsewhere in the world simply reflects the better and quicker reporting of recent times. A flood in Sudan or China has tremendous impact when we see pictures of it on our television screens or on the front page of the newspaper.

ICE AGE THREAT

There appeared to be a slight dip in temperatures in the 1960s and 1970s, which gave rise to scare stories about an impending ice age which seemed to be supported by the new ice core research from Greenland. We now look upon that temperature dip in between 1960 and 1980 as a minor northern hemisphere fluctuation in a general trend of rising temperatures. However, the interest in climate change grew with disastrous harvests in several areas of the world in 1972. This may have been a special case when one year's weather did change the course of world history. Grain prices shot up as precious surpluses were literally eaten up. Soon other commodity suppliers were re-analysing their position. In 1973 it was the oil producers, perhaps increasingly aware of their own strength as a result of the lesson of 1972, who were demanding more for their product. The southern fringe of the Sahara, the Sahel, suffered from several dry years in the 1970s and again in 1984. Famine was worsened in some regions by civil war, but the spotlight was again on climate. Those people who in the 1970s were so boldly predicting an imminent ice age would presumably explain their recent about turn by saying that human activities (in releasing greenhouse gases) have overtaken the natural course of events.

RECORD DECADE

World-wide, the 1980s was the warmest decade this century. The globe is now about 0.5 C (0.9 F) warmer than it was in 1900. Again this may not seem much, but it could represent life or death for marginal crops and marginal species of insect, bird or mammal.

In Europe we are probably almost rivalling the levels of the eleventh to fourteenth centuries. If we look at the six warmest years of the period 1900 to 1989 *world-wide*, then we find that they are *all* in the 1980s. One warm year is pure chance, two is coincidence, but six really does look statistically significant. However, we have a long way to go before we understand the true ice age of 15,000 years ago, the postglacial peak of warmth and the Little Ice Age around AD 1700, so we certainly cannot claim total understanding of the present warmth. Chapter 11 describes some of the mechanisms of possible climate change and, perhaps rashly, gives some forecasts for the future.

Chapter 2

UNDERSTANDING WEATHER

CONSTITUENTS OF THE AIR

THE ATMOSPHERE is the gaseous envelope that surrounds the Earth. If we ignore water vapour and perhaps pollutants, then the mixture of gases is pretty well homogeneous all around the Earth and up to a great height. Certainly the weather-bearing layers can be considered as a uniform mixture.

We usually list the constituents of dry air in descending percentages. Nitrogen is the most common at 78% by volume of dry air – it is a colourless, tasteless, odourless gas, essential to plant life, it liquefies at –196 C and freezes at –252 C, so there is no chance of either happening naturally! Next most common is oxygen at 21% – another colourless, tasteless, odourless gas which liquefies at –183 C and freezes at –218 C. Oxygen is, of course, vital to life and it is perhaps surprising that it constitutes little more than one fifth of each breath we take. Argon comes next at only 1%. This is known as an 'inert' gas because it does not react with any other element. It is harmless and virtually irrelevant.

These three make up near enough all of the dry atmosphere and only trace gases remain to be listed: carbon dioxide, neon, helium, ozone, hydrogen and krypton. Perhaps we should also list the pollutants which we produce, but which vary in abundance. The main ones are carbon dioxide (which is also present naturally), sulphur dioxide and various nitrogen oxides. These are produced by power stations, factories and vehicles; ozone, which occurs naturally at very high altitudes, can also be produced by chemical reactions between other pollutants at or near the Earth's surface, particularly over cities. Methane is formed by decomposing vegetation.

I have, of course, omitted water vapour, which in a typical sample of air would have come third in order behind nitrogen and oxygen. It is usually dealt with separately because it varies widely in amount from less than 1% up to 4%, being more common near the Earth's surface. In addition to being present as vapour and causing humidity, water also occurs as a

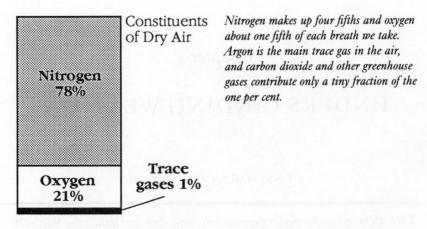

Constituents
of Dry Air

*Nitrogen makes up four fifths and oxygen
about one fifth of each breath we take.
Argon is the main trace gas in the air,
and carbon dioxide and other greenhouse
gases contribute only a tiny fraction of the
one per cent.*

liquid, forming fog, cloud droplets and rain, and as a solid, causing snow
and hail, so we cannot ignore it!

VERTICAL STRUCTURE

As we look upwards at the clouds, it is interesting to ponder on the
changes of pressure and temperature with height. The atmosphere
extends up perhaps 150 km (100 miles) or so. It is difficult to say where it
stops because it gets thinner and thinner, gradually merging with space.
Even at 300 km (200 miles) there is sufficient gas to exert a slight drag on a
spacecraft which would thus eventually be brought back to Earth.

The lowest meteorological satellites are at about 800 km (500 miles)
although short-lived space-vehicles can be in lower orbits.

The pressure at the surface is usually around 1000 mbar (millibars).
The exact value depends on the weight of air in a vertical column of
atmosphere stretching up from the Earth's surface into space. Pressure
decreases upwards but not at a constant rate. Because air is compressible,
there is more in a cubic metre near the ground than there is in a cubic
metre at a great height, and so the graph of height against pressure is
roughly exponential. Half of the atmosphere is below the 500 mbar level at
18,000 ft (5500 m). Three-quarters is below the 250 mbar level at about
36,000 ft (11,000 m), and this lowest 75% is about all we are interested in
for producing our weather in the British Isles. For one thing, there is little
water vapour above this height.

We can contrast this compression of gases under gravity with the water
in the ocean. Water is near enough incompressible, so oceanographers (or
dam-builders) deal with a steady, fairly uniform increase of pressure with
depth.

Why does it get colder with altitude? This question is less simple than it sounds. The simplest answer is that the Sun's radiation (i.e. heat) passes through the atmosphere and heats the ground. The ground gets hot, and heats the air, so we would expect the highest temperatures at the point where the radiation 'hits' the surface. This is only part of the story though. Because the pressure decreases upwards, any upward-moving parcel of air expands and cools so the full answer to the question must include an explanation of 'adiabatic lapse rates' which comes later in this chapter.

There is another temperature peak in the atmosphere at an immense height where a small percentage of the Sun's incoming radiation is intercepted near the top of the atmosphere in the ozone layer. So, at its simplest, we have reasonably high temperatures at the ground and again at the height of 50 km (30 miles) with low temperatures between, near the tropopause at around 40,000 ft (12,000 m) at which height our jet airliners fly.

THE BOUNDARY LAYER

The boundary layer of the atmosphere is defined as that layer which is directly affected by the Earth's surface. Its depth varies from one occasion to another (depending on air stability and wind speed) and from one area to another (depending on the height of hills and ruggedness of terrain). Stability is the tendency of the atmosphere to resist vertical air motion. An 'unstable day' is one when a lot of rising and descending air movement occurs.

In the British Isles the boundary layer is often said to be about 2000 ft (600 m or so) but the variability is enormous. Scientists can analyse the effect of the Earth on airflow and on temperature separately.

For a modern car racing along a motorway there are two obvious features that affect the airflow: the overall aerodynamic shape of the car and the smoothness of its paintwork. If the smooth, shiny paint were replaced with a rough surface like sandpaper then the airflow in the localised boundary layer above the bonnet would be altered. Similarly if we add a loaded roof-rack the overall shape of the car would be spoilt. These examples provide analogies with the meteorological boundary layer: the vegetation in a flat field makes the Earth's surface 'rougher'; a hill alters the whole pattern of the airflow. Both examples can be lumped together to explain why wind speeds are lighter at the Earth's surface than above the boundary layer at, say 2000 ft (600 m). We explain this in a form of verbal short-hand by ascribing it to the 'friction' of the surface.

The temperature aloft is also directly affected by the temperature at the surface when thermals rise on a sunny day. Rising air is replaced by pockets of descending air so the atmosphere becomes well mixed. This

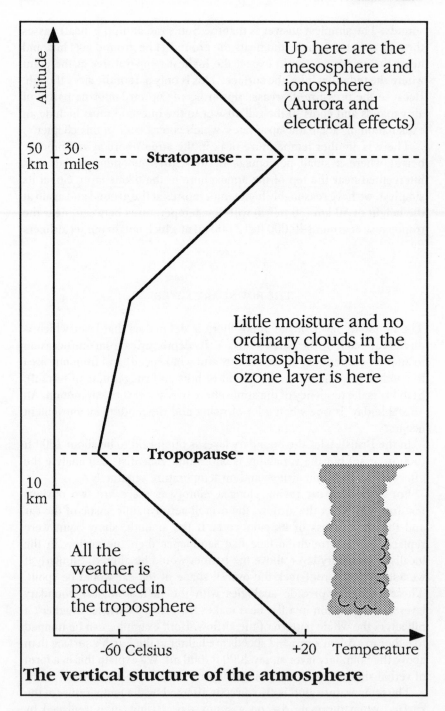

The vertical stucture of the atmosphere

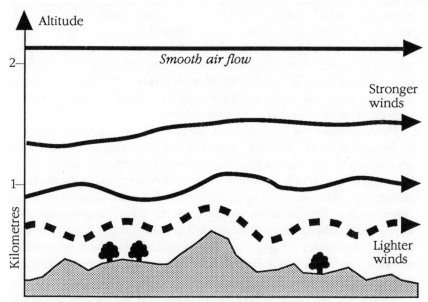

When strong winds are blowing over hilly terrain, the surface wind will be lighter but more gusty than the smoother but stronger airflow aloft. The lowest part of the atmosphere is sometimes referred to as the boundary layer.

mixing process takes place in the boundary layer, which is therefore much deeper by day than on a calm night.

A difficulty arises on days with 'deep instability' when thermals from the ground join together to form huge cumulonimbus clouds which extend to the tropopause several miles up. One could argue that this is all occurring within the boundary layer. At the other extreme there are those who concentrate on the lowest 200 ft (60 m) of the atmosphere and claim that this is the most vital part of the boundary layer. It is here that the transfer of heat, momentum and moisture between the surface and the atmosphere occurs.

If you fancy studying the boundary layer for yourself, then all you need is a tall mast with instruments at various heights plus plenty of logarithmic graph paper. Coupled with a vivid imagination you will soon find that your readings fall into straight lines, or am I being cynical?

TROPOSPHERE AND TROPOPAUSE

The troposphere is the lowest major level of the atmosphere; the layer in which by-and-large it gets colder as you go upwards. It starts at the Earth's surface, incorporates the boundary layer and extends up to the tropopause, which can be considered as a fairly well-defined 'lid'. A 'pause' is a boundary whereas a 'sphere' indicates a deep layer.

All the 'weather' and virtually all the clouds are created in the troposphere, and if we could just understand this one main layer it would be a major achievement. A meteorological book that spent 99% of its text on the troposphere might be considered well balanced, and most of the remainder on the next layer, the stratosphere.

The tropopause varies in height, being lower in the polar regions and at its highest near the Equator. This can be most simply explained by considering the convection process. Near the Poles there is little surface heating and therefore not much in the way of convection, so the depth of atmosphere which is stirred up is quite small. Near the Equator the huge cumulus and cumulonimbus clouds keep the whole troposphere well mixed and 'bubbling' like a saucepan full of boiling water. Whenever this stirring takes place, a 'lapse rate' is established whereby it gets colder upwards – and the troposphere is defined as the region where temperature falls with altitude.

Suffice it to say that a cumulonimbus cloud near the Equator can reach 50,000 ft (16,000 m) and this is roughly the height of the tropopause in Equatorial regions. The temperature here will be around – 80 C (-112 F). Thus, surprisingly, the coldest temperatures in our atmosphere are usually found high aloft over the Equator.

Near the Poles the tropopause is at about 26,000 ft (8000 m) and has a temperature of –40 C (-60 F). Over the UK it averages 33,000 to 39,000 ft (10,000 to 12,000 m) with a temperature of about –55 C. Interestingly, if we get a blast of northerly wind in winter or spring, then even in southern Britain we will have the (vertically compressed) polar profile. Under these circumstances any cumulonimbus clouds will be near the ground, of less depth but very vigorous. People in Scotland may say that 'the sky looks much lower' in outbreaks of Arctic air. Conversely, a tropical-type airstream will bring a much higher, colder tropopause, with perhaps more chance of high cirrus and cirrocumulus clouds.

To give a sense of scale we should remember that Mount Everest at 29,000 ft (9,000 m) does not reach the tropopause and that even transatlantic jets will barely do so. Concorde and some military aircraft do regularly fly through this 'lid' and into the rarefied air of the lower stratosphere.

THE STRATOSPHERE

If we ascended through the atmosphere, the stratosphere would be the second major layer. It lies above the troposphere, where the 'weather' happens, and below the mesosphere. Its lower boundary is the *tropopause* and it extends up to the *stratopause* at 50 km (30 miles).

In our imaginary journey through the stratosphere the pressure would fall from 200 millibars to 1 millibar and the temperature would rise from, say, –60 to about 0 C. There is very little moisture up there but nacreous or 'mother of pearl' clouds occur at around 24 km (15 miles), though sightings are rare.

When daily measurements have been made, for example by rocket, it is found that sharp day-to-day rises of temperature occur over Polar regions in the late winter or early spring, typically in February and March in the northern hemisphere. These events are known as 'sudden stratospheric warmings' and are presumably a manifestation of a subsiding airflow.

The explanation of the warm air up near the stratopause is that much of the ultraviolet light from the Sun is first intercepted here, and with such a thin mixture of gases, it doesn't take much energy to heat up substantially. For this reason the temperature maximum is at a greater altitude than the level of maximum ozone.

Ozone is relatively abundant in the stratosphere, especially around 15 to 30 kilometres (10 to 20 miles). It is created by the photochemical reactions caused by sunlight but can soon 'decay' back into oxygen. This natural process is disrupted by manufactured gases such as chlorofluoro-carbons (CFCs), which have the effect of reducing the ozone content (there is more about this in Chapter 11). Although the CFCs are mainly released in the densely populated and industrialised regions of the northern hemisphere, the circulation of winds in the stratosphere carries them around the globe. Neither this circulation nor the interchange of air between the stratosphere and troposphere is properly documented. We do know from recent measurements that the ozone is especially depleted in the Antarctic spring (i.e. October), and also that ozone-rich air is brought down into the troposphere behind cold fronts.

There appears to be a 'window' for the interchange of air between the two major atmospheric layers where the polar front jet stream occurs in mid-latitudes. This may also be where fine volcanic dust finds its way up and down through the tropopause – perhaps it is not such an effective lid to our tropospheric weather machine after all.

THE ENERGY CYCLE

If we consider the Earth–atmosphere system as a whole, then the amount of heat received from the Sun in a year is exactly matched by heat escaping into space. This is, of course, assuming for the moment that no climatic change is taking place, i.e. the greenhouse effect is temporarily ignored.

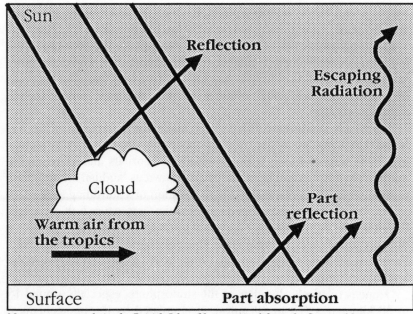

Measurements made in the British Isles of heat received from the Sun and heat escaping from the Earth show an imbalance. We lose more than we receive from the Sun with the shortfall being made up by 'imported heat' from the tropics.

However, if we set up an instrument (a radiometer) in Britain to measure the incoming heat from the Sun and compare it with a similar instrument measuring the outgoing heat from the Earth, then we find that there is a discrepancy. There is more heat escaping than coming in and the British Isles should be cooler than they in fact are. The same applies to all the temperate and polar latitudes north of about 38°N (which runs roughly through Spain). The apparent shortfall of incoming heat is compensated for in three ways. First, by warm air moving up from the tropics. Second, through the action of ocean currents: the Gulf Stream and North Atlantic Drift bring warm water from the tropics, and the Canaries Current takes cold water away southwards. Third, by the movement of latent heat: energy expended in the tropics to evaporate moisture is stored in the water vapour and brought north by the winds, where it is released as the vapour condenses into rainfall in our latitudes. The tropics are therefore net exporters of energy and the temperate latitudes are net importers.

Some of the Sun's heat is reflected by the clouds and some by the Earth's surface, and a little of it is absorbed by the atmosphere before reaching the Earth. The outgoing heat may also be intercepted, for example by a blanket of clouds. This energy cycle or 'radiation balance' is usually displayed in complex diagrams. A simple version is included here. Roughly speaking, half the Sun's energy gets through to heat the Earth's surface. The heat received from the Sun is utilised within the Earth–atmosphere system, but over the year as a whole, over the Earth as a whole, pretty much the same amount escapes into space as arrives at the top of the atmosphere. Direct input from geothermal sources such as volcanoes and from our own generation of heat are both negligible.

However, the effect of human activity on the composition of the atmosphere is another matter altogether. What used to be an energy balance may now be an imbalance. If the greenhouse effect is now warming us up, we are going through a transition phase when a little more heat comes in each year than escapes. If we then stabilise the level of carbon dioxide and other pollutants in the atmosphere, the heat balance will also eventually stabilise and once again energy received will equal that which escapes – though this new equilibrium will be at a higher temperature. More on this later in Chapter 11.

PRESSURE PATTERNS

The Earth's atmosphere is constantly in motion. Even on those rare occasions when calm conditions exist over Britain, there will be strong winds somewhere within a few hundred miles. These winds represent a lot of untapped energy. So where does all the energy come from? The ultimate source is the Sun. When we use windmills, wave generators or the more direct method of solar panels, we are tapping the energy of the Sun. And since we take such a tiny percentage it makes no difference to the atmosphere – indeed we eventually feed it back into the atmosphere as heat when we use the energy.

The Sun's warmth can be felt on the face, but how is this heat turned into wind power? Different latitudes of the Earth are heated at different rates and there are also contrasts between land and sea. These temperature contrasts result in differences in air density between areas, which in turn give rise to the pressure variations so beloved by meteorologists. (Where would we be without our highs and lows?) It is these pressure gradients that generate the winds.

A human can sense and therefore estimate temperature and wind speed and direction but not atmospheric pressure. Yes, one's ears 'pop' going downhill in a car and a few people claim to be able to detect pressure falls because their corns ache or their rheumatism gets worse, but really the changes that are important with respect to the weather are proportionally very small. For example, a fall of just 2 mbar from 1024 to 1022 mbar in one hour is in fact quite substantial and would usually only occur when a depression is approaching quite quickly. Yet to meteorologists the chart of highs and lows is the basic working tool. A chart with recently received observations will soon be 'drawn up' with isobars (lines joining points of equal pressure). A forecast chart will usually be a prediction of the pressure pattern, often with 'fronts' added. From this you can forecast the wind speed and direction and then you have the starting point for predictions of cloud, rain and temperature. Hence the obsession with pressure patterns.

THE ROTATING EARTH

If the Earth were not rotating, the winds would simply blow with the pressure gradient from areas of high pressure to areas of low pressure. Indeed, if the Earth were not rotating the whole atmosphere would operate in a totally different manner. Quite apart from the absence of day and night as we know them, there would be a vastly different arrangement of weather zones around the Earth from the Equator to the Poles. With our rotation (anticlockwise as you look down on the North Pole) an artillery shell fired in the Northern hemisphere will apparently be deflected to the right with reference to the Earth's surface. In other words, if you do not allow for the Earth's rotation, then you will miss the target.

Put simply, it is because the Equator is travelling more rapidly from west to east than is, say, London. The artillery shell fired from the Equator northwards to London has a rapid sideways motion which it retains – thus missing the target. If you stand on a moving roundabout and throw a tennis ball at a lamp-post, then you will miss the post if you do not allow for your sideways motion.

Scientists allow for this rotation by introducing the 'Coriolis effect'. Buys Ballot's Law accurately describes the result: 'If you stand with your back to the wind in the Northern hemisphere then the low pressure is on your left.'

This leads us on to the myth about the bathwater always running out anticlockwise in the northern hemisphere. The theory is all right but the reality is flawed because a bath is too small for the Coriolis effect to be significant and because of pre-existing water movements. If we filled up the Albert Hall with water, excluded all draughts and let it stand for a week – then, given a plughole right under the centre, the water would disappear in an anticlockwise spiral.

The studies that scientists have conducted of our atmosphere and those of other planets such as Venus and Jupiter show us some of the other effects of rotation. Notably there is a tendency for high rotational speeds to be linked to atmospheres with many (latitude related) zones. For the

Earth they can be summarised as the polar high-pressure zone with weak anticyclones, the travelling lows around latitudes 40° to 70°, the sub-tropical highs around 30°N and 30°S, and the Equatorial low-pressure zone which is responsible for the tropical rain-forests. These zones move north and south with the seasons, but the British Isles are firmly situated in the zone of travelling lows.

Further explanations of these weather zones are given in Chapter 3.

GEOSTROPHIC WIND AND SURFACE WIND

Pilots, yachtsmen and others who are well-versed in technical terms will have heard of the 'geostrophic wind'. This is the theoretical wind which blows along straight parallel isobars. In practice it is a very good approximation to the real wind in the 'free air' just above the friction layer at say 2000 to 3000 feet (600 – 900 m). Ironically, we use the surface pressure pattern to estimate the geostrophic wind, then we say that this represents the wind at 2000 feet, and then we use it to predict the surface wind!

Consider the case where there is a large area of low pressure to the north of Scotland. The isobars across Birmingham run from west to east, parallel and near enough straight. The meteorologist measures the distance between the isobars and can then calculate a precise value for the geostrophic wind, say 270 degrees 20 mph. If it is a clear night with a stable atmosphere then the *surface* wind will be backed by roughly 40 degrees and the speed will be a quarter of the geostrophic value, say 230 degrees 5 mph, thus blowing somewhat inwards towards the low pressure. At this time the air flow is smooth, horizontal and 'laminar', and we might say that the surface air is at least partially 'de-coupled' from the flow at 2000 feet.

By midday, after a few hours sunshine, cumulus clouds have formed and the air is fairly unstable with updraughts and downdraughts occurring. The geostrophic wind is still 270 degrees 20 mph as measured by the pressure pattern (and this can be confirmed by balloon measurements). Now, however, the low level air is 'coupled' to that aloft by the updraughts and downdraughts and the surface wind will be say 260 degrees 10 knots (i.e. backed by only 10 degrees from the geostrophic wind and with the speed half of that free air value, or just over).

In the evening the thermal currents cease, and provided that the pressure pattern remains constant, the wind will back and decrease, gradually reverting to 230 degrees 5 mph. These changes are the simple diurnal response to the change in stability.

Whilst tightly-packed isobars usually mean strong winds, a cold land surface can make it less windy at the surface than the pressure gradient would suggest. When the wind is light in strength on a sunny afternoon, then you can be fairly sure that it will fall calm at sunset.

For those who want to delve further, the geostrophic wind should be regarded as a balanced wind. In our example of the westerly flow over Birmingham, the pressure gradient from south to north is exactly balanced by the Coriolis 'force' which is trying to deflect the westerly wind to the right and acting from north to south. The geostrophic balanced flow occurs when these two forces are equal and opposite. The meteorologist, in trying to calculate the wind precisely, must allow for the distance apart of the isobars, the exact direction of the isobars, the latitude (in this case of Birmingham) and the air density. Even then there will be slight errors in the estimate, for example due to the curvature of the isobars. We can use the analogy of an athlete on a straight running track who represents the geostrophic wind. One person is trying to pull the athlete to the left (the pressure gradient) whilst another is pulling to the right (Coriolis), and these two opposing forces cancel each other out.

WEATHER ON OTHER PLANETS

Observations of the weather on other planets provide a reminder of the major influences on terrestrial weather. The things that can vary from one planet to another are the force of gravity, the density and composition of the atmosphere, the speed of rotation and the distance from the Sun. Each planet has many differences from the Earth, but often there is some aspect where a comparison is valid.

Jupiter rotates in about 10 hours, which is very quick considering its massive size. Its atmospheric cloud patterns are therefore split up into many latitudinal belts. We could compare these belts with the mid-latitude westerlies, the subtropical deserts and the tropical rain-band. Jupiter, however, also has the Great Red Spot. This is an almost permanent feature, and really too large to be compared with even our biggest depressions.

Venus is close to the Sun but has permanent total cloud cover compared with our worldwide coverage of half cover. Its atmosphere is acidic, its surface very hot, around 400 C (750 F) and there is an atmospheric pressure approaching 100 times that of the Earth. From a viewpoint on a satellite, Venus has a higher reflectivity than the Earth, with an 'albedo' or reflectance of 0.65, whereas our planetary albedo is around 0.35. In other words, more than half of the light falling on Venus is reflected, as indeed one might expect of a totally cloud-covered planet. Its high temperatures occur because it is closer to the Sun but also because the heat is trapped from escaping by a 'runaway greenhouse effect'.

Mercury has no atmosphefe so it could be considered as a happy hunting ground for a meteorologist wishing to 'get away from it all'. The lack of gases to hold the heat means that the sunny side is very hot, and that the dark side is relatively cold despite the planet's proximity to the Sun.

Mars provides the best parallels with our terrestrial climate. It is much further from the Sun and thus generally cooler, but its rotation period is very similar to ours, being just over 24 hours. Day-time equatorial temperatures can probably exceed 20 C (68 F). Also, since it does have at least a thin atmosphere the Martian nights don't cool down too much, perhaps reaching −100 C (-148 F) or so by dawn. Mars spins on its axis with a tilt of 25° from the vertical, compared with the Earth's 23.5° tilt, therefore it has seasons like ours and also has white polar ice caps superficially similar to those on the Earth. When the Martian North Pole is turned more towards the Sun (equivalent to the British summer) the ice cap shrinks from latitude 60°N back to a small remnant near the Pole. Similarly, later in the year (which lasts 687 days on Mars) the South Polar ice cap will get the benefit of the Sun's warmth and will shrink. Our Antarctic ice cap is far thicker and fortunately doesn't melt significantly in summer.

VERTICAL MOTION

We are all familiar with the horizontal flow of the wind but the vertical motions have just as dramatic an effect on the weather. Most of our cloud formations are formed by rising air. It is no coincidence that British mountains have up to six times as much rain as a sea-level site. When it rises air has to expand to equalise its pressure with the air at the higher level, and this expansion results in cooling.

Cooler air can hold less moisture than warm air. We can see this in practice when a kettle boils: a jet of hot moist air spurts out of the kettle's spout and almost immediately cools, with the moisture condensing into a visible cloud of steam. Our breath will similarly condense on cold mornings. The difference in the case of air rising in the atmosphere is that here the cooling is induced by pressure reduction. Any air containing moisture will, if forced to rise sufficiently far, form cloud − and for very moist air the smallest hill may be sufficient.

Air may rise very slowly, as in a large frontal cloud sheet where the rate of ascent may be measured in millimetres per second. At the other end of the scale the upward speed in a cumulonimbus over a tropical country may be as much as 30 m per second (60 mph). The dramatic effects are apparent from accounts by pilots of gliders or light aircraft who have been caught in such upcurrents and been lucky enough to live to tell the tale. Evidence of downdraughts only slightly less awe-inspiring comes from the gusts that often precede or accompany thunderstorms. These gusts stem from downdraughts or 'downbursts' which hit the ground and then spread out horizontally. Less dramatic are the huge areas of very gently descending air which occur above anticyclones (high pressure systems) and usually give cloudless skies unless fog or low cloud are trapped in the lowest 1000 ft (300 m) or so. The subtropical high-pressure zone is a permanent example, with descending motion or 'subsidence' the norm over many desert regions of the globe. Subsiding air always suggests clear skies.

We in Britain have many opportunities to study rising air and therefore cloud. However, very often there is a compensating downward flow not too far away. We could say that every cloud has a compensating downdraught!

UNSTABLE CONDITIONS AND LAPSE RATES

Why does it get colder as we go up a mountain? This question can only be answered by studying 'lapse rates' in the atmosphere and the rate of cooling of rising air parcels, which unfortunately makes the answer rather technical.

Inside a room, if one 'bubble' or 'parcel' of air is warmer than another, it will rise as a convection current due to its lower density. In the atmosphere much the same is true, but the parcel will not carry on rising for ever because it cools down as it moves up through the sky due to the decrease in pressure. The explanation for this cooling lies in the expansion of the parcel. The work performed in expanding is offset by a fall in temperature. In this theoretical treatment it is assumed no heat is gained or lost by the parcel as it travels up through the air – such a treatment is described as 'adiabatic'. The rate at which the bubble or parcel cools as it rises is known as the 'dry adiabatic lapse rate'. 'Dry' because we are considering an unsaturated parcel, 'adiabatic' because there is this assumption that no heat is exchanged with the surrounding air outside our bubble, and 'lapse rate' simple describes the reduction in temperature as we go upwards. The dry adiabatic lapse rate (DALR) is 10 Celsius per kilometre [3 C (5.4 F) per 1000 ft]. The difference between the atmosphere and the room is that indoors the vertical distance between the floor and the ceiling is so small that there is no significant drop in pressure as the bubble of warm air rises – this is convection at its simplest. In the atmosphere our bubble may ascend a kilometre from the Earth's surface and suffer a reduction in pressure from 1000 to 900 mbar. The work done in expanding will be offset by its temperature falling from, say, 15 C to 5 C. Suppose we were to release balloon-borne equipment outside now, and we discovered that the lapse rate in the atmosphere was greater than 10 C per kilometre – we should describe today's atmosphere as 'absolutely unstable'. In practice such conditions could not exist for any length of time without vigorous air currents rushing to restore the balance.

Thus far, we have only considered unsaturated air. When a convection current carries on rising and forms a cloud it will become saturated. Calculations must now allow for the condensation of water vapour into liquid water, which entails a latent heat calculation.

Because of the latent heat released as moisture condenses, a rising saturated parcel of air cools at a slower rate than a dry one. The saturated adiabatic lapse rate (SALR) is roughly 6 C (11 F) per kilometre, varying somewhat at different atmospheric pressures. If we release another balloon and collect a vertical profile of temperature which shows that the atmosphere on this occasion cools at less than 6 C per kilometre, then we describe that environment as 'absolutely stable'. No convection can take place even if the air is saturated.

An atmosphere where the lapse rate is between DALR and SALR is more problematical. A dry (unsaturated) parcel exists in a stable state. A saturated parcel needs only a nudge to make it rise. Such circumstances are described as 'conditionally unstable'. Unfortunately for the forecaster these difficult marginal cases are all too common!

INVERSIONS

Whenever we read about pollution, or try to understand cloud sheets or the concept of stable air, then we come up against the term 'inversion'. This is a layer of the atmosphere where it gets *warmer* as you go upwards.

A typical inversion is about 1000 ft (300 m) deep, sometimes less, and there are three basic types. First of all, the 'nocturnal inversion' forms right near the surface on a clear calm night when the ground cools down. Secondly, a 'subsidence inversion' occurs in a high-pressure area when air is descending. It may be anything from, say, 1000 to 7000 ft (300 to 2000 m) above ground. Thirdly, there is sometimes a 'frontal inversion' when warm air is moving high aloft.

And how do they affect the weather? They prevent vertical motion, so they stop pollution from escaping upwards. If there is a cloud present then it is often just a shallow layer with the inversion as the upper lid. The three inversion types can be associated with fog, stratocumulus and altostratus, respectively.

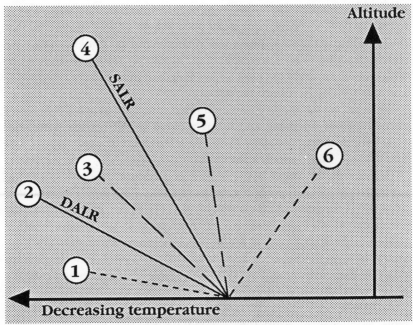

Six possible profiles of lapse rate:

(1) Absolute instability

(2) Dry Adiabatic Lapse Rate (DALR)

(3) Conditional instability

(4) Saturated Adiabatic Lapse Rate (SALR)

(5) Absolute stability (small lapse rate)

(6) Absolute stability (inversion)

When the temperature is measured with balloon-borne equipment on a sunny day the temperature will decrease quickly with altitude, roughly following lapse rates 1, 2 or 3. On a cloudy, rainy day lapse rate 4 may occur, whilst on a clear night profile 5 or 6 is likely in the lowest part of the atmosphere.

IS THE AIRMASS STABLE?

The conditions of stability and instability in the atmosphere can be roughly illustrated by drawing a comparison with everyday objects. A stable airmass can be likened to a book lying on a table – if you lift it and then let go, it will return to its original position. An unstable airmass is

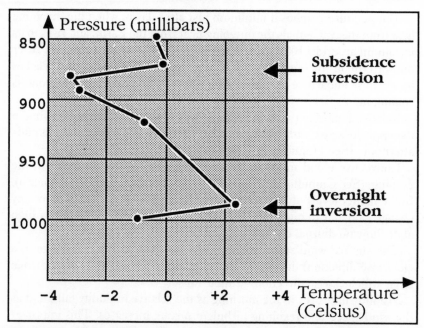

An example of changing temperature with height, as measured by balloon-borne equipment at midnight. There are two layers where it gets warmer with altitude. The first is caused by night-time cooling of the air right at the surface. The second occurs at 880 millibars (4000 feet) where warm air is descending or 'subsiding'. This type of subsidence inversion is common in anticyclones.

more like a helium-filled balloon caught in a bush – if you give it a nudge, then up it will go.

Since the stable airmass is one that tends to resist vertical changes, the airflow is very much horizontal. Any clouds which exist are spread out in huge sheets across the sky, fairly uniform from one place to another and changing little with time. Similarly, if the air is dry and cloud-free, then there may be a huge area enjoying clear, sunny weather. Stable conditions are typical of high-pressure regions. In winter, even when cloud is present, there will be too little cloud depth and insufficient vertical motion for anything more than drizzle to fall.

DAY AND NIGHT VARIATIONS

We can summarise the typical diurnal variations of temperature, humidity, wind and so on by thinking of a day with largely clear skies at an inland location.

Let us examine each parameter one at a time and look at the 'normal' response to daytime heating and nocturnal cooling.

Temperature reaches it minimum just after dawn, when the incoming heat from the Sun equals the outgoing heat from the Earth, and rises to its maximum around 1400 GMT when there is once again a balance. After mid-afternoon the outgoing radiation gains the upper hand and reaches its greatest imbalance at sunset when heat is flooding out, but none is coming in.

Relative humidity reacts in a simple way to temperature but moving in the opposite sense with highest readings at dawn and a minimum in mid-afternoon. (See Humidity in Chapter 6.)

Convective cloud forms in the morning and usually disperses in the evening. (See Cumulus and Cumulonimbus cloud sections in Chapter 6). In the higher levels of the atmosphere clouds like cirrus hardly show any change from day to night (and indeed the temperature and humidity high aloft show no diurnal changes).

The surface wind speed will typically increase and veer (change in a clockwise direction) during the morning and decrease and back (change in an anticlockwise direction) around sunset.

Visibility improves in the morning as the relative humidity falls, and as the wind speed and resulting turbulent mixing increases. This improvement is slowly reversed during the evening. (See Chapter 6.)

Barometric pressure reacts in a surprising way, rising very slightly in the morning to a peak at 1000 GMT (i.e. local 'Sun' time), falling until 1600 GMT, back up to another peak at 2200 GMT and down to a second minimum at 0400 GMT. These regular diurnal pressure changes are small in the British Isles, usually 0.2 to 0.5 mbar, and will not be detected on a household barometer. The first two turning points could be thought of as reacting to the Sun, but the whole diurnal pressure pattern is perhaps better thought of as a double-peaked variation travelling around the Earth in phase with the Sun. The movement of highs and lows usually makes these tiny diurnal changes, at least in temperate latitudes.

INSIDE A CLOUD

In the early days of meteorology it was known that rising air would cool and that its water vapour would condense into tiny droplets, and this provided an explanation for rain. During the late nineteenth and early twentieth century, however, scientists became aware that the rate of growth of droplets by condensation would be too slow to account for medium sized or large raindrops. In theory, clouds should take 20 or 30 hours to produce any rain. Collisions between tiny cloud droplets are unlikely if all the droplets are small and of a fairly uniform size, because they would all have a similar very slow fall-speed. Another mechanism had to be sought which could explain rain.

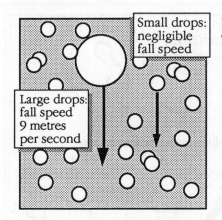

Small drops: negligible fall speed

Large drops: fall speed 9 metres per second

Once large drops have formed they will collect small drops along their path.

Then in 1933 the Bergeron theory demonstrated the role that ice crystals can play in the growth of snowflakes (which may subsequently melt to give rain at the ground). This explanation is generally satisfactory in the temperate and polar regions of the Earth. However as meteorologists began to study the tropics and the oceans in more detail the arguments opened up again. Precipitation falls from clouds whose tops do not even reach the freezing level. Such events, known as 'warm showers', are common in the tropics and over the seas and coasts of temperate latitudes. Salt particles also must play a part in the growth of precipitation, and electric charges probably 'help' droplets to collide. Once you can produce even small raindrops, then you are on your way. The rest is easy.

A typical raindrop will be 2 to 5 mm (0.08 to 0.2 in) in diameter and falls at about 9 m (30 ft) per second. At diameters greater than about 8 mm (0.3 in) the air resistance distorts the drop so much that break-up is inevitable. Once large drops have been created (perhaps held up for a time by air currents within a cloud) then smaller droplets will be gathered by collision due to differences in fall-speed. Break-up of large drops causes raindrop multiplication and heavy rain can result.

In the summer months in Britain, large raindrops are often particularly noticeable when they fall from medium level clouds on a hot afternoon. The first few drops may spread out on a path to the size of a two-penny piece. Such 'full-size' raindrops are sometimes the precursor of thundery weather. Certainly to meteorologists they are evidence of unstable conditions in the atmosphere.

AN INTRODUCTION TO AIRMASSES

For the meteorologist under training, one of the earliest items to study is the 'airmass'. This is a large body of air showing little horizontal variation

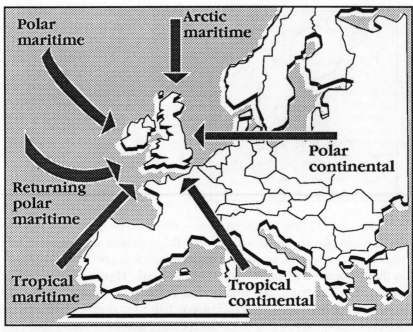

The six basic airmasses which affect the British Isles.

in temperature or humidity. It is separated from an adjacent body of air by a frontal zone.

From childhood those of us who grew up in the northern hemisphere will have had some idea of northerly winds being cold and southerly winds being warm. A small change of vocabulary will enable us to call these 'Polar' and 'Tropical' airmasses. If we also distinguish between moist and dry air, then we can add the label 'Maritime' and 'Continental' and we now have four possibilities: Tropical Continental is warm and dry; Tropical Maritime is warm and moist; Polar Continental is cold and dry; and Polar Maritime is cold and (fairly) moist. These four fundamental airstreams are responsible for most of the weather that we experience in the British Isles, though in practice we need to add one or two more, such as Arctic Maritime and Returning Polar Maritime, to make up the full set of possibilities.

Although to a certain extent the reasons for the characteristics of each airstream are self-evident, it is as well to imagine what has happened over the previous week or so. Air that has been hanging about over the Sahara in June will have grown hotter each day. As it got hotter, its relative humidity will have decreased. Probably some moisture would have been lost from the low-level air – perhaps as dew or perhaps convected away upwards. After, say, four days being heated, it spends three days *en route* for Britain. A little moisture may be added over the Mediterranean but its journey across Spain or France won't alter its properties too much. Some further slight modification will occur as it crosses the English Channel, but it will still arrive as a hot, dry airmass – a Tropical Continental. The characteristics of its source region are largely maintained and the modification that occurs will depend on the nature of the underlying surface that it crosses and on its speed of travel.

Tropical airstreams, whether Continental or Maritime, will be lighter (less dense) than Polar airmasses and will tend to rise over them. Thus the 'front' can be born. A front is a boundary between two airmasses and more specifically a boundary between a Tropical and a Polar airmass, because there must be a density contrast for a meaningful demarcation to exist.

Looking at a weather chart of the northern hemisphere we can distinguish the Polar air by its low temperature (and in practice often by its low dew point) from the Tropical air. This boundary runs all around the world at about latitude 50°N. It is called the Polar front. Some stretches are well marked; elsewhere the distinction is weak, for example in the middle of an anticyclone. But let us now consider airmasses on their own, without any fronts to complicate things. The concept of airmasses is invaluable and from a forecasting point of view, once we have learnt what a particular airmass brings in the way of weather, then we have a starting point for each forecast. We learn the conceptual model of, say, the Polar continental, then we have no need to 're-invent the wheel' when it happens again. The old saying 'every wind has its weather' sums up airmass meteorology nicely.

TROPICAL MARITIME

Tropical Maritime air usually approaches the British Isles from the southwest. It source region is the sub-tropical Atlantic Ocean, typically the Azores area, although occasionally it may have come almost directly from the Caribbean. If these sources make us think of sunshine, warmth and coconut palms then the dull, clammy, overcast, miserable weather that actually arrives on our shores is rather a disappointment. The reason for this discrepancy lies in the modification that takes place during its passage across the Atlantic. All the way, it is being cooled from below as it passes over progressively cooler ocean. Yet whilst it cools down, little of its moisture content is lost, so it reaches Lands End or western Ireland near enough saturated.

Sea fog is common in these Tropical Maritime southwesterlies. If by some lucky chance the cloud base is a couple of hundred feet up, then sea-

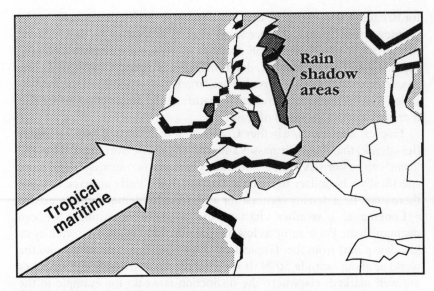

Southwesterly winds usually bring a tropical maritime airstream.

level sites will be saved from the fog, but as soon as the airmass hits rising
ground, then hill fog and drizzle will again be the order of the day.
Bodmin Moor, Dartmoor, Dyfed, western Ireland and western Scotland
can be shrouded in mild, damp conditions whether it be winter or
summer.

Further inland, in the summer half-year at least, the low stratus cloud
may be burnt off by the Sun and it could turn out to be quite warm,
though still humid. In the lee of hill or mountain ranges the 'föhn effect'
may be operating with sunshine and well-broken cloud. (The föhn effect
is described in Chapter 5.) Favoured locations like North Wales, Northumberland, the Moray Firth and Aberdeen area can bask in spring-like
weather on a January day because the mountains undo much of the
damage wrought by the three-day journey across the Atlantic, removing
some of the moisture and restoring largely cloud-free conditions. When
Colwyn Bay or Inverness is the warmest place in Britain, you can generally
reckon there is a southwesterly airstream. That no coconut palms grow in
either location is a reminder that it doesn't happen all the time!

Dew points in a Tropical Maritime airmass will be high, usually around
15 C (59 F) in summer, 9 C (48 F) in winter and the nights will be mild
and damp, and very noticeably so in mid-winter. In December and
January the overcast skies mean little variation in temperature between
day and night. Stratus and stratocumulus clouds will be of limited depth,
so drizzle is more likely than rain. The air cooled by the ocean at the
bottom of the atmosphere can be contrasted with the warmer, subsided air

out of the sub-tropical anticyclone which occurs aloft at perhaps 5000 ft (1500 m) so meteorologists would describe this as a stable profile.

Weather charts usually show that a warm front has passed through and a cold front is expected. Tropical Maritime air fills the 'wedge' between the two fronts on the southern side of a depression. This wedge is known as 'the warm sector'. In winter it is a classic synoptic situation and easily recognised as you open your door on a mild, clammy morning.

TROPICAL CONTINENTAL

Tropical Continental air comes with southeasterly or southerly airstreams. The source is France, Spain and the Mediterranean and originally the Sahara. Little wonder that it is hot and dry. In summer even easterly winds from Central Europe or the Ukraine area of the Soviet Union could be included in this category as the Continent becomes so hot at this time. Conversely, it is difficult to get a true Tropical Continental in midwinter for even France has become cold.

The air picks up some moisture over the Mediterranean or perhaps the Bay of Biscay but with the short sea-crossing of the English Channel little further moistening occurs. Dew points are therefore fairly low, often only 8 C (46 F) in summer even when the temperature reaches 25 C (77 F). Skies are typically cloudless and just a shade 'milky' with pollutants. Moisture from the Mediterranean, or originally from the sub-tropical Atlantic, may have found its way to medium levels in the atmosphere. Altocumulus castellanus clouds can develop like high-level turrets, showing their convective nature. Sometimes these castellanus clouds are the forerunners of a tremendous thunderstorm which can occur by day or night. When the latter is the case they are a memorable event and meteorologically difficult to explain. Strictly speaking, an airmass cooled from below on its northward journey should be stable. However, convection takes place from medium levels and is not triggered directly by surface heating; such events are always a risk with a deep southerly airstream (for reasons connected with convergence and the changes in stability of different layers). However, the majority of Tropical Continental airstreams do give a marvellous heatwave. The old weather saying 'three hot days, then a thunderstorm' to describe a typical British summer is not far wide of the mark, for often the heat-wave will end in this manner. More recently an adapted version has been suggested which is 'three hot days, then a water shortage'.

Spain and France will have provided a little pollution but not too much because their industrialised areas are widely scattered, and whilst there may also be desert dust and fine soil particles, these will often be spread through a considerable depth. So, these factors, coupled with a lack of moisture, mean that the visibility will be moderate to good and often described as a 'slight heat-haze'. The heat does not cause the haze, they are simply two separate characteristics of the same airstream.

Stretches of coast with a long sea-track, such as the Aberdeen area, may be shrouded in fog or low cloud but the majority of the country will be basking in sunshine. The summers of 1976 and 1990 brought several surges of Tropical Continental air.

POLAR CONTINENTAL

A Polar Continental airmass is one which originates in Scandinavia or Russia. It reaches us when northeasterly or easterly winds become established and therefore comes when there is a high-pressure area somewhere to the north of Britain, often over Scandinavia itself. Polar Continental airmasses are mainly a feature of the winter half-year when an easterly from Poland or even a southeasterly from Germany or Switzerland can be included in this category. Note that there is an overlap here with the Tropical Continental airstream since Central Europe is cold in winter and provides a 'Polar' airmass which in July we might term 'Tropical' – labels are never perfect.

Temperatures in Polar Continental are below average except perhaps in the lee of mountains which may shelter the Porthmadog to Aberystwyth coast of Wales, along with northwest England and western Scotland. Clouds are generally well broken in most areas of the country. Dew points are low, often below freezing, in this Continental airstream, especially when it has come by the Calais to Dover 'short sea-track' route.   Air that has crossed from Denmark to Scotland provides a 'long sea-track' version and is cloudy, cold and raw – showers of drizzle, snow or snow grains are possible near the east coast of Scotland.

Visibilities vary, generally being very good when the air comes from Scandinavia but moderate or poor when the air originates in the polluted region of central or eastern Europe.

Even in April or May the North Sea is still depressingly cold and does little to modify the airmass, apart from adding a little unwelcome moisture. Holiday-makers should avoid the east coast in a spring-time Polar Continental.

Perhaps the classic example of a gale-force Polar Continental airstream was that of 10 – 16 January 1987. The winds from the east-northeast were ferociously strong and bitterly cold, permeating houses and garages and causing frozen pipes. The airstream was so cold that even the North Sea was sufficiently warm by comparison to start off vigorous convection.

Those places such as Kent and East Anglia which had onshore winds endured snow and severe drifting. Along the south coast any promontory that stuck out into the easterly blast caught its effect. On the Isle of Wight, Torbay, the Lizard and even the Isles of Scilly, palm trees and sub-tropical shrubs were killed or severely damaged. Further north the anticyclone was nearer at hand and the wind less strong.

It is the south which is particularly chilled by Polar Continental airstreams; the north has more problems in northerly airstreams.

POLAR MARITIME

The usual westerly Polar Maritime airstream has originated in Canada or Greenland, then swung around in a great arc behind a depression, thus being warmed and moistened somewhat by the sea surface. This is our commonest airstream – coolish, especially in summer; fairly moist, but because of its polar origin not able to carry too much moisture; clean, because there are no pollution sources upwind; and unstable (in meteoro-logical parlance), because the air started off cold and has been heated from below.

Cumulus clouds, cumulonimbus clouds and showers are the order of the day. In winter the Atlantic starts most of the convection and the showers will batter the coasts by day and night, spreading inland if the winds are strong. The Scottish and Welsh mountains will shelter the eastern side of Britain, though with a northwesterly wind some showers will get through the Cheshire Gap to reach Birmingham and perhaps London. With a westerly, the winter showers can cross Glasgow and central Scotland to reach Edinburgh and Fife; others converge in the Bristol Channel and hit Cardiff and Avon; Lancashire and Cumbria get little protection from the scattered hills of Ireland. Even Dublin, though east-facing, can be reached by these westerly showers.

In spring and summer, convective clouds will tend to be set off by day-time heating inland. Now the shelter of the western mountains is less important, and showers or short-lived thunderstorms can occur almost anywhere. Indeed, since the highest temperatures will often occur in the east, the highest risk of a vigorous cumulonimbus is there.

Since the air is clean, visibility is very good and the blue of the sky will be deep with conditions generally good for photography – though often changing quickly. Rainbows are perhaps at their most likely late on a spring afternoon with a Polar Maritime airstream, just as a shower moves away eastwards.

ARCTIC MARITIME

When a low has crossed eastwards over Britain, wind will swing round clockwise (i.e. veer) to a northerly point and true Arctic air may reach us. Dew points will be low, well below freezing in winter and only just above in summer. Snow showers will hit all exposed north-facing coasts in Ireland and Scotland in any winter or spring month. If the wind gets round to due north, the showers sweep down the east coast as far as Norfolk. Norwich may have snow showers which can even be accompanied by thunder.

The Highlands of Scotland will usually take the brunt of a 'screaming northerly' with blizzards in winter and spring. Glasgow and Dundee are well sheltered with an Arctic airstream but the Scots will notice the low humidities which it brings.

Those who are pedantic about their meteorology will say that Polar air is separated from the very cold Arctic air by the 'Arctic front'. Elsewhere on the Earth this is undoubtedly true, for example near Japan where there is a huge north–south temperature contrast. Around the British Isles the evidence is weaker and it is usually a trough or line of showers that heralds the arrival of the true Arctic air.

RETURNING POLAR MARITIME

The expression *Returning* Polar Maritime indicates air which has originated in the polar regions, then travelled well south but is now (because of the pressure patterns) returning northwards.

The classic Returning Polar Maritime airstream comes when a large depression is situated somewhere to the northwest of the British Isles. Once the warm and cold fronts have passed through, then we are in a Polar Maritime airstream of some sort. If the winds are still from between south and southwest we should call this a Returning Polar Maritime. The air was originally cold but with a long sea-track across the Atlantic the lower layers have become warmer, moister and more unstable. Almost any mixture of weather is possible now, especially on exposed coasts and hills. With the high moisture content, stratus clouds and hill fog can occur; with the instability, cumulonimbus cloud and showers can occur; with the inherently polar air aloft the showers can include hail and thunder. Even inland this same awkward cocktail can plague forecasters. The stratus that has lifted and dispersed may re-form in a heavy shower, and the extra heating inland in the summer half-year keeps them guessing. What effects will surface heating have on this particular Returning Polar Maritime? No two airmasses are ever quite the same. When things go wrong for the short-period 'airfield' forecaster, it is quite often this airmass that is to blame. Southwest England and Wales will have the first taste of a Returning Polar Maritime and such airstreams are especially notable in autumn, since the air can hold plenty of moisture and the sea is still warm enough to start convection.

Further north and east, with some shelter from the mountains, conditions tend to be better and east coast areas may well be quite warm with only broken convective clouds. East Anglia and Kent will be closer to the high pressure that usually exists over Europe and may come off best. Night-time in the sheltered east and northeast should be clear, dry and pleasant.

Dew points are quite high, especially near southern coasts, but despite the moisture, visibility will usually be good due to the cleanliness of the air. Only if winds become very light can inland fog form where evening showers have moistened the ground.

People in the southwest may regard this as the *bête noire* of airstreams, combining as it does some of the worst features of Polar and Tropical Maritimes.

WARM FRONTS

A front is defined as a boundary between two airmasses, and a warm front is such a boundary where the warm air is advancing. Because the warm airmass will be either Tropical Continental or, more likely, Tropical Maritime, it is usually moving northeastwards (in the northern hemisphere). This then will enable us to picture the typical warm front, associated as it is with an active temperate latitude depression.

Ahead of the front is old polar air of some description – certainly cold, probably reasonably dry with a correspondingly low dew point. Then comes the warm, moist Tropical Maritime airstream with its high dew point. The tropical air is warm and therefore of low density, so it rides up over the Polar Maritime. The frontal zone or mixing zone is therefore a sloping affair with the Tropical Maritime being forced upwards along an inclined plane at a slope of about 1 in 150 (though diagrams inevitably look steeper).

Along this frontal mixing zone are found the traditional warm-front clouds: cirrus, cirrostratus, altostratus and nimbostratus – each lower in altitude than its predecessor. As the clouds get lower, so they tend to get thicker and richer in moisture.

Note that the warm front itself is drawn on the weather chart where the frontal boundary meets the surface of the Earth. If we imagine the sloping front with one end touching the ground and the other end raised, then we

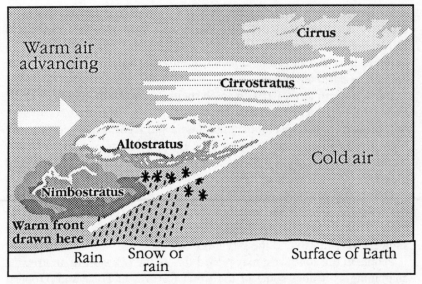

A warm front can often be recognised by the high clouds which precede it. The cloud-sheet progressively lowers and then snow or rain commences.

The true slope of the front is about 1 in 150, with the cirrostratus cloud perhaps 4 miles above the ground and up to 600 miles ahead of the surface position of the warm front.

get some idea of the vertical layout. A balloon released below the raised end will ascend through the frontal cloud, maybe cirrus or cirrostratus at 20,000 ft (6000 m).

Amateur forecasters can update their ideas as the warm front progresses and amend the professional predictions in the light of their own observations. An active warm front shows itself by the fairly steady progression of thickening and lowering cloud with few breaks, by the falling barometer and the wind from a southerly point. After two to three hours of rain the barometer will steady, the wind will veer slightly and the rain turn to drizzle – this is the passage of the warm front, to be followed by the warm-sector conditions of the Tropical Maritime airstream.

COLD FRONTS

The cold front is a boundary between two airmasses where the cold air is advancing. Because cold air is heavier or denser than the warm air which precedes it, the polar air undercuts the tropical air and a sloping boundary is formed. In contrast to the warm front, the cold front slopes backwards from its surface position.

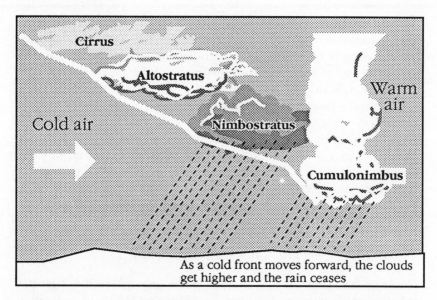

Cirrus

Altostratus

Warm
air

Cold air

Nimbostratus

Cumulonimbus

As a cold front moves forward, the clouds
get higher and the rain ceases

A cold front can often be recognised after it has passed through. This illustration shows the 'classic' type of cold front, but sometimes a shallower more 'drizzly' type occurs. The cold front is drawn on a chart where the warm air reaches the ground, roughly beneath the cumulonimbus cloud in this diagram.

Instead of a vertical boundary between warm air and cold air, the arrangement is more like a wedge with a slope of about 1 in 60. If we imagine pushing a broom along the ground we get some idea of the layout. First of all, there is little warning of its impending arrival, though a couple of subtle hints may occur: a brief unexpected break in the overcast stratocumulus of the Tropical Maritime sky (known to pilots as 'sucker's gap'), a slight fall in a previously steady barometer or a slight backing of the wind. Then the front arrives with a heavy burst of rain from a small but vigorous cumulonimbus cloud, embedded within the general frontal cloud. As the cold front passes the wind veers and usually increases, the barometer 'kicks' upwards and the stratus clears, at least partially. Rain may continue, accompanied by a pall of medium-level nimbostratus and some patches of low 'stratus fractus' cloud. Soon a bright clearance is visible on the northwestern horizon, which makes a bold reminder of the passage of a classic cold front when it occurs towards sunset. The bright, clear air advances, though perhaps not without one last burst of rain. Finally, the true Polar Maritime air arrives with its patchy sunshine, cumulus clouds, lower dew point, rising barometer and veering wind. Not every front follows the classic pattern. We now recognise 'split fronts' where the final clearance is from low drizzly cloud to broken skies. Just as the warm front (leaning forwards) gives so many signs of its approach, so the cold front (inclined backwards) gives so many indications that it has already passed through. This may be of less use to the amateur forecaster but it does serve to confirm the synoptic situation and he or she can now predict the typical Polar Maritime conditions – brighter, showery weather – with a certain amount of confidence.

The expressions used on radio and television to describe the contrast between the Tropical Maritime air ahead of the cold front and the Polar Maritime air behind it are legion. The tropical air is mild, humid, cloudy, damp, in summer-time even sultry. The polar air is clearer, brighter, fresher, cooler, more invigorating, showery or blustery. The visibility improves as the humidity drops; the wind may be considerably stronger but if the transition occurs by day, then at least the Sun should come out.

THE WARM CONVEYOR BELT

Conveyor belts carry things around. In the atmosphere it is heat and moisture which are carried along on faster-moving ribbons of air acting as conveyor belts. One of the concepts which became accepted during the 1970s and 1980s was that of conveyor belts associated with frontal systems. The warm conveyor belt is a southerly or southwesterly stream of air which runs along just ahead of a *cold* front bringing the moisture which feeds the frontal rain. It rises as it tracks northwards from perhaps 3000 ft (900 m) to 18,000 ft (5500 m) or more. Best of all, from the point of view of acceptability, you can sometimes see on a satellite picture the narrow cloud band which represents this airflow.

COLD FRONT WAVES AND WARM FRONT WAVES

Every now and then a 'cold front wave' makes the forecaster's job a nightmare. Four times out of five, a cold front will pass through fairly steadily at, say, 20 mph (30 kph) and the airmass transition from Tropical Maritime to Polar Maritime will be made in a straightforward manner. (It may even follow the text-book tradition in every respect!) The forecaster's job is simple and he or she 'tells' the weather with an easy confidence.

But there is one potential hazard – the cold-front wave. What this does to your forecast sometimes seems plainly unjust. Instead of clearing away as usual, the cold front seems to hang back and take a final swipe at its human foe. A final ripple or wave runs (typically northeastwards) up the front towards the main centre of low pressure.

Imagine a rope held stretched between two people. The more south-westerly of the two gives an upward flick and an undulation or wave runs

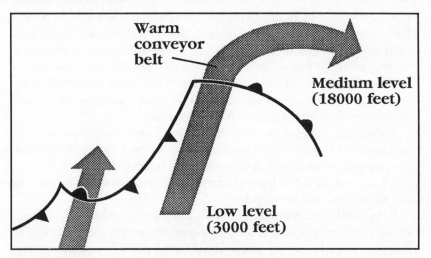

A typical 'warm conveyor belt' blows northeastwards just ahead of a cold front, and rises from low levels to medium levels as it does so. A further warm conveyor belt is depicted here to the west.

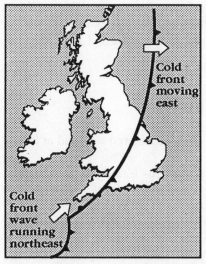

A forecaster in Birmingham might expect the weather to clear up quite quickly, but the cold front wave will delay the clearance.

along the rope towards the northeastern person, who represents the primary depression; so a cold front wave or secondary low runs along the front. The clearer Polar Maritime air will arrive eventually, but only later when the wave has moved out of the way.

So if we have been affected by this delayed clearance where were the warning clues? Probably they were three-fold. First, the surface chart would perhaps have shown only a small and *decreasing* flow of wind across the front, and remember, it is the winds that blow the cold air forwards.

For a forecaster in Birmingham the key observations would have been from southwest Ireland and Cornwall where the pressure would have been steady instead of rising, and the winds southwesterly instead of veering westerly. The surge of advancing cold air just wasn't available.

Secondly, an earlier satellite picture perhaps might have indicated a suspicious bulge in the elongated band of cloud that made up the cold front somewhere to the west of the Bay of Biscay.

Third, radar rainfall displays might have shown an extra westermost rain band, with radar echoes running northeastwards rather than making the eastward progress which they had a few hours before.

All of these are subtle hints of course, but in retrospect . . . but then we can all forecast well with hindsight.

If the development of a cold front wave is pronounced and a new centre of low pressure is expected, then the super-computers will probably pick it up, but often the wave is poorly developed – possibly little more than a ripple – and only a temporary feature. This is another example of the difficulty in predicting 'mesoscale' phenomena more than a few hours ahead.

Warm front waves can also occur. They run east-southeastwards with the upper winds, away from the primary depression. They are less common than the cold front perturbations, but just as difficult for the forecaster. In winter they can bring thickening skies and snow ahead of the main belt of precipitation.

OCCLUDED FRONTS

An occluded front, or 'occlusion', is often considered as a kind of hybrid between a warm and cold front.

If we look at the normal sequence of events leading to its formation, then this seems reasonable. The parent low, when it first forms, is referred to as a wave depression because its warm and cold fronts form a shallow wave shape. However, the cold front swings rapidly southeastwards then eastwards around the low and catches up the warm front, which is considerably held back by friction. As the cold front catches up with the warm front, the warm Tropical Maritime air is undercut and lifted off the ground. Now we have a complex structure with three airmasses involved.

Some meteorologists differentiate between 'cold occlusions' where the final westerly Polar Maritime brings really cold air, and a 'warm occlusion' where the easternmost Returning Polar Maritime airstream is the coldest. In either case the observer on the ground will not notice much change in dew point as the occluded front passes through because all the warm tropical air has been lifted aloft.

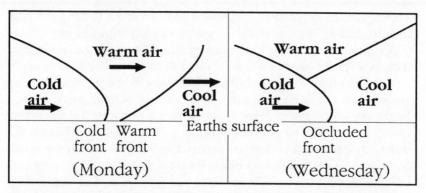

The classic method of occluded front formation. On Monday the cold front is catching up with the warm front. By Wednesday it has done so, and the warm air has been undercut and lifted aloft. The resulting single band of cloud and rain is known as an occluded front or 'occlusion'.

Watching the sky, the classic occlusion looks like a warm front as it approaches, with thickening cloud and increasing rain intensity. As it moves away eastwards or northeastwards, the sky may look much as it does during a cold front clearance with a fairly sudden rear edge to the departing cloud mass and a return to broken cumulus cloud.

Unfortunately, this wonderful theory is blown apart by a feature known as an 'instant occlusion'. Meteorologists can analyse a chart of the Atlantic and find an ill-defined trough to the north of a depression. A few hours later a satellite picture will show a well-developed band of cloud and rain much resembling an occluded front, but without the history of warm and cold fronts to explain it. Complex theories can partially unravel such features and their formation is likened to that of 'comma clouds', also seen by satellites. But there is a lot we don't yet know about occluded fronts.

POLAR LOWS AND COMMA CLOUDS

Mesoscale weather phenomena are intermediate in size between a cumulus cloud and a depression.

When we think about a weather chart, we tend to concentrate on highs and lows. Even a medium-sized low is 800 km (500 miles) across, and highs are bigger still. These are called 'synoptic' features. They have a lifetime of perhaps two to five days and may affect an area for a day or so. But what of smaller features?

We are all familiar with showers, a few kilometres across and lasting for quarter of an hour. A shower could be considered as a 'small mesoscale event'. There is, however, a big gap in the size-spectrum between the shower and the depression, and we are now in a much better position to understand the 'large mesoscale' features which occupy this gap.

A classic example of a wintertime mesoscale event is the 'polar low'. This is a small low-pressure area, say 100 m (60 miles) across, which comes down from the north bringing blizzard conditions. Polar lows are embedded in northerly airstreams. Brief warning of their arrival is given by the sky – perhaps an hour or two of falling pressure and thickening cloud – so satellite pictures are a big help in forecasting. Then, in the worst cases, a three-hour blizzard occurs. Coastal areas are often worst hit because the polar low derives its energy from the difference in temperature between the moderately warm sea and the very cold air above. As it moves inland, tracking southwards or southeastwards, it tends to weaken and the low 'fills' (i.e. gradually disappears).

The Northern Isles are particularly prone to polar lows. On 7 February 1969 a ferocious blizzard brought visibility below 20 m (66 ft) in Shetland and a gust of 136 mph (217 kph) to Orkney.

Another mesoscale feature is the 'comma cloud' (named after its shape on satellite pictures) which can affect part of Britain when a showery, westerly airstream covers the country. Not dissimilar to a polar low in its formation, it brings perhaps a two-hour spell of rain but is generally less violent than its northerly counterpart. An expression often used in forecasts is 'showers, some prolonged, perhaps merging into longer spells of rain' to describe this unstable type of westerly regime.

Satellite pictures and radar rainfall displays are vital in the location and tracking of mesoscale features – indeed these were largely the methods by which they were discovered and analysed.

Mesoscale phenomena are difficult for television forecasters to deal with. They are rather small to show on weather charts, they change character quickly and their life cycle is measured in just hours. This relationship between size and longevity runs throughout meteorology from a raindrop to an anticyclone. Small features do not last for long.

LIFE CYCLE OF A DEPRESSION

'Depressions' or 'lows' are important features of our weather and all too common, some might say, for they tend to bring rain and strong winds. Like meteorologists they have a life cycle: they are born, then develop, grow old and fizzle out. The description which follows is of a temperate latitude depression in the northern hemisphere, but a similar process can take place in southern latitudes, for example near the Falkland Islands or Tasmania.

A depression will tend to form where there is a large temperature

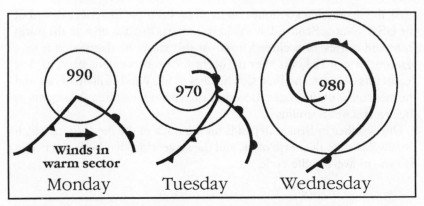

The life cycle of a low pressure system which forms as a deepening open wave depression on Monday, starts to occlude on Tuesday and fills on Wednesday.

contrast across an area, usually with warm air to the south or southeast and cold air to the north or northwest. This can happen almost anywhere between latitudes 35°N and 60°N but is perhaps most likely where the underlying surface tends to enhance the temperature contrast, so the area off eastern USA where the continuation of the Gulf Stream flows northwards is a notable formation region. In winter the cold surface of North America provides a huge temperature contrast with this warm ocean water.

Cold air starts pushing southwards and warm air pushes northwards and this creates a vortex spinning in a cyclonic sense (i.e. anticlockwise in the northern hemisphere).

It is difficult to understand why the depression forms just here but the flow of the jet stream in the upper atmosphere must be correctly placed to induce vorticity or 'spin'. And it is difficult to understand why the atmospheric pressure *falls* but the low-level convergence of the air is exceeded by the high-level divergence: more air is taken out of the system at high altitudes than flows in near the surface, so there is a reduction in 'column mass' and a fall of pressure at the surface.

The rotation of the Earth dictates that most synoptic features of middle latitudes will move roughly eastwards. So now we have our depression, deepening and moving east. The boundaries between the advancing warm air ahead of the low (the warm front) and the advancing cold air behind the low (the cold front) are where much of the rain occurs. These airmass movements gradually change the character of the depression, which deepens and will often later turn east-northeast. The central pressure which was only, say, 990 mbar in the early stages may be down to 970 mbar; the winds around it have increased from Force 6 to Force 8 over the North Atlantic.

As the depression continues on its route from the eastern seaboard of the USA towards Scotland, the cold front starts to catch up with the warm front and causes an occluded front. At this stage the depression is very vigorous. About 18 hours after the occlusion process commences, the low reaches its deepest, and then slowly starts to fill. Winds will moderate and the movement of the system becomes sluggish. Quite often this occurs as the low reaches Scandinavia.

Our weather in Britain depends on the track of the depression, which usually passes to the north of us, and the stage which has been reached in its two- to five-day life cycle.

FAMILIES OF DEPRESSIONS

We shouldn't think of depressions as being one-off events because there is often a sequence or 'family' of lows. Although a typical temperate latitude depression has a life cycle of about five days, there are many variations on the theme. Sometimes a secondary depression will form on the cold front and last only a few hours. On other occasions a huge system will slow down between Iceland and Scotland and survive for a week before it finally fills and can no longer be located on our weather charts of plotted observations.

A common sequence of events when the jet stream around the northern hemisphere becomes vigorous is for a family of depressions to cross the Atlantic one after another. Depending on their size and speed, they may come racing across at 24-hour intervals. If we are lucky the rain may occur at night and the days can bring reasonable weather as transient ridges cross the country. Sometimes with really deep lows, our weather chart looks more like a dartboard than a weather map. Once the first depression has crossed Scotland, taking the gales away towards Scandinavia, another approaches – commonly taking a slightly more southerly track.

The strongs winds will normally be some sort of westerly, as a depression crosses Britain, and places where the gale can blow straight in from the sea catch the worst of it. Shetland, the Hebrides and western Scotland are near to the main highway, the M1 of depression tracks. Western Ireland, Wales and Cornwall are vulnerable to a low that keeps well south and is still at the vigorous stage.

Quite often after a family of four or five depressions bringing stormy conditions, a large ridge will build which heralds the start of a settled spell. If it develops into a near-stationary high then the mobile westerly spell is at an end and a blocked spell is coming. Computers can often predict this change from mobile to blocked type; the slow but prolonged rise of the barometer confirms the prognosis.

The deepest depressions occur in the winter half-year and a centre of 916 mbar was recorded in December 1986 just south of Iceland. In 1984, two successive deep lows crossed the area to the south of Iceland on 10 and 13 January. However, active depressions can also occur in July and August as the summers of the middle 1980s remind us.

ANTICYCLONES

An anticyclone or high is looked upon (in Britain) as being a good feature of the weather chart, and this is broadly true because it brings dry conditions. At a superficial level, we can consider the chart as a battle-ground between the 'good' anticyclones, which are large but slow-moving, and the 'bad' depressions which skirt around them, trying to force them away eastwards. Farmers, of course, like an occasional depression rather than a summer drought, so the concept of good weather is not a universal one.

How high does the pressure need to be for us to call it an anticyclone? There is no precise answer to this question but there will rarely be a centre of less than 1016 mbar on the charts. Traditionally we draw isobars at 4 mbar intervals and a typical well-developed high has a 'closed' (i.e. roughly circular or elliptical) isobar of 1028 and a central pressure of 1030 mbar. Summer anticyclones tend to be over the relatively cool ocean areas or perhaps the North Sea. In the winter they are more likely to form over the cool Continent and specially over the vast land area of the Soviet Union. The 'Azores High' is a semi-permanent feature and often a ridge or extension from this area of the Atlantic will build sufficiently to bring us a summer dry spell. Conversely, the European or Siberian high, if it develops westwards in winter, will bring cold easterly winds. These slow-moving systems can be contrasted with the mobile anticyclones that occur temporarily between our travelling depressions. A large ridge will bring similar weather to an anticyclone.

A high brings dry weather in summer because the air within it tends to be converging at very high levels in the troposphere and gently descending over the general area of high pressure. This subsiding air holds little moisture and is warmed (by compression) as it descends. Unfortunately, in winter the warm subsiding air is often prevented from quite reaching the ground by a cold surface layer. It may be frosty and foggy in the bottom 300 m (1000 ft) even when there is warm dry air above, perhaps making mountain tops for once warmer and sunnier than low ground.

Explanations which simply say that cold air is dense and this creates high pressure are grossly over-simplifying a complex subject.

The dominant physical process in a summer anticyclone is the incoming heat from the Sun, which the clear skies allow; the dominant process in winter is the outgoing heat from the Earth, again because of clear skies, hence the frost and sometimes fog. Perhaps in winter the 'good' weather really does come with depressions, which can at least bring in mild air from the Atlantic.

THE POLAR FRONT JET STREAM

The polar front jet stream could arguably be called the most important fast-flowing 'river of air' in the world's atmosphere. The jet streams are often said to have been discovered during the Second World War as aircraft sought to fly at greater altitudes. Certainly British meteorologists and aviators played a part, and the Americans supplied the name 'jet stream'. Actually though, the strong winds aloft had long been suspected by watchers of cirrus clouds moving rapidly across the sky, but the height of such cloud was still in some doubt. We use an arbitrary lower limit of 60 knots (110 kph or 70 mph) to define a jet stream. and they can blow at three or four times that speed.

It is now known that the polar front jet stream in the northern hemisphere circles the Earth, albeit in a somewhat discontinuous manner, usually lying between 40°N and 70°N. It is broadly westerly, though this does not preclude meanderings (known as Rossby waves), which provide sections of southerlies and northerlies, and very rarely a short easterly stretch. The jet tends to be strongest in winter.

The cause of this jet (and others) is a temperature contrast. Southern Europe is relatively warm and the pressure at a height of 30,000 ft (10,000 m) is 300 mbar. If you ascend to the same height in the colder, denser air over northern Britain, then the pressure is perhaps 280 mbar. Thus a pressure difference exists, and therefore the wind blows. Just as at the Earth's surface the southerly wind which is suggested by the pressure gradient force is deflected to the right by the Earth's rotation and becomes a westerly, so the same rule applies at high altitude.

Aircraft flying from New York to London will generally benefit from strong tail winds. Going back the other way the pilot will expect headwinds. The true headwind component will vary enormously from day to day and week to week. Even if a very powerful jet stream persists for several days, a small change in aircraft track or altitude can reduce the loss of time and the extra fuel involved.

Because temperature contrasts are the cause, it should come as no

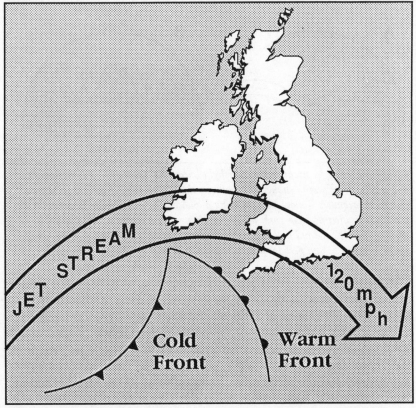

A jet stream may blow at 120 mph but the weather system beneath it will usually move much more slowly, typically at one third of its speed. This diagram shows the typical relationship of the jet stream to a frontal system.

surprise to find that the jet streams blow at their strongest roughly parallel to active weather fronts.

ROSSBY WAVES

Scientists have given the name 'Rossby waves' to the meanderings of the polar front jet stream, after the man who first explained them. Just as a river tends to meander, so does the mid-latitude jet stream. The immediate character of British weather is largely determined by the position and strength of the jet on any particular day. A strong jet stream usually means mobile 'zonal' west-to-east movement of the weather systems, with depressions rushing across the Atlantic. A weak jet stream implies a more slow-moving or blocked 'meridional' type of weather, where northerlies or southerlies predominate (although these are also easterly spells too).

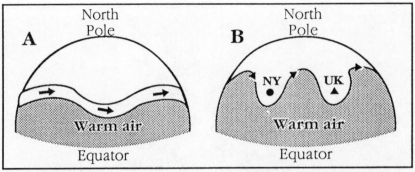

A persistent strong jet stream with only slight 'meanders' (as shown in Diagram A) will usually bring a mild changeable winter to the British Isles. A weaker jet stream with large meanders is more likely to bring a cold winter. In Diagram B, an outbreak of cold air is affecting New York, whilst simultaneously a separate 'cold plunge' is affecting the UK. Iceland will be experiencing mild weather with this distribution of the Rossby Waves, and perhaps five such waves will exist around the North Pole.

In the middle part of this century weather systems were predominantly of the mobile type, with strong westerly jet streams, and so they were during the mild winters of 1988/89 and 1989/90.

The Rossby wave pattern of the northern hemisphere is vital to our weather and our climate. It varies from week to week and perhaps from century to century. It is caused by the rotation of the Earth (which does not change) and the temperature contrast between the Equator and the North Pole (which may change, either naturally or due to human activity). The pattern can explain why New York often has a winter cold snap at the same time as Britain. New York is in one southward meander of the cold air, whilst we are in another.

BLOCKING PATTERNS

Why was February 1986 cold whereas February 1988 was mild? The answer lies in the difference between blocked and mobile weather patterns.

The mobile spell of weather is one where westerlies predominate. Depressions, or families of them, move eastwards across the Atlantic and perhaps across the British Isles, or else they narrowly miss us to the north, and the main polar front jet stream, also a westerly, lies somewhere near at hand. In winter this mobile type of weather will be unsettled, but at least it will be mild since it brings air from the Atlantic – whether Tropical Maritime or Polar Maritime. February 1988 was mainly of this type, and notably mild.

In summer, a mobile spell will bring disappointing changeable weather, but with frequent rain for the farmers. The summers of 1984 to 1988 were of this type. Warm spells in summer are usually associated with stagnant anticyclones or southeasterly Tropical Continental airstreams.

A blocked regime, on the other hand, is one in which the depressions are slow-moving, and at least one major anticyclone will be not too far away. In winter, this tends to bring calm conditions and therefore cold weather. The weak incoming heat from the Sun by day is exceeded by the outgoing heat at night and the British Isles therefore cool down. Contrast this with a westerly airstream which continually brings mild air in from the semi-perpetual source of the Atlantic.

Meteorologists define three technical types of blocking pattern: the 'diffluent block', where the jet stream is split with one weak branch far to the north and another branch far to the south; the 'meridional block' where the huge meanders of the jet stream are of just such a size that they do not destroy themselves but happily maintain their existing positions; and the 'omega block', where there is one exaggerated meander to the north.

And how long does a blocked pattern last? That, unfortunately, is a very difficult question. We wouldn't call it a block unless it lasted at least a couple of days, and there seems to be no upper limit to the length of time for which a blocked regime can persist. The cold winter of 1963 and the hot summer of 1976 were examples of long-lasting blocked patterns, though both cases did have some brief interruptions. Thus the answer to the question of duration is somewhere between two days and perhaps two months.

The timing of the breakdown of a blocked weather pattern is important, since the weather we experience will then often undergo a major shift. Computers usually, but not always, get it right. Obviously forecasters watch the weather charts of the upper atmosphere which show the meandering of the jet streams with great interest. We must study the whole of the northern hemisphere because the changes in the upper winds now taking place over Japan and the Pacific will affect North America and then ourselves within a very few days.

WARM AND COLD ADVECTION

Southerly winds will normally blow warm air towards the British Isles and meteorologists describe this as 'warm advection'. Similarly, northerlies usually bring 'cold advection'. The word 'advection' comes from the Latin for 'blowing towards' and can also occasionally be used to describe the movement of moisture.

Looking upwards at the sky we can quite often see different cloud types moving in different directions. There is an interesting relationship between the winds at low levels and the winds high above. If the winds veer (i.e. change in a clockwise sense) with increasing altitude, then warm advection is occurring. If the winds back (i.e. change in an anticlockwise sense) with height, then cold air is being advected. This rule for the northern hemisphere is consistent and scientifically valid but not easy to explain.

Winds near the surface are determined by the pressure gradient, and Buys Ballot's Law states that if you stand with your back to the wind in the northern hemisphere, then the low pressure is on your left. In just the same way if you could stand on top of a 30,000 ft (10,000 m) mast with your back to the jet stream, you would find the cold, dense air on your left. Ahead of a warm front, the low-level winds are southwesterly and the winds aloft veer with height through a layer up to, say, 300 mbar (around 30,000 ft) where a strong northwesterly jet stream is blowing. We can even think of the low-level southwesterly winds as blowing the jet stream slowly sideways. This is what advection is all about. The air is gradually warming up through this deep layer of atmosphere, perhaps by 3 C in a 12-hour period. Obviously the whole layer will not warm up at a uniform rate and the most rapid warm advection ahead of an approaching warm front will occur first at high altitudes and then at lower altitudes as the front gets near. Indeed, the cloud will lower in the same progressive manner. Outdoors in the summer we can use the different motion of clouds at different levels to tell us something about the weather to come. Winds veering with height suggest perhaps an approaching warm front, whereas those backing with height suggest that a cold front has already passed through and cooler, showery air may soon be on its way.

And what if the winds are constant in direction with increasing altitude? Well, there isn't always an easy answer but probably not too much is changing.

Incidentally, these rules cannot be used with low stratus cloud. This occurs in the boundary layer where the wind direction is affected by friction. Our antipodean colleagues have a completely reversed set of rules: a British meteorologist would find it much easier to adjust to western Canada than to New Zealand.

CONVERGENCE AND DIVERGENCE

Rising air is the cause of clouds and rain, so any mechanism which can force the air upwards must be of interest. Convergence is one such mechanism.

If a sea breeze is blowing into Cornwall from the north, and another

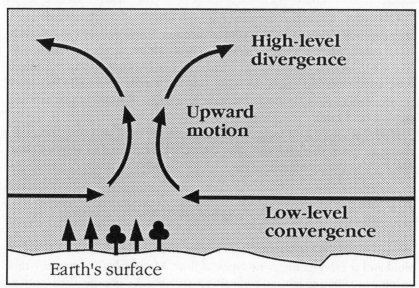

When the air is converging at low levels in the atmosphere then it is forced to rise, and must almost inevitably be diverging high aloft (above say 18,000 feet). We can think of the tropopause as forming a lid on the whole system and on all our clouds and weather (at about 36,000 feet).

sea-breeze is blowing into Cornwall from the south, the two airstreams will meet. Where does the air go? Upwards will usually be the answer. However, the convergence mechanism is not just a small-scale feature, it can also occur over a huge area, for example in a developing depression.

Imagine an exact cube of plasticine or soft clay lying on the floor (which represents the Earth's surface). If you squash the clay inwards from the four vertical sides, then it gets taller – this is analogous to convergence and upward motion in the atmosphere. If we start with another cube of clay and pull outwards in all directions, then the height will decrease which represents divergence and downward motion in the atmosphere. This latter process takes place in an anticyclone. Gently sinking air occurs over the middle of the high and air flows slightly outward around the edges.

So far we have not mentioned an upper limit to the rising of converged air, but if you imagine the tropopause acting like a glass lid at the top of the atmosphere, you can see that air converging at low levels will rush upwards, hit the lid and then spread out. So, low level convergence causes rising air and results in divergence high aloft.

This is the process going on when a depression is deepening rapidly, and the rising air produces a huge region of cloud and rain. Most of the convergence is happening below 500 mbar [18,000 ft (5500 m)] and most of the divergence is happening above that height.

Of course in practice the winds are not usually blowing inwards from four cardinal points towards a central location. Convergence can be much more subtle when a westerly airstream is blowing towards an obstruction like the Pennines. Similarly, the wind could be blowing into an imaginary cube at 30 mph and out of the other side at 29 mph. This still represents an accumulation of air inside the cube and suggests more of that upward motion (and rain).

If all this seems a bit technical then we can fall back on a simple notion: rising air leads to cloud and rain, whereas descending air implies clear skies.

VORTICITY

Water tends to meander and form eddies and whirlpools; the air is also a fluid and it exhibits the same types of flow. Meteorologists measure this turning or spinning motion and call it 'vorticity'. We use the word 'vortex' to describe a large atmospheric whirlpool like a depression, but even a gently curving airflow has significant vorticity.

Since the Earth is also spinning, we have two components to deal with – that which exists as a result of the rotating Earth and the extra assessment of the air over, say, the British Isles. This 'relative vorticity' can be cyclonic or anticyclonic, i.e. anticlockwise or clockwise, respectively, in the northern hemisphere.

It could be argued that a tiny eddy around a building has a spinning motion, but this is more in the realms of local turbulence because other nearby eddies will be spinning in different directions and turbulent flow is random. Rather, the concept of vorticity is used to describe the processes going on in anticyclones, depressions, comma clouds and troughs.

Vorticity is talked about qualitatively when scientists discuss the long life of features like hurricanes or the weird cloud spirals seen on satellite pictures downwind of mountainous islands such as the Canaries and Hawaii. A sequence of satellite pictures often provides a fascinating array of downstream pressure areas known as Von Karman vortices near such islands. These eddies and atmospheric meanders may be many miles across, but they are analogous to the whirlpool behind a rock in a fast-flowing river.

The concept of vorticity is built into our forecasting computers, which can compute the vorticity of the air all over the Earth at many different levels up through the atmosphere. One of the more surprising results to come out of the equations which describe air movement is the link between cyclonic vorticity, convergence and rising air. This is the scientific trio which causes rain.

Having said that we consider vorticity to be a medium- or large-scale feature, it is obviously also important in our attempts to understand tornadoes and dust devils which are small-scale events.

The best place to see vorticity in action is in a liquid. Rivers, streams, washing-up bowls and baths are all suitable places to view this phenomenon. The bath is particularly good as you can introduce barriers to fluid motion. A brick can simulate Greenland. A shampoo bottle can represent the Canary Islands creating downstream vorticity. Finally, when you pull the plug out, you get an excellent example of a vortex.

OCEANOGRAPHY

More than half of our weather comes from the Atlantic, so weather people must take an interest in another science – oceanography.

In oceanography, there are many parallels to meteorology. The oceans have watermasses just as we have airmasses. Mediterranean water can be traced far out into the Atlantic by its 'signature' of temperature and salinity. A deep current carries it out through the Straits of Gibraltar even when Atlantic water is flowing into the Mediterranean nearer the surface, like two winds of opposing directions at low and high levels. There are boundaries akin to fronts in the oceans.

A large anticyclone in the atmosphere has its equivalent in the ocean which is known as a 'gyre' (pronounced with a soft 'g' to rhyme with 'fire'). Let us look at one of the most important gyres, and start by considering the weather feature which helps cause it.

There is a semi-permanent anticyclone near the Azores commonly known as the 'Azores High'. Winds blow around it in a clockwise fashion and the ocean currents, driven by the wind, follow suit. This leads to the warm northward-flowing Gulf Stream near Florida which extends across the ocean at 40°N to 60°N as the northeastward-flowing North Atlantic Drift. It then turns southwards past Portugal and West Africa as the now relatively cool Canaries Current and then flows westwards towards the Caribbean to complete the huge gyration or 'gyre'.

The currents carry heat with them and the North Atlantic Drift keeps the British Isles relatively mild in winter because our usual westerly winds have just come in from the sea. Because the currents can warm or cool the air, they affect the temperature pattern of the atmosphere and therefore the wind pattern. The winds in turn determine the ocean's movement, so atmosphere and ocean are to some extent locked together. They exchange heat, moisture (rainfall and evaporation) and momentum (i.e. winds cause currents).

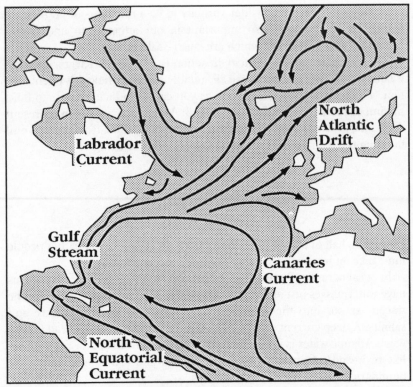

The ocean currents in the North Atlantic are the result of the wind circulating around the semi-permanent Azores anticyclone. Like the winds, the currents are affected by the Earth's rotation.

Whilst the great gyres are like anticyclones, there are also smaller vortices like depressions, though these are less important in oceanography.

Just as the atmosphere has two great layers – the troposphere where all the weather happens, overlaid by the stratosphere – so the ocean has an upside-down two-layer pattern of warm surface water underlain by cold, deep water. In the atmosphere the great boundary is called the 'tropopause', whereas in the ocean it is the 'thermocline'.

Typically the thermocline is relatively shallow at 20 to 200 m (60 to 600 ft), below which is the deep, cold water. Some might say that the top section of the ocean is more akin to the boundary layer or mixing region of the atmosphere, because when strong winds occur the resulting ocean waves cause mixing (just as strong surface winds cause mixing in the lower atmosphere).

Occasionally cold water, perhaps from melting ice, finds itself overlying warm water and then upside-down convection occurs in the ocean.

Salinity can be a big complicating factor in the ocean whereas it is humidity which is the 'added ingredient' in the atmosphere.

We have seen that the oceans and atmosphere interact, therefore we cannot forecast one without the other. In the future the best atmospheric computer simulations must include a simulation of the oceans.

Chapter 3

WORLD WEATHER

INTRODUCTION TO WORLD WEATHER

THERE ARE numerous academic books devoted to the climates of the world, many of them following the now widely accepted classification of the climatologist Köppen. Any attempt to summarise the world's climates in a few pages must therefore resort to a broad-brush approach.

If you look up the climate statistics for a particular place you will find that things are far more complicated than I have implied. On the other hand, simple explanations have their use as the first step to full understanding. World-wide, we end up with six circulating 'cells' of air motion above the ground. At the surface we find four desert zones and three rainy zones.

HADLEY CELLS

If the Earth were solely covered in water and not rotating, then the wind system would be much simpler. Air would rise over the warm Equator, flow northwards across our hemisphere and sink near the North Pole. The movement in the southern hemisphere would be a mirror image, with descent over the South Pole.

Because the Earth rotates, the hypothetical single circulating cell per hemisphere is split into three. The air which rises over the Equator sinks at latitude 25°N or 30°N over the Sahara. This descending dry, warm air then splits in two with half of it flowing southwards to complete the 'Hadley Cell'. The British scientist George Hadley first proposed the existence of this type of circulation, though he suggested *only one cell per hemisphere* rather than three. His name is now usually applied only to the major cells on either side of the Equator.

The second cell exists at mid-latitudes with low-level air flowing northwards until it reaches the polar front (roughly over Britain) where it meets the cold air flowing out at surface level from the third cell near the North Pole.

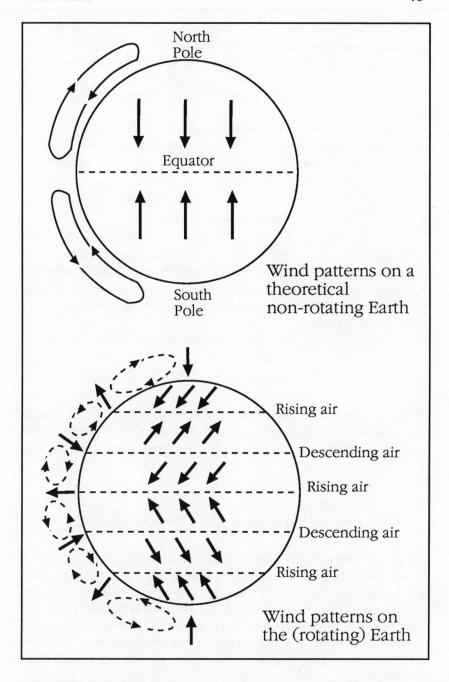

North
Pole

Equator

Wind patterns on a
theoretical
non-rotating Earth

South
Pole

Rising air

Descending air

Rising air

Descending air

Rising air

Wind patterns on
the (rotating) Earth

*George Hadley proposed a simple pattern of air rising at the Equator and descending
near the Poles. In reality there are three cells in each hemisphere. Descending air
implies low rainfall and therefore desert climates.*

Due to the Earth's rotation, the southerly winds (e.g. over Europe) are deflected to the right and become southwesterlies. The northerly winds in the Arctic are also deflected to the right, and become predominantly northeasterly. The winds in the major Hadley Cell just north of the Equator also become northeasterlies and are known as the 'northeast trade winds'.

In the southern hemisphere there is a mirror-image pattern consisting of southeast trades, temperate latitude northwesterlies and Antarctic southeasterlies. (Deflection by the Earth's rotation is to the left here.)

FOUR DESERT ZONES

This pattern of air movement leaves us with four regions of descending air: over the North Pole, at latitude 25° to 30° N, at latitude 25°S to 30°S and over the South Pole. These regions are deserts (though there is so much ice and so little evaporation that it is perhaps inappropriate to call the Poles by that name).

THREE RAINY ZONES

It also provides us with three regions of rising air with abundant rainfall: our temperate latitude depression zone at 40°N to 70°N, the equatorial rainy band and the other temperate latitude depression zone around 35°S to 60°S.

COMPLICATIONS OF SEASONS AND LANDMASSES

All we now have to do to complete the explanation of the world's rainfall is to add two sentences of caution. First, the three zones of rainfall move north and south slightly with the seasons, reaching their northernmost position in July or August. Second, the distribution of landmasses and mountain ranges confuses the otherwise simple pattern which would emerge. (The landmass of Asia is particularly influential since it induces the monsoon regime which is essentially an enormous sea-breeze mechanism.)

Having set the scene, we can now look briefly at the World's weather zones, starting in the Arctic and then moving southwards to the Equator, before examining a few special issues such as flooding and hurricanes.

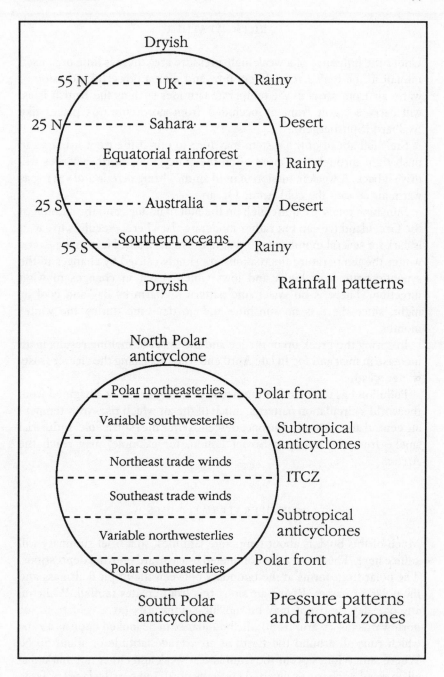

A simplified diagram of rainy and desert zones (above), with their meteorological causes (below). The UK gets its rain from the polar front whilst the equatorial rain-forests lie under the inter-tropical convergence zone or ITCZ.

ARCTIC WEATHER

Under the influence of a weak high-pressure area there is little organised rainfall in the high Arctic. Every now and then a powerful incursion of warm air from areas in the temperate latitudes such as the British Isles, will carry a warm front or occluded front north towards places like Svalbard (Spitsbergen).

Snowfall ahead of the system may turn to rain if the front manages to push right through, but more often the anticyclonic northeasterlies will drive it back. A weak incursion of mild air may bring drizzle and sea fog as warm air crosses the cold Arctic Ocean.

Sunshine totals are quite high on the mountain tops and the summit of the Greenland ice cap but rather moderate elsewhere. Needless to say, it is dark for several months of the year in the high Arctic. Here in the Arctic winter the temperature fluctuations are simply caused by changes in the synoptic pattern of highs and lows which result in changes of wind direction. There is no systematic pattern of warm by day and cool by night, since there is no sunshine and no day-time during the winter months.

In spring the break up of the ice and the onset of melting results in an increase in mist and fog in late April and May, replacing the clearer frosty winter weather.

Pollution has increased in the Arctic because, as can be imagined from the world's circulation patterns, much of the air which rises over temperate central and northern Europe, descends over the North Pole. Industrial smoke from the northern Soviet Union, for example, may reach the Arctic.

TEMPERATE LATITUDES

Much of this book is about temperate latitudes, so a brief summary will suffice here. This is the zone dominated by eastward-moving depressions. The polar front forms at the boundary between the tropical airmass and the polar airmasses. Rising air along this front creates rainfall. While on any one day the front may be moving southwards (as a cold front) or northwards (as a warm front), the boundary can be looked upon as a zone which runs all around the Earth at an average latitude of about 50°N. Where anticyclones occur the front is very weak and either not marked at all on weather charts or diverted far to the north (up near Iceland) or far to the south (down near Portugal). As with all weather zones, the temperate latitude westerlies and the associated polar front jet stream tend to edge a little further north in summer and further south in winter.

Places on the western sides of continents are subject to a fairly steady stream of eastward-moving depressions. Further into the landmasses the climate becomes more continental with colder winters and hotter summers. The winters are drier because the depressions have shed much of their moisture on western coasts and hills. In summer, convective rainfall is more of a feature due to the hot land surface, so in continental areas of the so-called temperate latitudes, considerably more than half of the rainfall comes in showers during spring and summer. This is the pattern in Central Canada, Eastern Europe and Soviet Central Asia.

MEDITERRANEAN WEATHER

Warm wet winters and hot dry summers make up the classic pattern of Mediterranean climates. From November to March some of the temperate latitude depressions track far enough south to give rainy spells. In Portugal and North Africa this gives the typical mild winters, but on the northern shores of the Mediterranean where northeasterly winds can blow, cold weather turns up from time to time, notably in Turkey, northern Greece, Yugoslavia and on the north Italian plain.

In summer the sub-tropical high-pressure belt is far enough north to cover both the Sahara and much of the Mediterranean, at least up to latitude 40°N. Descending air is the cause of this sunny weather, and advice on when and where to find it can be found in the chapter on holiday weather. The Mediterranean climate zone is often thought of as being ideal for wine production but grapes, especially white grapes, can withstand the frosts of Germany and the southern Soviet Union.

Further across in the same latitude band, the eastern sides of the continents have different 'east margin' climates. Here there are drier winters, but in summer moist air is drawn in from the adjacent seas to give more in the way of convective, thundery rain or showers – for example, in the eastern USA, China and Korea.

DESERTS

The Sahara is the world's largest desert. On the Tropic of Cancer at latitude 23.5°N the weather is almost totally dry. Winter rainfall from the temperate latitude depressions never gets down this far south. Summer rainfall from the equatorial rainy zone never gets this far north. Descending air predominates. Just very rarely some little patch of moist air ends up over very hot uplands, such as the Hoggar Mountains of Algeria, and gives a shower at, say, Tamanrasset. This should not be taken as suggesting that there is only one weather event per year. The remnants of old cold fronts may move south to give a dust-storm. Powerful heating by the sun sets off dust devils. Nights are cold in January because the desert sand cools rapidly. Sunshine averages 4000 hours per year in the eastern Sahara, but sometimes the blue skies are spoilt by patches of altocumulus or cirrus cloud high aloft, moving eastwards in the sub-tropical jet stream.

THE EQUATORIAL RAINY ZONE

This region can be called the 'equatorial rain-band' but it is normally referred to by meteorologists as the 'Inter-tropical Convergence Zone' or the 'ITCZ' for short. It encircles the Earth just about on the Equator, crossing Brazil, Zaïre and Singapore, and giving these regions their classic tropical rain-forest climate.

The ITCZ essentially marks the 'thermal equator' or perhaps more revealingly the zone where the northeast trade winds of our hemisphere meet the southeast trade winds of the southern hemisphere. Convergence of these winds forces the air upwards. Rising air implies cloud and rain, and the equatorial rain-forests get plenty of both.

The ITCZ moves with the Sun and reaches its northernmost position in July and August and its southernmost position in January or February. In some parts of the world, it moves only slightly with the seasons; in other regions, particularly over the interiors of the continents, this movement is quite marked because the landmass responds quickly to the changing angle of the Sun with the seasons. Thus over the oceans it tends to lie between latitudes 10°S and 10°N, whereas over Africa in January it gets down into Botswana and Zimbabwe at 20°S and by July it has reached north to the southern fringe of the Sahara (the Sahel) at 15°N and also into India, where it gets mixed up with the southwest monsoon rains.

Let us now dispel two myths about tropical rainfall brought back by travellers and colonialists of earlier times and subsequently embroidered. The first myth is that the rains in a certain location always commence on a fixed date. This is far from true over most of the tropics, though there are some areas, for instance like India, where one can predict the onset within a week or two.

The second myth is that each day brings a shower or thunderstorm at a fixed time, often quoted as half-past four! Whilst it is true that inland convective rain is most likely in the afternoon, there will be many occasions when showers break out earlier, say around midday, and on other days a thunderstorm may arrive after dark, having drifted in from

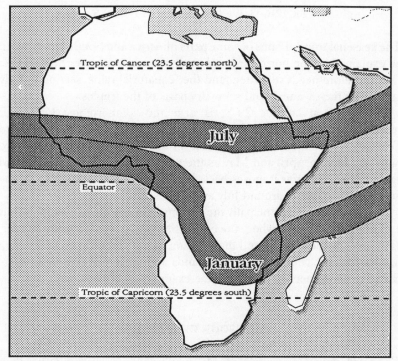

In January the tropical rainy zone is well south of the Equator but as the Sun moves north, so the rains move northwards and by July they lie across Mali, Southern Chad and Ethiopia.

elsewhere. On coasts and islands this diurnal pattern is even more complex with night-time storms set off by the warm tropical seas.

Finally, it is apparent from the climate statistics of tropical locations which lie pretty well under the ITCZ, such as the Amazon rain-forest of Brazil, that even the rainy season can be reasonably sunny, and rain does not occur on every day. In Tanzania, for example, it may rain on average on just one day in three, and seedling plants can suffer in the strong sunshine before another showery day comes along to provide water. Here, if the television forecaster mentions 'good weather' then he or she may well be talking about rain.

The area between the Tropics of Cancer and Capricorn is the only region of the Earth where sizeable weather systems regularly move from east to west. The general motion of any large clusters of thunderstorms will usually be westwards at 10 to 20 mph (15 to 30 kph), though there are plenty of exceptions.

Any notion that the tropical rain-forests have predictable weather should be forgotten. The forecaster's task is particularly difficult there.

TROPICAL WET AND DRY CLIMATES

The seasonal tropical rains of some parts of Africa and South America can be explained by the northward and southward movements of the ITCZ. One therefore needs to understand the 'equatorial rains' section to fully appreciate the savannah and semi-dry parts of the tropics.

Zimbabwe, at latitude 20°S, is near the southernmost limit ever reached by the ITCZ and there is just one rainy season, November to February. Nairobi in Kenya is almost on the Equator and there are two rainy seasons: in April and May as the rainband moves northwards, and again in November as it moves back south. Ethiopia at latitude 15°N has just one rainy season around July and August.

We are describing principally the regions between the two Tropics (but excluding those places where the equatorial rains persist virtually all year, as in parts of West Africa and the Amazon basin). Tropical cyclones are a feature of some countries, mainly islands and those places with an east-facing coast. Appendix VI gives some examples of climate data.

MONSOON CLIMATES

The word 'monsoon' actually means 'steady wind' or 'season' rather than 'rainfall', with which it has generally become associated. Southeast Asia and India have the classic monsoon climate. In winter a huge anticyclone develops over Asia, northeasterly winds blow out from the high and the weather is relatively cool, but dry and sunny. This is the period of the northeast (dry) monsoon.

As spring turns to summer, the heat builds up over Asia and a huge area of low pressure develops, centred roughly over the Tibetan plateau or Afghanistan. Low-level winds are sucked in towards the centre of this huge 'heat low'. Over India, Burma and Thailand, for example, these are moisture-laden southwesterlies, which give copious rainfall from June to October. This is the southwest monsoon or 'rainy season', and is especially wet where hill ranges force the moist air to rise, as at Cherrapunji in eastern India.

The monsoon rains do not set in everywhere simultaneously, but progress gradually northwards across India in a roughly similar pattern each year. When the heat low develops early and the sub-tropical jet stream jumps to a position north of the Tibetan plateau, then the monsoon rains will probably start earlier than the standard date for any particular location. In Hyderabad, the onset is expected around the 7 June whereas further north in Delhi it does not arrive until the latter half of the month.

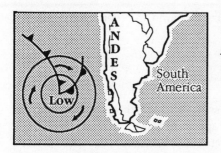

In the mid-latitudes of the southern hemisphere, depressions usually track from west to east (as they do across Europe) but the winds blow around the low in a clockwise direction in the southern hemisphere.

An alternative way of looking at the Southeast Asia monsoon is to regard the heat low as an extreme northward displacement of the ITCZ right up into China.

A less-marked monsoon affects West Africa from Nigeria westwards.

THE SOUTHERN HEMISPHERE

The situation in the southern hemisphere is largely a mirror image of that in the northern. Jet streams still blow from west to east since this is the direction of the Earth's rotation, so the depressions still move mainly from west to east in the temperate latitudes. The big difference is that winds blow in the opposite direction around a low (i.e. clockwise 'down under') because all the air movements are now deflected to the *left* by the Coriolis force. To put it another way, the pressure gradient would once again suggest a wind blowing straight into the low pressure, but the deflection to the left makes the circulation clockwise.

A southerly wind in our hemisphere equates to a northerly one below the equator, but a mobile westerly airstream is still a mobile westerly. Our mild southwesterly in the British Isles is matched by a mild northwesterly in Tasmania.

As regards climates, there is less land in the southern hemisphere and less desert, though the Atacama and Namib deserts would be thought of as equating to the Mexican desert and the Sahara.

Mediterranean-type climates occur around latitude 35°S in Central Chile, around Cape Town, Perth (Western Australia) and Adelaide. The British climate is roughly equalled by Southern Chile, and Falklands, Tasmania and the South Island of New Zealand, around latitudes 45°S to 50°S.

The southern hemisphere tends to have more mobile weather as there are fewer mountain ranges and landmasses. Antarctica is a large cooling influence and 'squeezes' the climate zones a little closer to the Equator. The Falklands at latitude 52°S are rather like Shetland at 60°N and the

Mediterranean type of weather occurs at around 35°S compared with, say, 38°N.

HURRICANES

A hurricane is an intense low-pressure area which originates over the tropical oceans. It should have wind speeds of at least 64 knots (119 kph or 74 mph) to earn this title. The diameter of a hurricane is usually about 500 km (300 miles), so it is comparable in size with a smallish temperate latitude depression, and of course the winds blow around it in the same direction – anticlockwise in the northern hemisphere.

A hurricane may have its origins in an area of thundery rain over West Africa. The cloud cluster responsible for this rain moves westwards over the Atlantic Ocean at latitude 10°N, and at this stage it may either disperse, or else start drawing in more moist air and developing a circulation. By the time it has moved westwards into mid-Atlantic the tropical storm may have reached the hurricane stage. Turning slightly away from the equator it heads west-northwest to menace the Caribbean islands and the Gulf of Mexico. If the hurricane crosses an island, the inhabitants will receive an onslaught of ferocious northeasterly winds and heavy rain; huge seas will pound the coast. Then they have an hour or so of respite if the 'eye' passes directly overhead. An eerie calm with fairly clear skies exists in this 30 km (20 mile) centre of low pressure, soon to be followed by tremendous southwesterly winds which moderate slowly over a period of hours.

A hurricane feeds off the warm oceanic water at a temperature of 27 or 28 C (around 82 F), and if it moves inland, for example into the southern USA, it will soon be a spent force. Coastal cities like Galveston, New Orleans and Miami are at risk from June to November, but especially during August to October.

Sometimes hurricanes change track with little warning. Quite often they curve away northwards, then turn northeast towards western Europe, but by now they are extra-tropical in character. The October 1987 storm in southeast England was not a true warm-cored hurricane, rather it was a very fierce temperate-latitude depression with wind speeds approaching hurricane force, but the effect on trees in Kent and Sussex was certainly similar!

TYPHOONS AND OTHER TROPICAL CYCLONES

Whilst I have described the life cycle of a hurricane in the tropical North Atlantic, there are many other areas of the World where the same sort of

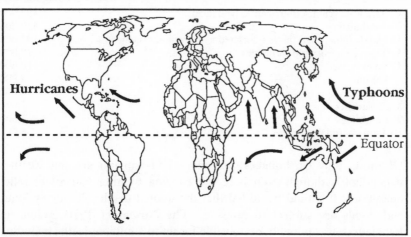

Typical tracks of tropical cyclones. They occur over all tropical oceans except the South Atlantic where the water is too cold to allow them to form. They move westwards, gradually turning away from the Equator.

fierce tropical cyclone occurs. Those that approach the Philippines and Southeast Asia are known as 'typhoons', while in the Indian Ocean they are simply called 'cyclones' and in Northern Australia they are 'cyclones' or 'willy-willies'. The fact that tropical cyclones never occur right on the equator is proof that the Earth's rotation is an influence, and that the Coriolis effect is a vital factor in their formation.

Names are decided before the season commences for each tropical cyclone area, with the first hurricane starting with the letter 'A'. Originally only girls' names were used but in the interests of equality meteorologists now alternate between girls' and boys' names.

Because of the requirement for a warm ocean surface (and latent heat can be considered the 'fuel' of the tropical cyclone) they have a definite season. In the northern hemisphere the season extends from May to November and in the southern hemisphere from around December to March. The peak time for the Caribbean and Southeast Asia is probably in September. The record of low pressure in the eye of a typhoon is 870 mbar recorded in November 1975.

Whilst tropical cyclones are bad news in most respects, there are areas where they bring much needed rainfall to refill the reservoirs and replenish groundwater.

WORLD WEATHER DISASTERS

An analysis by Bindi V. Shah in 1983 of the world's natural disasters between 1947 and 1980 showed the following death tolls:

1	Tropical cyclones (hurricanes, typhoons)	499,000
2	Earthquakes	450,000
3	Floods (other than those associated with tropical cyclones)	194,000
4	Thunderstorms and tornadoes	29,000
5	Snowstorms	10,000
6	Volcanoes	9,000
7	Heat-waves	7,000
8	Avalanches	5,000
9	Landslides	5,000
10	Tsunami (tidal waves)	5,000

Of these, only earthquakes, volcanoes and tsunami are not weather dependent – though even here the ensuing weather will affect relief operations. It should be added that the quoted death tolls for cyclones and floods are subject to question. The November 1970 cyclone in Bangladesh was possibly responsible for up to a million deaths including subsequent famine and disease.

Tropical cyclones occur over the oceans, mainly between latitudes 5° and 25°, occasionally reaching to 40°N or 30°S. Satellites help us to track them, and they are to a fair degree predictable, though enormous damage to property is inevitable. Their greatest threat to life is from flooding by the sea in low-lying coastal areas where communications are poor and escape is difficult, such as Bangladesh, India and coastal China.

Earthquakes are not caused by weather and do not have any known effect on the atmosphere. The earthquake near Wrexham at 2.48 p.m. on 2 April 1990 was 5.2 on the Richter scale. No one was injured. There was a report of lightning occurring at the same time as the 'quake' but this was presumably just coincidence.

Floods, other than those caused by cyclones, can be of perhaps three different types. Flash floods may be very localised and occur in hot weather with brief but intense rainfall. In the British Isles this means summertime and mainly in the south, but all of the tropics and many temperate continental areas are at risk. Widespread floods can occur where snow melts (as in Britain at the end of the 1947 winter) or alternatively after straightforward prolonged rainfall (of the type which occurs in Wales, Scotland and the Lake District). Usually some special factor plays a part in causing a tragedy: a narrowing river valley, a collapsed bridge, a burst dam or a crowded place with no rapid escape route.

Thunderstorms and tornadoes are caused by vigorous cumulonimbus clouds and therefore share a common cause with flash floods, and sometimes occur at the same time. Whilst meteorologists can forecast which days will be *prone* to these events, it is impossible to say where they will occur. Inland, the afternoon is the peak time of day when temperatures are high and cumulonimbus clouds are at their most intense. In the

United States observers watch out for and report tornadoes as they form and run northeastwards. (There is more information about tornadoes in Chapter 6.)

Snowstorms are, by and large, predictable though of course there are marginal occasions when rain turns to snow. Wind is the killer element here. Few people die as the result of a few inches of level snow, but a huge wind-blown snowdrift blocks roads and railways, and blizzards reduce visibility to near zero and cause the wind-chill effect.

Heat-waves (like fog, smog, cold weather and hypothermia) are largely self-evident problems. Perhaps they are at their most disastrous when they are outside the normal expectation for the area. (Similarly cold weather can be a killer in Italy where many houses have no heating.)

Avalanches occur on slopes with gradients between 28° and 45°. Areas of forest will often prevent them from sweeping down on to villages and roads, but off-piste skiers are sometimes caught out. The danger signs are a heavy fall of new snow (often on a north-facing slope) and rapid changes of temperature. Locals usually know the portents and the regular avalanche zones. The worst British disaster was at Lewes, Sussex, when a mass of snow crashed down on some houses on 27 December 1836 killing eight people.

Landslides are usually started by heavy rain. Such was the case in the coal-tip disaster at Aberfan, South Wales, on 21 October 1966. Earthquakes and volcanic activity are also potential triggers of landslides.

A tsunami is unfortunately also known by the expression 'tidal wave'. Since it is caused by an earthquake, or just occasionally by a major landslide, the Japanese name is preferred. An under-sea earthquake will generate a high-energy wave. In the open ocean this wave will perhaps be only a few inches (say 10 to 30 cm) high, but moving at an incredible speed of up to 1000 kph (600 mph). Ships may not notice it, or will only feel a slight jolt as it passes. However, when the tsunami reaches shallower water, the huge energy which it carries is transformed from speed into height. It becomes evident as the wave steepens and breaks, inundating coastal areas.

Chapter 4

BRITISH WEATHER

THOSE WHO enjoyed the 1989 and 1990 summers may be wondering how they compared with previous vintage summers. Many of us remember 1976 but there was also 1983, which might be labelled 'the forgotten summer'. Previous fine efforts have been 1975, 1959 and 1947.

Official statistics for the summer season cover June, July and August. If we consider 1989 data for London (which shared the 'good' summer with most of England, Wales and also southern and eastern Scotland) then temperatures were not up to the levels of 1983 or 1976. July was the hottest month with average temperatures 2.7 C (4.9 F) above normal, though May, June and August were also well above the long-term average. However, sunshine is what 1989 was really about. The June to August period gave 811.5 hours in London compared with 810.2 hours in 1976, so on that score it really was a record summer, beating all central London records back to their commencement in 1929. A further thought: if we included May and September in our definition of summer then the 1989 sunshine totals would look even more remarkable.

Just as 1975 and 1976 had provide two consecutive 'scorchers', so 1989 was followed by 1990. The most notable event this time was the heatwave of July and early August which culminated on 3 August 1990 with eggs literally frying on the pavement. (This happened in Salisbury when an egg lorry crashed!) The drought was severe though not equalling the 73 rainless days at Mile End in London from 4 March to 15 May 1893. From the point of view of water supplies, the real problem was consecutive hot, dry summers with (in Southern Britain) an intervening dry winter, as in 1975-76.

Those who are still at school will no doubt remember these blue skies, and even next century will still be saying 'I remember the summer of 1990'. But why do we tend to remember summers of our youth as hot and sunny? Anyone who thinks the summers of the 1960s were good has a faulty memory and is looking back through rose-coloured spectacles. I believe that the solution to this enigma may lie partly in the fact that our memories are selective. If the weather is fine then we are more likely to go out boating, making visits, or playing sport, and will therefore have a more memorable day. Staying indoors and reading a book is hardly the sort of pastime which will stick in the mind 20 years later. We also tend to have more opportunity to enjoy the warm days when we are young, with the long school holidays and short school days.

At Portmeirion in North Wales, there is a small monument to vintage summers erected by the eccentric architect Sir Clough William-Ellis. The comment on 1976 was 'nonesuch' suggesting that, for *prolonged* high temperatures at least, it will be a difficult summer to beat.

HEAT-WAVES AND HUMAN COMFORT

Many people quote the British record as 38.1 C (100.5 F) at Tonbridge in Kent on 22 July 1868. This, however, was not measured under standard modern conditions and it is considered that the reading would have been a couple of degrees lower in a Stevenson screen. This left the argument open, for several places claimed temperatures around 36 C (97 F) in June 1976, including Plumpton in Sussex on 28th. Then, on 3 August 1990, a new record was established of 37.1 C (98.9 F) at Cheltenham.

What temperature can we expect on the hottest day of the year? For Edinburgh the answer is 25 C (77 F), for Cardiff 28 C (82 F) and in London 29 C (84 F). Contrast this with Seville in southern Spain where a once-a-year high of 44 C (111 F) is typical.

And when will the hottest day be? This is more tricky. 21 June provides the highest elevation of the Sun, but high temperatures do not depend solely on one day's heating of the atmosphere. Days in June, July and August are all possibilities. Highest summer temperatures usually occur inland, or just occasionally on a coast with an offshore wind. Almost inevitably in the British Isles, it will be a southeasterly Tropical Continental airstream or with a stagnant anticyclone.

When we sweat, either profusely or just in a slow process known as 'insensible perspiration' we are attempting to cool ourselves by evaporating moisture from our skin into the air. Since evaporation will be much slower on humid days, humidity is an important factor in human comfort. However, it is meaningless if considered on its own without the temperature: a relative humidity of 95% is not uncomfortable on an autumn morning with 10 C (50 F), while a humidity of 50% is very sticky and unpleasant if the temperature is 30 C (86 F).

Many comfort indicies have been proposed, but all incorporate both temperature and humidity in some form. Wind speed is also a factor for the stationary human being, but is often ignored in these formulae, as is sunshine.

In tropical rain-forests and monsoon regions we experience an energy-sapping combination of high temperatures and high humidity. The Arabian Gulf around Bahrain is also a notable candidate for discomfort in the months of July and August, when temperatures of 38 C (100 F) and 50% relative humidity are not uncommon. Death Valley, California, is another unpleasant spot, though here high temperatures predominate over moisture.

In the United States the most common evaluation of human discomfort is the Temperature–Humidity Index or THI which equals two-fifths of the sum of the dry-bulb and wet-bulb thermometer readings (in Fahrenheit) plus 15. Death Valley holds the record of THI with 98.2 which has been reached twice with 119 F (48 C) and 31% relative humidity on 27 July 1966 and 117 F (47 C) and 37 % relative humidity on 12 August 1970.

Our British THI values come nowhere near these levels, but the 1948 Olympics were held under very humid conditions, and most summers include at least one day of 'clammy' Tropical Maritime air, perhaps approaching 27 C (81 F) and 50% relative humidity.

WEATHER FOR HAY FEVER SUFFERERS

Hay fever, an allergic reaction to the pollen of various grasses, is something which involves medics, botanists and meteorologists. Pollen is a fine, powdery substance discharged from the anthers of flowers. It is the male element which fertilises the ovules. Grain sizes depend on the species, but pollen is sometimes visible as a yellow powder when settled on cars.

An allergy is said to be an 'unusual reaction' to food, bites or, in this case, pollen, but since there are vast numbers of sufferers in the British Isles, it is not all that unusual. It is now suggested that air pollution may play a part in making hay fever worse, perhaps explaining the apparent increase in the number of sufferers. The term 'acid air' has been coined to describe these polluted conditions.

Some plants rely on insects to distribute their pollen, whilst others have more elaborate mechanisms. For grasses though, it is mainly the wind which carries the pollen far and wide, to the dismay of hay fever sufferers. The pollen grains are light enough to remain air-borne in a moderate wind and only a flat calm will lack the necessary turbulent air motions to transport the pollen from the fields to the sufferer.

Individual plants vary in the rate at which they develop through the

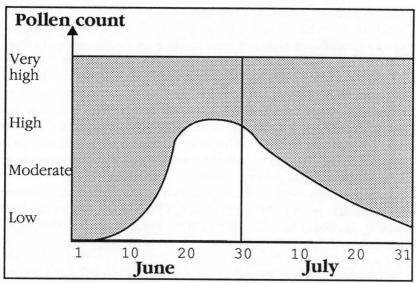

A simplified graph of grass pollen in the air over southern England. The day to day weather will cause large variations. Sunny days will produce very high readings whilst cold, rainy days will suppress the pollen count. In northern England and Scotland the peak will be reached later, usually in early July in an average year.

spring and early summer, with some plants naturally pollinating slightly earlier than others. Also, a south-facing bank or other warm location will bring them on more quickly, so there is neither a sudden start nor abrupt cessation to the hay fever season. Usually it will be a couple of weeks earlier in the south of Britain than in the north. Given the free time, a sufferer might spend June in Shetland and return to southern England in July when the season is on the wane: in a normal year the peak of the season tends to be towards the end of June in the South and in early July in Scotland. Grasses do not start pollinating before June even in the earliest of years, but many hay fever sufferers are also allergic to other things, for example tree pollen. It is therefore difficult to name dates for individuals who may also have a range of lesser allergies which start earlier. During May the London plane tree and the yellow fields of rape are possible culprits.

Grasses tend to release their pollen on sunny mornings, and wind speeds are usually higher during the day-time than at night. It follows that a sunny morning is bad news, whereas a cold day with heavy rain will clear the air. Rain can physically wash pollen out of the air or prevent it from becoming air borne in the first place.

The influence of wind speed is rather variable, since if you live amongst grassy fields there will frequently be pollen in the air even in light wind conditions. In a city, well removed from the source, it is breezy sunny days which are the worst since the pollen grains will be blown in from rural areas. Generally, the higher up a tall building you go, the less pollen there will be. Only strong winds and the associated turbulent movement of the air can carry pollen to the top of a city tower-block. Closing windows will obviously help to some extent.

Trains on rural lines can be bad for hay fever sufferers because the grasses are shaken by the passage of the locomotive and some of the pollen may subsequently find its way in through open carriage windows on a warm morning. The 'pollen counts' sometimes quoted in the media are simply the number of pollen grains collected from a certain volume of air, usually one cubic metre. Forecasts use both meteorological and botanical information to predict whether the count will rise or fall. A value above 50 may be regarded as high, though it rather depends upon where the sample was collected.

SUNSHINE RECORDS

Not only was the summer of 1989 a 'good one' but the calendar year of 1989 was the sunniest in central London since we started taking readings in 1929. During the 27 October we passed the previous record of 1762.5 hours sunshine duration which was recorded in 1976 and we went on to reach 1914.8 hours.

The league table of 61 years in London from 1929 to 1984 inclusive shows that the top ten for duration of sunshine in chronological order have been 1929, 1933, 1949, 1959, 1967, 1970, 1973, 1975, 1976, 1989. This may prompt a couple of comments. Firstly, the sequence of years ending in 9 might show some sort of cycle. Secondly, there seems to have been more sunshine in recent times than in the middle part of the century. To the first of these suggestions the response must be that it is pure coincidence. After all, we cannot have a proposed ten-year cycle of sunny years without a proposed cause – and although the sunspot cycle is ten to twelve years, there is no obvious link between sunspots and cloud amount. The second point about increased sunshine in recent decades is more persuasive and probably is, at least in part, the result of the Clean Air Act of 1956.

The London Weather Centre uses a sunshine instrument which might be regarded as old-fashioned, but it does provide a long-term standard for comparison. The Campbell-Stokes sunshine recorder has a glass ball about 15cm (6 in) in diameter which focuses the Sun's rays on to a card upon which it burns a trace. No moving parts are needed since the Sun moves around the sky and produces a long brown burn across the card which is clipped into a holder. There are a few uncertainties in estimating the sunshine duration for one day, because a discontinuous burn is more difficult to judge than that from a cloudless day. Also, one always loses the first few minutes and the last few minutes of the day when the Sun is near the horizon (within about 3°) and the strict definition is 'duration of bright sunshine'. This loss of low-angle Sun means that you cannot achieve 100% of possible, and in practice even a cloudless day falls well short of the theoretical maximum in December.

A comparison of the 30 years from 1929 to 1958 and a corresponding period since the Clean Air Act began to take effect for 1959 to 1988 shows the averages to be 1356 and 1513 hours per year respectively. Exactly what proportion of the increase is due to the Act and how much to broader climatic change (or indeed to pure random variation) is impossible to say. Random variation is the obvious argument when dealing with fluctuations by individual years, but becomes a weaker argument when dealing with 30-year periods. One conclusion is that the transfer from domestic coal burning with smoke emitted at roof-top level to a system of power where the emissions are mainly from high-level stacks outside our cities has improved our urban localities (but led us to forget the global impact).

CROP CIRCLES

One subject to receive a lot of attention recently is the circles that have appeared in fields of corn, especially in Wiltshire and Hampshire but also at other locations throughout the World.

Various theories have been advanced to explain their origin (and I have added my comments on their likelihood): human hoaxes (very probable), helicopter downdraughts (improbable), natural problems with the crop such as fungal attacks (improbable), tornadoes (improbable), fair-weather whirlwinds (possible), hurricanes (ludicrous), 'plasma vortices' containing some sort of electrical force (??) or aliens from outer space (no comment).

The circles themselves are flattened areas in a crop of either wheat or barley usually about 20 m (60ft) across with the corn lying flattened in one direction, which may be either cyclonic (anticlockwise) or anticyclonic (clockwise). Often there is a refinement such as a small separate outer ring or 'annulus' perhaps a couple of yards across in which the corn may be lying in the opposite direction. There may occasionally be two or four outlying smaller circles placed symmetrically about the main one. They appear between May and harvest-time, are sometimes visible from nearby hills, and of course are very apparent from the air.

Looking at the suggested causes one by one, the human hoax theory does seem very attractive, although it is claimed that the circles are too perfect. Initial access to the circle might be difficult without leaving a trail were it not for the tractor wheel marks or 'tram lines' which occur during crop spraying. These would allow determined hoaxers to find their way to the middle of a cornfield without leaving a noticeable access path.

The downdraught from helicopter rotors is too turbulent to lay down the corn in such an organised manner, and this would also apply to Harrier jump jets.

Natural problems like drought would hardly cause the crop to fall over in a perfect circle and the same argument applies to a fungal attack. Of course fungi can make circular marks like fairy rings on a grassy lawn, and proponents of this theory also suggest that the underlying soil could have been subject to alteration, for example by a prehistoric construction such as a stone circle which has somehow previously gone unnoticed.

Tornadoes are associated with thunderstorms. They are about the correct size and can sometimes be seen to have a contra-rotating outer sheath and occasionally little mini-tornadoes outside that. Unfortunately they are usually moving along at 20 mph (30 kph) in a northeasterly direction. They are associated with bad weather and do not hang about making perfect circles.

Fair-weather whirlwinds are the best meteorological bet. These occur in fine sunny weather usually between midday and about 4 p.m. They are circular whirlwinds which are often strong enough to lift hay and other light litter. Also, they tend to occur in calm conditions and might therefore remain slow-moving over one field. It has also been suggested that the hills can trigger such vortices and this would support the notion of a stationary whirlwind. However, having said all that, the circles do seem rather too perfect and it seems unlikely that a fair-weather whirlwind would have such an abrupt outer edge that it left the adjoining corn perfectly untouched. A hill-induced vortex would not remain absolutely stationary either.

This leaves only hurricanes, which are a ludicrous suggestion since they are hundreds of miles across, and one can only assume that those suggesting this cause must have meant tornadoes.

So, I think that the cause of such perfectly circular phenomena is unlikely to be meteorological. We must await further evidence before we can decide whether there is some other natural cause or if they are all the products of hoaxes.

SAHARA DUST

About once a year on average, Sahara dust arrives in Britain. Usually this dust is noticed on parked cars after rain has fallen. Pale beige is the most common colour but falls of brown or reddish tints have also been reported. In the Alps red snow has fallen.

We tend to think of desert sand as being similar to that on a British beach, but in reality it is usually much finer and more powdery. When a strong wind blows and creates a so-called sandstorm, it is the finer particles which tend to remain airborne, so often the term dust-storm is more appropriate.

Heavier grains of sand have a substantial fall speed and will fall out of the atmosphere long before they reach northwestern Europe, so it is truly a dust which arrives here. The typical size of the particles we see on a car will be about 10μm (micrometres) in diameter. This is one-hundredth of the size of the millimetre divisions on a ruler. When rubbed between the fingers the deposit feels very much more like dust or finely powdered pepper than granular sand.

Having become airborne, usually over Morocco, Mauritania, Algeria or Tunisia, the dust is carried northwards with the airstream and may be forced to rise over the Atlas Mountains of northwest Africa.

Probably the dust will reach a height of 10,000 to 16,000 ft (3000 to 5000 m) as it crosses Spain or the Majorca area of the western Mediterranean. Certainly pilots have reported dust at this sort of height, and the time taken to reach the British Isles ties in with the wind speeds at these altitudes. Satellite pictures occasionally show up an ill-defined smudge which helps us to locate a dust cloud.

The most common route is with a strong southerly, which can bring the dust perhaps 2600km (1600 miles) in 40 hours. Often such a broad, persistent southerly airflow at medium altitudes will occur just ahead of a frontal system. As the dust reaches the British Isles it may pass below the rain-bearing clouds. Any sizeable raindrops falling from the cloud will wash dust particles out of the atmosphere. The bonnet of a car after light to moderate rain is the best place to see the deposit. If no rain falls, then the dust will usually pass over; if the rain is heavy, then the air will be washed clean and the car too will tend to be washed clean by the later part of the rain storm. Much dust may have fallen but heavy rain destroys the evidence by taking it into the gutter or down the drain.

A few simple checks will help avoid mis-identification: the car should be clean before the dust fall; it should not have been driven since the dust fall or else road grime could be redistributed by the rain into a dappled pattern; the risk of dust blowing off nearby roofs should be borne in mind. The meteorologist will also want to check that the airflow aloft has been from the south.

Notable falls occurred in Britain in 1968 and again on 9 November 1984. Pride of place must go to 1987 which produced a bumper crop of reports, especially 17 August and 27 October. A recent notable case was

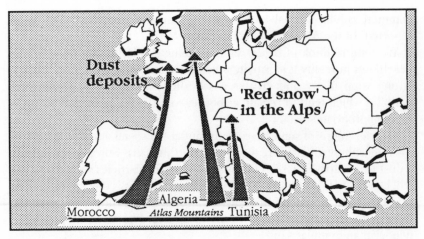

Typical tracks of dust from North Africa which may reach the British Isles within two days of a dust-storm in the Sahara.

on 7 May 1988. Sometimes the falls cover most of the country and many thousands of tons of material are deposited.

Other parts of the world have similar events. During the 1930s dust from the central USA reached Massachusetts. In Arabia and China too, there are dust-storms that keep skies milky-white for several days at a stretch – to the frustration of visiting photographers. Sahara dust has even been known to reach the Caribbean.

CHERNOBYL AND RADIOACTIVE DUST

In contrast to desert dust and volcanic ash, the microscopic radioactive particles or indeed gas that result from nuclear accidents are invisible. They are, however, easily detectable by equipment and so events like that at Chernobyl on 26 April 1986 give meteorologists a unique opportunity to study the dispersion of material.

The Chernobyl nuclear power station in the Soviet Union, near Kiev, suffered a massive but conventional explosion during the very early hours of the morning. What started as a local tragedy turned into an international event. An anticyclone existed to the east of Chernobyl and at first the winds took the gas and particles northwestwards towards Sweden. Here the increased levels of radioactivity led to the shut down of a nuclear power station near Stockholm, since the Swedes were unaware of the Soviet accident and thought they had a local leak. Over the next few days the main part of the cloud meandered southwestwards towards Switzerland, then turned northwestwards again to reach the British Isles on 2 and

3 May. Some of the material had been lost *en route* by dry deposition, but much remained in the air. Over Britain, for the first time in the life of the cloud, substantial rain fell from the middle levels of the troposphere and washed out some of the material on to the ground on 3 May. If one imagines a particle of less than 1 μm in diameter (a millionth of a metre or a thousandth of a millimetre) being hit by a comparatively huge raindrop, then you can understand the effectiveness of washout. The worst-affected areas of the British Isles were those that had substantial rainfall, including parts of the Yorkshire Pennines near Skipton, Cumbria, southwest Scotland, the Isle of Arran and the Highlands of western Scotland. It was perhaps fortunate that it was mainly upland areas which were affected by rain and therefore by radioactivity. This is of course little comfort to sheep farmers who were still suffering from restrictions on sheep movement four years later as the radioactive material re-cycled itself through the plant life.

This account of the Chernobyl material suggests that it was simply a matter of a cloud wandering across Europe, which is obviously a simplification. Some material escaped high into the troposphere reaching 30,000 ft (9000 m) altitude and beyond. This was carried eastwards by the jet streams to reach Japan on 3 May and western USA on 6 May. It would therefore have circled the Earth in about a fortnight, like the material from atmospheric nuclear explosions in the 1950s. (Some of that material persisted in the stratosphere for many years.)

We should beware of relying on Chernobyl as a model for any future accidents. It was surprising in that event how the British Isles, a thousand miles west of the source, should receive so much fall-out. Also, due to the meteorological situation, much of the material stayed in the lowest 5000 ft (1500 m) of the atmosphere (in total contrast to nuclear explosions). Perhaps the worst conditions for normal industrial accidents are calm conditions, as at Bhopal in India, where there was no wind to disperse the hazardous material.

WINTER GALES

Gales are more common in the British Isles in winter than in summer, because depressions are deeper and more vigorous in the winter-half of the year. This in turn is due to the greater temperature contrast between the Equator and the North Pole in winter than in summer. In January the polar region is bitterly cold whilst in July it is only moderately so. The Equator remains at pretty much the same temperature all year round and therefore the thermal contrast tends to reach a maximum around January.

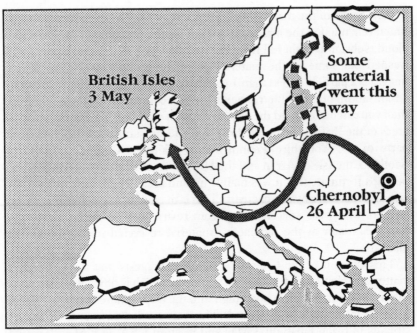

Most of the radioactive material from Chernobyl blew northwestwards at first. Some reached Scandinavia where it was drawn upwards into a jet stream which carried it eastwards across Asia. However, some of the material remained in the lowest part of the atmosphere and meandered westwards to the British Isles where rain intercepted the cloud and washed out most of the remaining radioactive particles.

Major gales are certainly biased towards the winter-time, as the roll-call of disasters shows.

The 'Great Storm' of 26-27 November 1703 wrecked literally hundreds of ships in the English Channel and the North Sea with huge loss of life amongst sailors. Tree damage was also extensive. Judging from reports at the time, the depression which caused these (mainly south-westerly?) gales crossed England moving northeastwards.

February 1962 brought two gales to Sheffield within four days. First on 12 February, then a second event on the 16 February when severe damage was localised around Sheffield, though most of Yorkshire was somewhat affected. In the latter event, the westerly gale was worse to the *lee* of the Pennines. This was for meteorologists an unusual but reasonably well understood case of a lee-wave gale. The air, having been forced up over the Pennines, curved downwards to hit the ground again at Sheffield.

Glasgow has suffered at least twice during this century from major gales. The first case was on the 28 January 1927 when eleven people died in the city. More recently on 15 January 1968 another westerly gale swept through in the early hours of the morning and nine people died, with widespread damage to buildings.

Ferrybridge power station lost five cooling towers in a gale on 1 November 1965. Certainly this was a strong blow, but subsequent investigations using wind tunnels showed that the air forcing its way between the first row of cooling towers actually caused a huge force on a second row of towers, and so it was the supposedly sheltered constructions in the back row which collapsed. The individual towers were reasonably satisfactory but their combined effect on windflow had been ignored.

On the night of 2-3 January 1976 came a memorable westerly gale for much of northern England, the Midlands and East Anglia when a deep depression crossed northern England into the North Sea. As usual with eastward-moving lows, the strongest winds were just to the south of the depression track. Coniferous forests in Norfolk were devastated and some 200-year-old cottages were severely damaged.

London's most famous gale came on 16 October 1987. This time the depression came up from Biscay, tracking across Devon, Birmingham and Yorkshire. The worst winds were southerlies on its southeastern flank, with severe gales in the Home Counties before dawn. That event and the Burns' Day storm of 25 January 1990 are described more fully in the next two sections.

All of these cases, with the exception of the local intensification near Sheffield, were caused by substantial depressions moving northeastwards or eastwards across Britain. This is the commonest cause of widespread damage, and is most likely between October and April with a statistical peak probability around December or January.

As a rough guide for inland parts of the British Isles a 70 mph (110 kph) gust will damage the odd tree and blow down a dubious fence, whereas a 90 mph (145 kph) gust will remove tiles and television aerials and destroy garden sheds and elderly conservatories.

THE OCTOBER STORM OF 1987

Meteorologists in southeast England were besieged with questions about the storm in the early hours of 16 October 1987. Millions of trees were uprooted and 19 people died.

Could it happen again? Yes, obviously it is possible for any weather phenomenon to happen twice. The chance of a gale of that severity happening in inland regions of the southeast are very small in any one year. If you take into account that it was largely a southerly gale rather than the usual westerly then the event becomes rarer still. If we also acknowledge that it came in mid-October after a mild and very wet spell when the

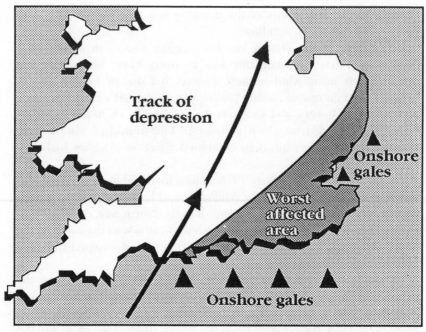

In the October storm of 1987 the depression crossed Devon and the Midlands but the worst gales were in the southeast.

leaves were still on the trees, then the chance of similar tree damage becomes remote – probably less than once in two hundred years (though return periods are a statistical minefield). The wetness of the soil was certainly an important factor in the laying waste of our woodland because the trees, still in leaf, were uprooted. Those in the north and west of the British Isles were somewhat bemused by the press interest in an event which largely passed them by. We should also acknowledge that gales of that severity are an almost annual event on the western side of Shetland or the Isle of Lewis.

What about the forecasting? Could it have been improved? Whenever an exceptional event occurs, meteorologists go back over it with a fine-tooth comb, and this minute dissection has been applied to the October storm. We don't refer to it as a hurricane because that term is reserved for a warm-cored vortex over the tropical oceans, although the expression Hurricane Force 12 is included in the Beaufort scale and the October storm winds reached Force 10 to 12 on that scale. None of the major computer models in the world predicted the severity of the pressure gradient and therefore the full wind strength just east of the depression, although the track of the low was reasonably well forecast.

Much of the subsequent review has focused on the lack of ship observations in the Atlantic to the west of Portugal at midday on the previous day and also on the way in which the computer interprets or assimilates such observations as are received. The computer needs the best possible starting point (i.e. a perfect analysis) to achieve a good forecast and in this case there were insufficient ships in the area. In the event the low deepened as it passed Brittany, reaching Devon at 0100 GMT, central pressure 955 mbar, and Birmingham at 0400 GMT with central pressure 958 mbar. It then continued northeastwards across Yorkshire filling as it went. The band of strongest winds was about 100 miles east of the depression centre and therefore crossed Sussex, eastern Surrey, western Kent, London and into Essex. With a southerly wind the coastal strip of Sussex was badly hit between midnight and 2 a.m. Inland the inevitable gustiness was the main cause of damage with London affected at around 4 to 5 a.m. Temperatures reached an amazing 19C during the gale. A gust of 99 mph (158 kph) was recorded at Gatwick in Sussex – remarkable for a low-level inland site.

THE BURNS' DAY STORM OF 1990

On Thursday 25 January 1990, there was widespread damage as a deepening low- pressure area swept across the British Isles. The centre of the depression which caused the gales was about 953 mbar as it crossed Ayr in Scotland, the birthplace of Robert Burns, on this anniversary of his birth. Ironically, Scotland was spared the gales which hit Ireland, Wales and then England.

When we get two great gales within 28 months then the first event is still quite fresh in the mind as we clear up the debris of the second. Comparisons are inevitable.

First of all, how did the strengths compare? Maximum gusts were in each case around 82 to 107 mph (132 to 172 kph), depending on location. However the great gale of 16 October 1987 was more unusual in that the strongest winds were confined to Kent, Sussex and Surrey rather than the more typical areas of Scotland, Ireland and Wales. Thus the strengths were not strictly comparable and the 16 October 1987 event was the statistically more surprising.

Another important difference was that the January 1990 tragedy covered five times the area of the earlier one with the result that 47 people died compared with 19. A bald calculation would thus suggest that 1987 was more severe within its very localised region. But another factor to consider is that with the Burns' Day storm the gale occurred in daylight, between 11 a.m. (Cornwall and Wales) and 4 p.m. (East Anglia and London), whereas in 1987 it was between 2 a.m. and 6 a.m. so most people were indoors (and some even slept through it).

On both occasions Scotland was unaffected and the whole aftermath must at times seem excessive to those north of the border who suffer gales frequently.

Gusts in the Burns' Day storm of 1990 included 107 mph (172 kph) at Aberporth (Wales), 102 mph (164 kph) at Culdrose (Cornwall), 98 mph (158 kph) at Hurstmonceux (Sussex), 97 mph (156 kph) at Boscombe Down (Wiltshire) and Cardiff Airport, 92 mph (148 kph) at Wattisham (Suffolk) and 89 mph (143 kph) at Waddington (Lincolnshire). However, damage is not always directly related to speed, there are other factors to consider: traditional buildings on the western side of the country are stronger; trees in exposed locations are more stunted or virtually non-existent, as in Shetland; and an important difference between the two storms is that on 16 October 1987 trees were still very much in leaf after a mild autumn and the ground was very wet, which prevented the roots from holding firm.

Wind directions on 25 January 1990 were from the southwest or west-southwest (the traditional gale directions) rather than southerly. This directional factor may explain why fences that had withstood the previous storm were blown down. Individual gusts react with the surrounding topography and buildings in a complex way. Eddying and suction cause damage on the lee side of buildings.

In each case the strongest winds were to the right of the depression track, i.e. to the south or southeast of the low centre. (Tip: look out for tightly-packed isobars on your weather chart to the south of an eastward-moving low. The strongest gales come when the depression is still deepening. If it is already very deep when out in the Atlantic then it will probably be a spent force by the time it reaches eastern Britain.)

And what of the aftermath? The usual human reaction to disaster seems to be to look around for people or institutions to blame, and both events were similar in this respect despite the fairly accurate prediction of the Burns' Day storm. Those looking for lessons to put into practice next time will point out that staying indoors is safer than going outside.

And are such gales getting more common? I don't know. Certainly the storm of Thursday January 1990 was in meteorological terms a much more 'typical' event than that of 16 October 1987, and neither of them matched the great storm of 1703.

COASTAL FLOODING

On 31 January 1953, disastrous floods affected eastern England and the Netherlands with 1800 lives lost on the continent and about 300 in the British Isles.

The cause was high tides coinciding with a 'storm surge' which drove the water to overtop and breach the coastal defences, especially in East Anglia.

If one was to stand on a sea wall observing for a whole month, one might see the water get to the foot of the wall three times. First of all a very high spring tide might reach it. Secondly, straightforward large waves driven by a strong onshore wind might achieve it. Thirdly, a 'normal' high tide might be higher than expected due to a storm surge, caused by a gale but probably not an onshore one. Only if the surge coincides with a spring tide is there likely to be trouble, rather like throwing two dice and getting two sixes. This type of tragedy has some parallels with the coastal floods caused by tropical cyclones, which are also cases of abnormally high tides due to deep low-pressure systems.

Tides depend principally on the Moon and are therefore predictable. The time and height of each high tide can be published many years in advance. However, the predicted tides can be in error by 30 cm (1 ft) and just occasionally by a metre (3 ft) or more due to a storm surge. Typically this happens when the sea is driven by gale force winds into a shallowing basin like the North Sea. Surprisingly the water is driven at an angle somewhat to the right of the wind direction (due once again to the ever-present Coriolis effect). A westerly gale near Orkney will drive water into the North Sea and a northwesterly will drive it southwards down the east coast of Britain. In a process which takes several hours it may then 'slosh' against the Dutch coast and back as a storm surge into the Thames estuary. If the extra component (of, say, a metre in height) occurs at or near the same time as high tide, then the Thames barrier will be lowered to prevent the sea water from moving up-river and flooding London.

Similar events can cause an extra-high tide in the Bristol Channel and enhance the Severn Bore, which moves up-river near Minsterworth towards Gloucester.

Negative surges or abnormally low water levels are a threat to super-tankers in shallow parts of the Straits of Dover. The largest ships could in fact be grounded if the negative surge were to coincide with low tide.

The Storm Tide Warning Service, situated at the Met Office HQ at Bracknell, warns the appropriate authorities of these storm surges. The main threat is near the equinoxes when spring tides are especially high, and in winter when gales are at their most intense, and thus the risk season runs from September to April. Low atmospheric pressure also plays a part because the sea level rises very slightly as the downward pressure of the atmosphere is reduced. A serious of gauges around the coast enables the Warning Service to watch the progress of the storm surges as they move down the east coast of Scotland then England. Increasingly there are requests to keep an eye on other coastal stretches of the British Isles.

SINGULARITIES AND BUCHAN SPELLS

Friday 23 September 1988 was very windy over Ireland, Wales and England, with gales on most western coasts and hills. This was also the date of the autumn equinox when the sun crossed the equator 'moving' southwards.

However the gale on this date raises the spectre of 'singularities' or 'irregularities'. These are recurrent weather patterns which are said to happen on just about the same day every year or at least with greater-than-chance frequency. The 'equinoctal gales' are one example. There is a well-established increase in windiness in the winter half-year and obviously an increasing risk of strong winds as the month of September progresses. After what is usually a relatively quiet period of weather in terms of gale frequency during June, July and August, the first strong 'blow' of autumn is likely in September or October. It will be all the more noticeable because no gales have occurred for three months or so. Therefore, almost any strong wind in September tends to get called an equinoctial gale, even if the date is out by a week or two.

'Buchan spells' are the most famous proposed list of singularities. Dr Alexander Buchan proposed that cold periods occur around 7-14 February, 11-14 April, 9-14 May, 29 June–4 July, 6-11 August and 6-13 November and also that warm periods occur around 12-15 July, 12-15 August and 3-14 December. However, his suggestions were based on data for southeast Scotland, mainly during the 1860s, and have been disproved by subsequent analysis. In other words, they seemed a good idea when the data was first available but they just have not stood the test of time. The glib response from advocates of the Buchan periods is that 'the climate has changed' to which there is little answer except 'therefore they are of no use'.

Proposals of singularities are a valuable contribution to scientific discussion into the nature of variability in weather. Often a ten-year analysis of one site will throw up a marked cold spell, say in mid-January. However, this may just be from the coincidence of it happening twice in the ten-year period. After a further 20 or 30 years the 'mid-January cold spell' will probably be statistically extinguished. And yet, it would be fascinating to find such a spell that really worked, and not unreasonable, because synoptic patterns to tend to recur at *roughly* the same time of year. Of all the recurrent spells or singularities suggested for the British Isles there is one which I feel may stand the test of time – the mid-September anticyclonic spell of 6-19th. (Note how wide the spread of dates is in this example!) This comes when the land is starting to cool at the end of summer and day-time convection is on the wane, but before the general storminess and vigorous depressions of winter. Central Europe sometimes shares this spell, and it can therefore be a good time to visit Germany or Austria. Having criticised singularities, I have concluded by describing one!

MILD WINTERS

The Met Office splits the year into four seasons, each of three months. This simplistic division provides us with a winter which runs from December to February inclusive. It unfortunately means that March thereby falls into spring-time, which is inappropriate in the north of Britain.

The winters of 1989 (i.e. December 1988 to February 1989 inclusive) and 1990 were around 2 to 3C (3 to 5 F) warmer than the long-term average. Aberdeen and Newcastle were amongst the places which had the greatest anomaly above average, which no doubt stems partially from the mountains which lie to the west of these cities, the frequency of westerly winds and the föhn effect (which is explained in Chapter 5).

The number of frosts was also dramatically reduced. In Manchester, for example, in winter 1989 the total number of frosts was 12 (1 in December, 4 in January, 7 in February). In Glasgow there were 6 frosts (0, 1, 5). In central London, as measured on the Weather Centre roof, which is a somewhat unusual site, there were no frosts at all in the official period. Winter 1989 equalled that of 1869 according to the Central England Temperature Series started by Professor Gordon Manley, with 1990 a close third. This series of records was researched by Manley back to 1659 and is now computed by averaging the readings from four stations in the Midlands.

CHRISTMAS WEATHER

Many people since Bing Crosby have dreamt of a white Christmas – children, skiers and meteorologists among them. For bookmakers it may be more like a nightmare, since they take bets from the public without anyone backing the (odds-on) converse.

But what constitutes a white Christmas? Most bets are struck on whether snow will actually fall on Christmas Day. This usually means at any stage of the 24 hours from midnight to midnight. Depending upon the bookmaker's rules, a short burst of sleet in an otherwise rainy period may qualify as success for the punter. Sleet is defined as rain and snow mixed in our version of the English language, so the snow certainly need not settle on the ground. (In the United States the word sleet is used for what we understand as hail.)

And where must the snow or sleet fall? Obviously any location could be selected. The summit of Ben Nevis would improve one's chances over the flat south of England. Unfortunately the observatory on Scotland's highest mountain is no longer in use! The London Weather Centre verifies the occurrence or otherwise of snow, sleet, etc., on its roof about 100 ft (30 m) up above High Holborn. An observer goes outside on the roof every hour to record the temperature, humidity, cloud base and visibility and look for any precipitation. During cloudy periods he or she will also check between routine hourly observations and especially so on Christmas Day if the temperature is close to or below freezing-point. The Supervisor and Senior Forecaster will also be keeping a lookout between mince pies and coffee.

During this century you could have 'collected' on a white Christmas bet for London in 1916, 1927, 1938, 1956, 1964, 1968, 1970 and 1976. These were occasions with sleet or snow falling but not necessarily lying, averaging about one year in twelve.

What happens if snow falls on Christmas Eve or before and is still lying on the ground? This doesn't count for most betting purposes, but it certainly does provide a beautiful sight and a traditional white Christmas. In 1981 snow was lying over much of the country from a previous fall, though the weather on Christmas Day itself was gloriously sunny. The roll-call of years with snow lying in Central London yields only five this century – 1906, 1927, 1938, 1970 and 1981. On higher ground away from the urban environment the list would be much longer, and even in parts of outer London 1917, 1923 and 1956 can be added.

COLD SPELLS

The record low temperature for the British Isles is –27.2 C (-17 F) at Braemar in Scotland on 11 February 1895 and again on 10 January 1982. This latter occasion brought widespread cold and many observing sites set new 'individual' records with –20 C (-4 F) exceeded quite widely even in southern England. Shawbury in Shropshire is also a notably cold site which has come close to the British record.

Just to put our cold weather in perspective, the world record is –89.2 C (-128.6 F) at the Vostok base in Antarctica. Canadian and Siberian sites are frequently below the all-time British record and '40 below' is reasonably common there. (40 below is – 40 in both Celsius and Farenheit scales.)

So what meteorological circumstances combine to produce a record?

Clear skies will enable the heat to escape (by the radiation process). Calm conditions will ensure that the air which has been cooled by contact with the ground remains near the surface and is cooled further. A long night will allow maximum time for cooling, so in Britain more northern sites in mid-winter stand the best chance. A surface of fresh powdery snow will act as insulating material and therefore prevent heat from the soil flowing upwards to spoil the record. Finally, a dry, pollution-free column of air above the site will allow maximum transmission of radiation out into space. In connection with this last point, upland sites have less atmosphere above them and especially less water vapour, so probably many cold nights occur on snow-covered plateaux but go unrecorded. We talk of frost hollows into which cold air can drain, but a shallow saucer-shaped area in an upland region is even more effective at collecting cold air on a really calm night.

Dry, sandy soils have many air spaces and thus produce much the same effect as snow in preventing heat from the soil being conducted upwards to the surface. Unexpectedly low temperatures can occur at dawn in sandy regions like the Breckland area of Norfolk and even in May and June quite sharp frosts are recorded at Santon Downham near Thetford.

WINDCHILL

Windchill is all about the combined effect of wind speed and low temperatures. Misunderstandings abound because, for example, the effect of windchill on a building will be quite different from that on a human being. Similarly we should define the clothing worn by the human being before we make a statement such as 'half of human heat loss occurs through the head'. This is obviously not true if we are standing naked in a snow storm. However, it may well be true if we are wearing several layers of efficient clothing but our head is bare.

Northerlies and easterlies tend to feel cold and raw, because they can bring simultaneous low temperatures and strong winds. Similar arguments apply on hills where windchill is normal in winter. December and January can bring a chilling blast of Polar Continental air from the east which has been cooled for several long nights over Europe and will usually have the necessary depth needed for the combination of strong winds and sub-zero temperatures. Mid-January 1987 saw this at its most lethal with –5 C (23 F) and a wind of 25 mph (40 kph) widespread over southern England.

Another factor in making the human feel cold is the humidity. If the air is dry (i.e. low wet-bulb temperature and dew point), then evaporation from the skin is more rapid, and our face particularly will feel cold. When climbing out of the sea or a swimming pool, our bodies act like a wet-bulb thermometer. Even on occasions when we think that our skin is dry there is still some 'insensible perspiration' or loss of moisture through our skin. More details on humidity can be found in Chapter 7.

Various tables and graphs have been produced showing 'effective temperatures' or 'equivalent temperatures'. The American 30-30-30 rule of survival states that with a temperature of minus 30 Fahrenheit and a wind speed of 30 mph, human flesh will freeze solid in 30 seconds. This valuable piece of information is passed to recruits (volunteers?) for Antarctic bases. Fortunately neither Arctic Maritime nor Polar Continental airstreams bring quite those conditions to the British Isles. Other tables giving effective temperatures including the Steadman version and the Sipple-Passel formula. One reason for the reluctance to use them in forecasts is that a true temperature of +2 C (36 F) may yield an effective temperature of −5 C (23 F) which could give the general public the impression that frost was expected when that was not the case. As a rough guide, for a temperature of 0 Celsius, i.e. freezing-point, winds of 10, 20 and 30 mph will give effective temperatures of −4, −10 and −14 Celsius respectively, depending somewhat upon clothing, and so on.

BLIZZARDS

A blizzard is a combination of falling snow and strong winds which cause the snow to drift and blow about.

It is also possible after a snowfall has ceased for blizzard conditions to be produced simply by the wind increasing to such an extent that the air is again filled with snow lifted from the surface. Under these circumstances, it may be impossible for the observer to tell if snow is actually falling or whether all of the airborne snow particles have been raised from the ground. Winds of about 15 mph (25 kph) will lift dry snow from the surface and send it snaking across the roads or fields near ground level – this is 'drifting snow'. Winds of 25 mph (40 kph) are necessary to raise snow high into the air and produce a significant reduction in visibility at head height and above – this is 'blowing snow'.

Dry, powdery snow with a temperature below freezing will be lifted much more easily than old wet snow which has compacted over a period of days.

In Scotland and other northern areas, a blizzard is most likely with a northerly airstream and especially with a polar low. On the mountains, blizzards are far more frequent than on low ground for two reasons: a greater percentage of the precipitation falls as snow, and also winds are

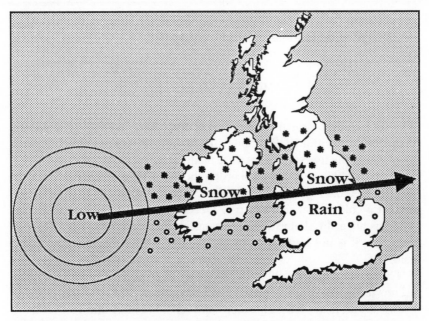

A depression which crosses the British Isles in winter will usually bring westerly winds and rain to those places lying to the south of its track, but some snow to areas lying north of its path.

stronger. The potential blizzard season also lasts much longer above an altitude of 2000 ft (600 m), perhaps from November to May. One of the worst things that can happen is the onset of a blizzard in the Cairngorms, the Lake District or North Wales during Easter week, when holiday-makers and part-time walkers are out on the hills. Onset at midday following a sunny morning will catch out those who are unprepared, especially as visibility can be reduced to less than 30 m (100 ft), with hill walkers then disorientated and apt to lose their way. In short, they will get lost, cold and demoralised.

Above 4000 ft (1200 m) snow can fall in any month of the year, though a true blizzard is fairly improbable even on Ben Nevis or the Cairngorms in July or August.

In the southern half of Britain, the classic blizzard scenario is one with some sort of easterly or southeasterly airstream blowing in from the Continent. A warm front or occluded front approaching from the south-west becomes slow moving, lying from, say, Bristol to the Isle of Wight. Everyone just north of this line will get a blizzard, whilst to the south milder air is established. The difficulty for the meteorologist is to predict the position of that front and its often slow and decreasing progress northeastwards. Certain stretches of road can become blocked with certain wind directions and those responsible for clearing the highways get to learn of these trouble spots by experience.

FAMOUS COLD WINTERS

The four coldest British winters this century have been 1963 (coldest), then 1947, 1940 and 1979 although the ranking order does rather depend upon where the measurements were made. If we take the last three, 1947, 1963 and 1979 in chronological order, there is a 16-year cycle. Obviously this will be seized upon by the simplistic lovers of such quirks of nature to predict a cold winter in 1995 (i.e. December 1994 to February 1995). There is not a shred of evidence to suggest a physical *reason* for a 16-year cycle, but it is not impossible by chance that winter may turn out to be cold.

Those who enjoy recalling the bitter weather of the distant past must acknowledge that for most places 1963 was coldest, but 1947 was perhaps snowiest with heavy falls, especially between 28 January and 10 March. A run of cold winters around 1979 to 1982 gave way to very mild ones in the late 1980s. Whatever the greenhouse effect does, some more cold winters are certain in the future. We should not let a couple of mild years colour our judgement.

A CHRONOLOGY OF BRITISH WEATHER EVENTS

This covers the period from 1659 to mid-1990. Seasonal temperatures refer to central England values but will usually be typical of most of the British Isles.

September 1666   The Great Fire of London followed a very dry summer, and occurred with strengthening winds which fanned the flames.
Winter 1684   Coldest on record.
26-27 November 1703   The Great Storm caused the loss of 8000 lives as a deep depression crossed England. Many of those who died were sailors in the English Channel and the North Sea.
Summer 1725   Coolest on record.
Autumn 1730   The mildest autumn on record (just beating 1731).
Autumn 1740   Coldest on record.
Winter 1740   Second coldest on record, behind 1684 but just beating 1963.
1740   Coldest calendar year on record by some margin.

Winter 1814   Bitterly cold with a frost fair in London, but officially ranked fourth, just behind 1963.

Spring 1837   Coldest on record.

26 October 1859   The *Royal Charter* ran aground on Anglesey and 400 drowned when a deep depression moved northeast across Britain taking a similar track to the storms of 1703 and 1987.

Winter 1869   Mildest on record equal with 1989.

Spring 1893   Warmest on record.

28 December 1897   The Tay Rail Bridge collapsed in a westerly gale as a train was crossing, and 75 died.

9 August 1911   One of the hottest reliably recorded days in British history though beaten on 3 August 1990.

28 June 1917   250 mm (10 in) of rain at Bruton (Somerset), second highest daily total behind Martinstown in 1955.

1921   Record dry year.

May 1923   Persistent snow storms in the Cairngorms.

28 January 1927   Westerly gales swept across Scotland with 26 killed. Glasgow badly affected.

6-7 January 1928   North sea floods, though not as severe as 1953, were 1.8 m (6 ft) above the predicted tidal level in London.

27-28 January 1940   Widespread freezing rain coated trees, overhead wires and roads in Wales and Southern England with ice (after severe cold on 21 January).

8 May 1943   Deep snow in Scotland.

Winter 1947   Cold and very snowy. Lost its place among the temperature records because the cold did not begin in earnest until the third week in January. Followed by snow-melt floods in March and April.

Summer 1947   Notably warm.

1949   Second warmest calendar year on record in central England behind 1989.

21 May 1950   Tornado runs from Berkshire to Norfolk between 4 p.m. and 8 p.m. with four people killed by lightning. Considerable damage in Leighton Buzzard.

15-16 August 1952   Disastrous flood at Lynmouth, north Devon.

5-8 December 1952   Worst London smog ever. Literally thousands died, many elderly or infirm. This triggered the Clean Air Act of 1956.

31 January to 1 February 1953   North Sea floods caused by a storm surge. About 300 died in Britain and 1800 in the Netherlands. Many lives were lost in the gales at sea including 133 from the Stranraer ferry *Princess Victoria*.

18 July 1955   British record rainfall for one day of 279 mm (11 in) at Martinstown, Dorset, beating the Somerset record of 1917.

6 August and 5 September 1958 Hailstorms at Tunbridge Wells (Kent) and Horsham (Sussex) respectively.

9 July 1959 Hailstorm at Wokingham.

Summer 1959 Notable warm summer included a 57-day drought (i.e. without measurable rain) in parts of eastern England from 14 August to 9 October.

12 and 16 February 1962 Sheffield suffered two severe gales within four days, the second enhanced by lee-wave airflow.

Winter 1963 The cold winter started in December 1962 and persisted right through to February. Third coldest behind 1684 and 1740.

1 November 1965 Cooling towers at Ferrybridge, Yorkshire, collapsed in gale.

15 January 1968 Westerly gales in Glasgow as a deep depression crossed the Highlands in the early hours. Similar to the 1927 event.

July to September 1968 Heavy rain caused various episodes of flooding. Leeming, North Yorkshire, had 35.7 mm (1.4 in) in 8.5 minutes on 2 July. Widespread floods in southern England on 10-11 July and 14-17 September.

7 February 1969 Gust of 136 mph (219 kph) at Kirkwall in Orkney as severe northerly spell commenced.

2 June 1975 Snow over Scotland and eastern England, lying for a time on high ground.

14 August 1975 The Hampstead storm gave 170.8 mm (6.7 in) of rain in a few hours with severe flooding.

Summer 1975 Notably hot and sunny.

2-3 January 1976 Severe gales in England as depression tracks eastwards overnight. Worst damage in the Midlands and East Anglia.

Summer 1976 Hottest on record. The run of hot days finally finished on the late August Bank holiday weekend. Hottest spells were 3-4 July and 26-28 July, with 36 C (97 F) widely reported.

Winter 1979 Cold and snowy in January and February, but nothing like as cold overall as 1963.

December 1981 Bitter cold.

January 1982 Bitter cold.

15 June 1983 Hail the size of cricket balls on the south coast of England.

16 October 1987 Severe gale (the October storm) hits London and southeast England in the early hours of the morning, uprooting vast areas of woodland. The depression track was northeastwards across Devon and the Midlands, thus very similar to the storms of 1703 and 1859.

Winter 1989 Notably mild, sharing first place with 1869.

Summer 1989 Warm and particularly sunny from May to September.

1989 Sunniest and warmest calendar year so far his century over much of the British Isles.

Winter 1990 Notably mild, just behind 1989 and 1869.

25 January 1990 The 'Burns' Day' storm. Severe gales over Ireland, Wales and England. Forty-seven die as deep depression moves eastwards across southern Scotland. As usual the strongest winds were some way south (or to the right) of the depression track.

Summer 1990 Warm and sunny, but most notable for the heatwave which culminated on 3 August with 37.1 C (98.8 F) at Cheltenham.

Chapter 5

LOCAL WEATHER

WHERE WILL FOG FORM?

THE THREE basic requirements for fog are clear skies, light winds and a sufficiently long night to allow the air to be cooled to its condensation point. In view of this last requirement, it is logical that the months November, December and January should be inclined to fogginess, since they have the longest nights. Occasions of clear skies and light winds are fairly evenly distributed throughout the year, whenever a high pressure settles down over the British Isles. Of course there doesn't have to be a high because a stationary low pressure could have light winds near its centre and so too could a 'col'. This last-named feature of the weather chart is the region between two highs and two lows where there are no isobars and therefore no wind.

When the fog is forming in the evening it usually does so over low-lying fields and river valleys. Here there is more moisture and less wind, and possibly also cold-air 'drainage' whereby dense air flows in from surrounding slopes. The expression a 'pool of fog' is therefore often appropriate during the formation period. At this stage it will be shallow, perhaps only a metre or two deep as it accumulates in the valley bottoms or over flat ground. The stars or Moon will be visible looking upwards through the fog. During the night, a second stage will be reached whereby the fog deepens and the stars are no longer visible. (For those scientists who like to study the heat balance of the system, the radiation is now escaping from the top of the thick fog rather than from the ground through the shallow fog.)

Motorists may notice that there is a contrast between the evening when the fog will usually form first on low ground, and the morning period when it may be dense and widespread but will tend eventually to lift away from the low ground. By late morning it may well be the higher stretches of road and the hills which are still in fog when on the low ground it has thinned. A lot depends on whether a slight breeze is stirring the atmosphere up. Fog most frequently occurs around dawn, which is of course the time of minimum temperature, and is least likely inland in the afternoon around the time of maximum temperature.

On the coast, with the complications of sea-fog, it is a completely different picture. The classic mechanism here is warm moist air drifting slowly over a progressively colder sea surface until it is cooled down to its saturation point. Since the sea temperature hardly changes from day to night, sea-fog can appear at any time.

The mountains of northwest Scotland are very prone to hill fog, but it is the lowlands of Scotland and more especially England which suffer with winter 'radiation fog' in high-pressure systems.

On a more local scale there are known trouble-spots. The M25 has been studied from the air to locate the fog-prone stretches. Gatwick seems to collect fog in a way which Prestwick Airport near Glasgow very rarely does. There is also a roundabout near my house where fog seems to form at the drop of a hat. No doubt the same kind of fog-prone localities have been noticed by motorists throughout the country.

COASTAL WEATHER

Coastal weather is often different from that inland. This will obviously not be true with a strongish offshore wind, but may well be the case if the wind is very light or blowing onshore or parallel to the shoreline. When we visit the coast and find that the weather is different there, our first reaction may be one of surprise but the climate of the coast is fundamentally different, including the clouds, wind, temperature and humidity.

Rainfall totals as measured in a rain-gauge are similar to those on low ground inland. This hides perhaps an increased frequency of drizzle and the unpleasant, near-horizontal nature of winter rain, driven sideways by a gale. And, writing of gales, they are very much more common at the seaside, with typically 20 days per year on our western coasts compared with perhaps 2 days per year of true gales inland. For this reason the coasts are not ideal climatologically for retirement, though gales are far less frequent on southern and eastern coasts than in the Northern Isles, Outer Hebrides or western Ireland. (Non-meteorological factors are probably much more important in the major decision on retirement location.)

Temperatures on the coast are lower in summer, especially in day-time, but higher in winter and especially at night. This amelioration of winter cold due to the proximity of the sea leads to the overall year-round warmth of the Isles of Scilly (where really high temperatures never occur!).

Relative humidity tends to be higher near the sea, but this is not a particularly unpleasant feature in the British Isles. The most marked differences in humidity tend to occur on summer days when high temperatures are recorded inland and the coasts are cooler. An extreme example of this effect comes in spring and summer when sea-fog clamps in at the coastal resorts while places a few miles inland are basking in sunshine and enjoying temperatures several degrees higher. This happens in anticyclonic weather on the east coast of Scotland and England, but also when moist southwesterly Tropical Maritime airstreams affect southwest England and Wales.

The coasts of the British Isles, and especially of southern England, do have one great climatological bonus. Here annual sunshine totals are at their highest, amounting to over 1800 hours a year on the Channel coast. Days which benefit most are those with southwesterly airstreams when the sea is clear of cloud, but cumulus forms inland due to the convection process. The coasts may then be a couple of degrees cooler than inland but the extra sunshine is ample compensation.

So where is the ideal site for a house? Perhaps it is a mile or two inland from the south coast, but sheltered from coastal gales by a small hill range. Here you should get most of the coastal sunshine without too many of the detrimental effects of higher wind speed and drizzle.

SEA-BREEZES

A sea-breeze can be defined as an onshore wind (i.e. blowing from the sea – we usually name the winds by the place from which they emanate) which is caused by a temperature differential between the sea and land.

What are the requirements for sea-breeze formation? The natural windflow due to high- and low-pressure systems must be weak, and the middle of an anticyclone is therefore an ideal region, but not the only one. The land must be significantly warmer than the sea, by say 5 C (9 F) or more.

By mid-morning, when the temperature differential has become established, the air over the land has warmed and expanded. We can think of it as a column of air which has got taller. However, the column of air over the sea is still the same height as it was during the night, since the sea temperature remains pretty well constant. A pressure difference therefore exists aloft – at 3000 ft (1000 m) or more – and the higher-level air flows from land to sea, which immediately induces a low- level flow from sea to land. This is the sea-breeze. On the beach, we experience the onset of the cooler, moist air in mid-morning. There are occasions which illustrate the whole mechanism when smoke from a coastal power station can be seen blowing inland, then rising and blowing seaward aloft. As the day goes on

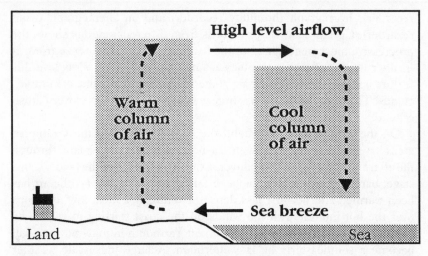

The sea-breeze system, with an offshore wind just aloft and a cool onshore breeze at the surface.

the whole system gets bigger and deeper, and gradually the surface sea-breeze extends further inland.

Sea-breezes occur in temperate latitudes like that of the British Isles from about March to September, but in the tropics all year round. On the coasts of Arabia, India, Florida or Africa, the sea-breeze can be 20 mph (30 kph) in strength. Most Mediterranean resorts are similarly affected in spring and summer, and quite often the sea will get rougher during the morning after a calm start. The cooling influence of the sea air is marked within a few hundred metres of the coast but becomes barely noticeable a few kilometres inland.

During the night, if the area is still under a slack, anticyclonic regime, a land-breeze may develop. In some regions land-breezes also become well defined, though these are more a feature of winter rather than summer. Observations from the Portuguese and Spanish coasts at 0600 hours on a winter morning sometimes show light offshore winds all around the Iberian Peninsula, blowing outwards from the cold interior. These land breezes are typically of 5 mph (8 kph).

THE SEA-BREEZE FRONT AND THE 'HEAT LOW'

The forward edge of the sea air often progresses inland in the British Isles at about 5 mph (8 kph) starting at 0900 hours and reaching 80 km (50 miles) inland by 1900 hours. At this stage it is weak and hardly noticeable except to an alert meteorologist armed with a thermograph (temperature recorder), hygrograph (humidity recorder) and an anemograph (wind recorder). Careful analysis of records from different stations shows the progressive movement inland of the leading edge or sea-breeze front. It finally runs out of steam and dies around sunset. Glider pilots love this feature because there is rising air, sometimes marked by a line of cumulus clouds. The best-organised sea-breeze systems tend to occur over flattish ground.

On the eastern side of Britain, the East Anglian and the Grampian areas have some similarities, with sea-breezes progressing inland through the afternoon and tending to converge due to the shape of the land. By this stage, barometric pressure has been falling over the land (as the air has been warmed and become less dense). Eventually a 'heat low' develops over the hot interior with the winds on the coast starting to veer. The easterly sea-breeze which set in at Great Yarmouth in mid-morning will become a southeasterly by late afternoon. A large mesoscale weather system has become established. Instead of a localised density current, we are talking about the windflow around a small depression, and a slightly different set of rules apply. When the first rush of sea air occurs in the morning, the rotation of the Earth is almost irrelevant, but by the end of the day a larger weather system has developed and the Earth's rotation is now beginning to be of some significance. This explains why the sea-breeze veers as the day goes on in the northern hemisphere.

In Spain a heat low develops every year in about May or June and tends to persist, even at night, right through to August, but there is usually not much weather associated with it. In Asia, the huge summer low-pressure area has the same basic cause.

THE PENINSULA EFFECT

Whilst in winter it is the warm sea which sets off showers, in summer it is the warm land. However, in some parts of the country, sea-breezes help the process by adding an extra convergence effect. These vulnerable areas for spring and summer showers are in peninsula locations where two sea-breezes approach from different directions. On an otherwise calm day the sea-breezes can meet head on and the only way the air can go is upwards. Enhanced convection and more showers can be the result in Cornwall, Dyfed, County Mayo, Galloway, Aberdeen and Norfolk. In the very hot weather in 1976, the sea-breeze from the east coast of England met that from the west coast over the Pennines, giving isolated thunderstorms.

The reverse side of the coin is where divergence occurs over the coasts. In these areas shower frequency is diminished and there are very few day-time showers over the sea in summer, adding to the pleasure of cross-channel sailing.

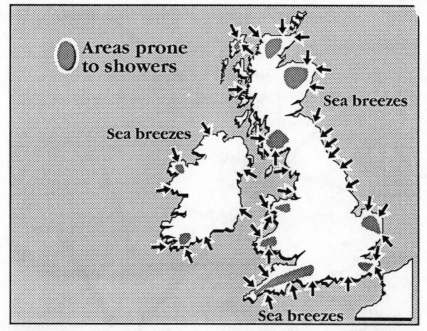

In spring and summer, onshore sea-breezes can cause convergence over a peninsula which results in showers. This mechanism will only work when winds are light at the start of the day.

FUNNELLING EFFECTS

In autumn and winter the sea is relatively warm. When a cool Polar Maritime or Arctic Maritime airstream blows in from the west or north then you have the classic situation of cold air over warm sea. Convection is the result, usually strong enough to give showers.

When a showery westerly airstream hits Wales, the showers will be intensified, but very few will penetrate into the English Midlands, since they have been cut off from the source of warm moist air over the sea. Rather like turning the switch of a boiling kettle off, when the source of power is removed, the bubbling soon dies away. By contrast, the showery westerly blowing up the Bristol Channel has everything going for it. The airmass is still over warm water and also it is being squeezed from each side as it pushes between Exmoor and South Wales. Extra convergence means extra uplift and more vigorous convection. The showers continue eastwards across low ground and manage to persist across Wiltshire but usually die out before London.

Elsewhere in Britain the same funnelling effect occurs. For example, with a northwesterly airflow the showers go sneaking through the Chesh-

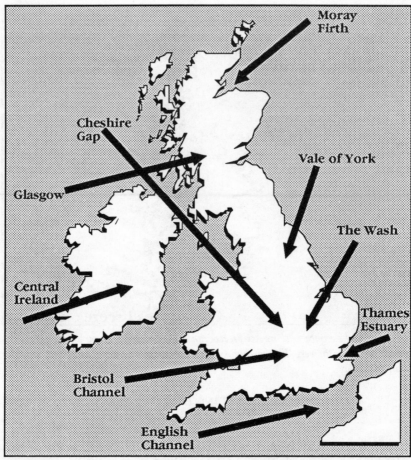

In autumn and winter strong winds can drive showers inland through estuaries and gaps in the hills.

ire Gap towards Birmingham, and with a northeasterly into the Moray Firth or the Wash. With an east-northeast wind in winter, London is exposed to drizzle or showers. With a westerly, Glasgow is vulnerable to showers.

SHOWER TRACKS INLAND

In this section, there is another myth which needs to be cast aside – that of the thundery shower 'following the river.'

Many of the mesoscale features observed in hill country have genuine scientific explanations, usually involving air being diverted horizontally around mountains or vertically over them. However, it is often claimed that rivers, woods and very minor geographical features play a part in shower development or movement. Usually such claims are mistaken.

Over a flattish area which is well inland, most of the variations in shower or thunderstorm activity are essentially random. (They must of course have an ultimate cause, such as a patch of slightly colder air which was once over a certain part of Canada, or more likely because of what happened to that air as it crossed Ireland.) In a fairly flat area like Bedfordshire or Cambridgeshire the showers do not follow streams, rivers, woods or shallow ridges. Instead they just carry on going wherever the wind is blowing them, developing or dying as the inflow of moist warm air increases or is cut off. Thunderstorms do not circle around and come back, though a second or subsequent cell may track along behind the first giving that impression. Often, if you stand outside watching an approaching shower, it will appear to split before it reaches you, with heavy rain passing on either side. Usually this is an illusion caused by two individual cells appearing to be a single cell when they are far away, and seeming to split when they are close enough to be observed more accurately.

For those reluctant to abandon the notion of thunderstorms following rivers, the difference in size should cause them to think. The cumulonimbus is perhaps miles across, whereas the river is only yards across. A twig will not usually divert a charging elephant!

MOUNTAIN SKIES

Mountain skies can be very different from those viewed from low ground. We tend to think of huge vistas, and indeed visibility may be good away from the sources of pollution. However, mountain views can by contrast often consist of just 300 ft (100 m) of hill fog especially in western Britain. Our western mountains are often cloudy, and hill fog is just cloud in contact with the surface.

The observatory on the summit of Ben Nevis which was operational in the late nineteenth century (and I take my hat off to those who observed there) showed just how unpleasant conditions are at an altitude of 4406 ft (1340 m). The summit is in hill fog over for over 70% of the time in the winter months. Living below a cloud sheet is bad enough but living *in* one is even worse.

What happens when a cloud is blown towards a mountain? The mountain range forces the airstream to rise but the cloud does not rise with the airstream. The most common case is for the cloud to continue horizontally and shroud the mountaintop with the cloud-base remaining level. However, there can be variations on this theme.

If the air at low levels is moist, and especially when the ground is wet and cold, a patch or roll of stratus cloud will remain 'stuck' on the upwind slope of the hill range. On other occasions when the Sun has been shining intermittently and the rocks are warm, the cumulus clouds will genuinely rise very slightly to clear the mountain summit. You can then stand on the peak and watch the ragged shreds of cloud racing past within a few metres. The more general rule for those forecasting hill fog in upland regions is that the cloud-base maintains its altitude above sea level. A sheet of stratoculumus at 2000 ft will obscure a mountaintop at 2100 ft rather than lifting over it. After all, the condensation level does not change if the airmass is homogeneous.

If the air high aloft is moist, then orographic clouds may form vertically above the mountaintops and will remain there in the uplifted air, despite the wind-flow through the cloud. These clouds can look like a pile of plates, or even like a flying saucer.

After a period of rain, many wisps of ragged stratus will hang amongst the mountain treetops, lifting and dispersing only slowly as drier air arrives. Drizzle or rain can continue on upwind slopes and summits all day when the area to the lee of the mountains is clear. It is not by chance that our high ground is much wetter and cloudier than the lowlands.

Mountains do not always get the worst of the deal, though. In calm conditions the cold air may drain into the valleys which then become foggy and polluted. Those on the mountaintops can bask in sunshine and look down on the murk below. The observer looking downwards on the fog away from the Sun may see his or her shadow enlarged through a depth of fog – this is called a 'Brocken spectre'. Another optical effect is the corona or halo of coloured light around the shadow which the observer may cast upon the upper surface of the fog, and this is known as 'a glory'.

Such days of calm mountain sunshine are fairly rare, and pretty much restricted to anticyclonic conditions. One wonders if they compensated the Ben Nevis observers for all the appalling weather they had to endure.

THE FÖHN EFFECT

Air rising on the upwind side of a mountain range will often give rain or drizzle. As it descends on the lee side of the range there will be warmth and clear skies. This is the classic föhn effect. (The word is also sometimes spelt *foehn* which gives a better clue to its correct pronunciation, though 'phone' is commonly heard.)

At its simplest, the föhn principle can be thought of as the air precipitating its moisture on the hills and giving cloud-free and therefore sunny weather on the lee side. More technically, the air which rises on the

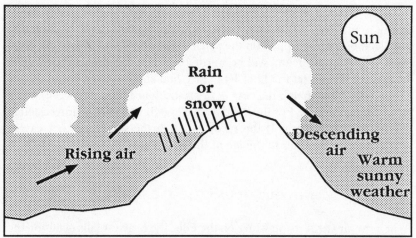

The Föhn effect occurs when rain or snow falls on the mountains and the descending air brings warm, often sunny conditions to valleys and plains in the lee of the hills.

upwind side is saturated and thus cools at the Saturated Adiabatic Lapse Rate (SALR) of about 2 C per 1000 ft (300 m). Having shed its moisture, the cloud base on the lee side of the mountains is higher and the descending air warms at the Dry (i.e. non-saturated) Adiabatic Lapse Rate (DALR) of 3 C per 1000 ft (300 m), and is therefore warmer when it gets back to original level. (The extra sunshine on the lee side will also add an additional degree or two.)

Wherever there are mountains and moist air, the classic föhn can work. A southerly flow over the Alps will give the 'south föhn' when it descends dry, warm and blustery into the valleys of Switzerland, Austria and Southern Germany. Occasionally a pool of stagnant cold air will remain in a valley while warm air flows overhead a couple of hundred feet up. This 'high föhn' unable to penetrate to the valley floor can result in higher temperatures on the ski-slopes than in the valley-bottom villages.

The Alps can also produce the 'north föhn' when the southern slopes and northern Italy become warm. Westerly winds across the Rockies generate the same response, called the Chinook or 'snow-eater', which can produce rapid temperature rises in Canada and the USA. On one occasion its onset caused a rise of 27 C (49 F) in two minutes at Spearfish, South Dakota, on 22 January 1943.

Scottish mountains generate the föhn effect too. With southwesterly winds it is Inverness and Aberdeen who benefit, with southeasterlies Inverness and the northwestern coastal strip, where Achnashellach has reached 18 C (65 F) in December. The North Wales coast can also do well and Aber equalled this value on 10 January 1971.

A variation on the classic mechanism is the 'subsidence föhn', which tends to occur in more anticyclonic conditions with the mountain range acting as a barrier to cold air. Cold, dense air cannot easily be forced to rise, so it becomes trapped on the *upwind* side of the mountains. Air from aloft, above an inversion, will be warm and when this descends it will be heated yet further (at the DALR) to give hot, sunny conditions in the lee of the hills. Note that in the case of this subsidence föhn, no precipitation need fall on the hills. For the holiday-maker (who may not be interested in the physical explanation!) the result is much the same in either case – warm, sunnier weather to the lee of the mountains.

WHY OUR MOUNTAINS ARE SO WET

When the air sheds its moisture on the hills, the heaviest falls occur on the upwind slopes and the very summit itself. Precipitation totals are already decreasing on the downward slope, except perhaps in occasional cases of snowfall, which may sometimes be blown further downwind before reaching the ground.

A lot of the 'extra' rainfall in our uplands is due to an inflow of low-level moisture. Small cloud droplets are 'zapped' by large raindrops falling from higher cloud layers. A raindrop may collect thousands of small droplets on its way down and grow so large that it splits into two and thereby induces raindrop multiplication.

The meteorologist's view of 'orographically enhanced rainfall' is that high-level clouds act as the 'seeder' and a strong moist low-level airflow is the 'feeder'. The only limit to this seeder–feeder mechanism is how much moisture the low-level winds can input into the system. Torrential rain is the result on upwind slopes in windy Tropical Maritime airstreams. This is the main reason why our British mountains are so wet. I remember being in Blaenau Ffestiniog in North Wales once, when this process went on all day.

RAIN-SHADOWS

It follows that if the air has shed most of its moisture as it rises, then little will remain for the valleys and lowlands behind the hills. *Their* annual rainfall totals are generated with different wind directions, or by convection or other mechanisms. Rain-shadows in the British Isles are principally in the east.

The Cairngorms have only half the rain of western Scottish mountains of similar altitude. Inverness, Edinburgh, Newcastle, York, Chester and Hereford are relatively dry. Places like Aberdeen and the Yorkshire coast catch much of their rainfall during autumn and winter northerlies when a depression becomes slow-moving in the North Sea. Convection is the main rain-producer in eastern Britain in summer. Perhaps a new weather saying could be developed along the lines of 'no frontal rain east of the hills in summer-time'.

OTHER LEE EFFECTS

Nine times out of ten the winds are lighter in the lee of the hills than on the upwind side because frictional drag slows the low-level airflow over the rough topography. On the tenth occasion something strange happens to the low-level air flow, and this is the 'lee-wave effect'. When air is forced to rise in order to cross a substantial mountain range, such as the Pennines, it may meet a resistance to this upward motion. Depending on the temperature and wind structure aloft, the high-level air may 'press back down' on the low-level air. As the air descends behind the mountain it is pushed downwards and 'squashed' against the ground. It responds by bouncing back upwards and thus a series of undulations occurs to the lee of the hills.

With a strong westerly wind the Pennines may cause as many as ten identifiable lee-waves which are visible as narrow cloud-bands on a satellite picture, each perhaps 8 km (5 miles) apart and therefore extending 80 km (50 miles) downwind to the Yorkshire coast. From the Rockies or Andes such downwind trains of lee-wave clouds may extend ten times as far.

If moisture is present, then every time the air rises a lee-wave cloud is formed, lying across the wind. Often lens-shaped or almond-shaped, at least in cross-section, they are usually designated stratocumulus lenticularis or altocumulus lenticularis. In the British Isles they typically occur between 3000 and 10,000 ft (1000 and 3000 m). Note that they do not move with the wind. At the upwind edge, cloud is continually forming in the rising air, while the downwind descending cloud-edge is continually dispersing. The undulations in airflow are 'standing waves' and the cloud can thereby stay in the same place relative to the mountains – which is very annoying to the mountain landscape photographer waiting for a patch of sunshine. The winds too are peculiar, strong and gusty where the air descends, light where the upward 'bounce' occurs. Occasionally the airflow is very complicated with rotor clouds and even reversed wind directions. The Helm wind occurs near Appleby in Cumbria in northeasterly situations with a special local cloud known as the 'Helm bar' when the wind has descended, gusty and turbulent, from the Pennines.

Lee-wave motion explains why in hilly country it sometimes looks as if

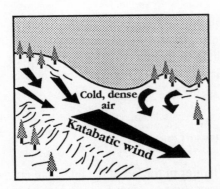

A katabatic wind blows downhill on a clear night.

it is going to clear up, but instead it keeps on raining. Alternatively you may get a sunny day under a persisting downdraught, when a nearby place stays cloudy all day underneath the lee-wave clouds.

DOWNSLOPE WINDS

On a clear, calm night when the air gets cooled, a downslope wind may start to blow. This is known to meteorologists as a 'katabatic wind' which is cold and therefore dense, causing it to flow downhill.

The downslope wind has some similarities to the sea-breeze. We can simulate the flow of dense air by using water in a laboratory tank. Warm, pink-coloured water is separated in the tank by a vertical, watertight wall from cold, blue-tinted water. When the dividing wall of, say, perspex is removed and we view from the side of the tank, we see the cold blue water advancing along the floor of the tank. At a higher level near the surface of the tank, the warm pink water flows in the opposite direction. When being used as a sea-breeze simulation, the blue water represents the advancing cold sea air and the pink flow in the opposite direction above represents the return flow. What it does is to illustrate the importance of density in local winds.

If the cold air is advancing downhill, as in the case of the katabatic wind, then the higher density provides a powerful driving force. On a winter night in a mountainous area the cold air will leave an upland plateau and flow downhill like a river towards the sea.

A small-scale katabatic wind can form in a field on a perfectly calm night. You may even be able to see bonfire smoke which, having lost its warmth, joins a gentle downslope flow of cold air. There can also be a corresponding day-time upslope air current known as an 'anabatic wind', but you really need to go to the Alps to see one of these in action.

In Britain, small localised katabatic winds occur in many hilly areas. A motorway or railway embankment may block a valley and prevent the natural drainage of cold air. The valley of the river Tyne is one place where a sizeable katabatic wind can develop as a westerly airflow, reaching Newcastle and eventually, on a winter morning, perhaps blowing offshore as a land breeze. On Rannoch Moor in the central Highlands a pool of cold air can develop which flows westwards to empty itself through Glencoe. On a tiny scale a garden fence may create a 'dam' behind which cold air will collect.

The northerly wind in France known as the Mistral is complex, but certainly augmented by katabatic winds flowing out of side valleys to join the main flow down the Rhône towards Marseilles.

In many hilly Mediterranean countries quite fierce winds can develop as cold air drains down from the mountains at night, perhaps funnelled through a ravine to reach nearly gale force in the early hours of the morning, rattling the shutters, before dying away with the sunshine of the new day.

However, it is the Antarctic which is the great place for katabatics. The icy slopes allow smooth airflow and momentum can build up to a severe gale accompanied by temperatures well below freezing and this may persist for 48 to 72 hours at a time. Our katabatic winds in Britain are quite feeble by comparison.

WEATHER INDOORS

It might be said that there is no weather indoors and certainly we would hope to exclude precipitation and cloud! Visibility too becomes meaningless over the short distances involved, unless one achieves a dense fog in the bathroom or perhaps in a freezer.

Atmospheric pressure is pretty much the same as that outdoors, although very small changes may occur in windy weather if the barometer is moved from one wall to another in a room with an open door or window.

Temperature and humidity are the main parameters which are different indoors from outside. Temperatures are obviously higher indoors due to heating in winter and relative humidities are very much lower for the same reason. Let us examine an example. The air coming into the house is carrying, say, 3 grams of water vapour per kilogram of air. At saturation point it could carry, say, 4 grams and its relative humidity is therefore 75%. It is now heated up indoors but no water vapour is added. It still holds 3 grams of water vapour per kilogram of air but its capacity is now perhaps 15 grams. The relative humidity is therefore reduced to 20%. Indoor plants may suffer, some types of furniture may be affected, static electricity can build up on carpets, etc. This low relative humidity problem is most likely in cold but dry winter weather – with a northerly airstream in Scotland and northern England, or with a southeasterly in southern parts. Ironically, in summer when the relative humidity outdoors tends to be lower, we may leave doors and windows open. If the temperature inside is the same as that outside, then the relative humidity will be little altered from outdoors.

If the Sun shines in through a window it will raise the temperature indoors a little above the external conditions. This 'free solar heating' is particularly useful in March when the Sun is quite powerful but the air outside is cold. Houses with large windows facing south will have a lower heating bill than identical houses orientated differently. A thick-walled granite cottage may take time to warm up on a summer morning and it can temporarily be cooler indoors than out. Opinions vary widely on the ideal temperature indoors, but it must depend on clothing, food intake, individual metabolism, and on whether we are watching television or being more active.

WEATHER UNDERGROUND

Challenged to come up with an example of someone who never needs a weather forecast, you might think that a person underground (whether for pleasure or for work) would come high on the list. Even here though, there are some weather factors.

Potholers or cavers need to know if heavy rain is expected because a sudden influx of flood water will raise water levels in underground caverns, with potentially fatal consequences.

The usual temperature in caves in the British Isles is around 11 C (52 F) but at great depths this increases. Humidities are often in the 90% range, as few caves are dry, though the rate of air change with the surface varies widely.

Coal-miners are less affected by weather but the conditions aloft play a part. The air taken in for circulation down the shafts and around the lower levels becomes gradually moister and warmer on its route around the pit as it passes machinery and wet rock surfaces. For those near the end of the air circulation a cool dry air intake is certainly preferred.

Coal-mines often require warnings of rapid pressure falls. When a depression is approaching or deepening then the atmospheric pressure decrease on the surface also occurs underground. Methane gas, known as 'firedamp', may leak out of the rocks bringing a reduction in air quality and a risk of explosion.

Finally, of course, temperatures above ground enhance or reduce demand for coal, though with a long 'lead-time' from production to use.

THE URBAN HEAT ISLAND

Cities and towns tend to be warmer than the surrounding countryside, and this warm zone is known as the 'urban heat island'. It often amounts to around a couple of degrees Celsius (3 to 4 F) extra, and occasionally to a 6 C (11 F) bonus for people living or working in built-up areas.

It might be thought that the extra heat is escaping through windows or under doors from poorly insulated buildings or those lacking draught-proofing. Obviously this is a source of heat, but usually only a small one. Heat from chimneys is marginal.

The main benefit comes from the fabric of buildings which heat up naturally during the day, and release their heat at night. Concrete and especially brick warm up nicely on a sunny day, and by sunset have a substantial heat reservoir which is mainly released during the evening and early part of the night. The buildings are therefore acting rather like a storage heater (in which bricks are again used, this time deliberately) which heats up using cheap electricity and releases its warmth later. Evidence that this is the major factor in warming the towns and cities is provided by comparing an urban site with a rural one. The biggest difference in temperature occurs three or four hours after dark following a sunny day. By the end of a winter night the output from the bricks and other building materials is almost exhausted. By mid-morning the streets of a city in the shadows of tall buildings can be decidedly chilly – perhaps even colder than open sunny fields elsewhere. Thus the city is usually, but not always, the warmest place around.

The wind speed during the night is an important factor, because strong winds diminish or even destroy the urban heat island by blowing in cooler air from the rural areas. With calm conditions even a small town can develop a heat island, and the main factors seem to be the density of buildings and perhaps the materials used for construction. In a light to moderate wind the size of the city becomes important.

One unusual effect of the urban heat island is that it may generate a breeze blowing in from the rural areas towards the city centre on otherwise calm evenings. This 'country-breeze' is actually caused by the city warmth and is analogous to the coastal sea-breeze. It can even set off showers over a city during the late evening when the air flowing in from the rural regions converges over the city centre, so there are some negative aspects to the urban heat island!

Chapter 6

SIGNS IN THE SKY

RAINBOWS

RAINBOWS are one of the more spectacular displays which nature provides. The basic requirements are simultaneous sunshine and falling rain, but the geometry also has to be correct with the Sun roughly behind the observer and the rain in front. The light from the Sun is bent (refracted) as it enters the raindrop, reflected from the back of the drop like a mirror, and bent again as it comes out towards the observer. At its simplest therefore, it could be said that each drop acts like a triple mirror, and the combined effect of millions of drops is to reflect some of the Sun's light back towards the observer. The white light of the Sun is made up of different colours and, as they enter and leave the raindrop, these different colours are bent by varying amounts and thus split up into red (on the outside), orange, yellow, green, blue, indigo and violet. Even more complex optics can be used to explain a secondary rainbow which is sometimes faintly visible outside the first, and has the colour order reversed.

Sometimes a waterfall will produce enough spray to create a long-lasting rainbow on a sunny day and they can be seen in some photographs of Niagara or of the Victoria Falls. For the more normal, weather-produced rainbows Honolulu is a favoured location with frequent afternoon showers over nearby mountains. The sinking Sun is in the right place for the geometry to work.

And what can we deduce about the weather when we see a rainbow? Probably it is a showery day with cumulonimbus clouds forming the rain shower, and areas of clear sky for the sun to shine through. Showery regimes in the British Isles are often associated with westerly airstreams and this tells us something about whether the shower is approaching the observer or has already passed over. If it is morning with the Sun in the east, then the observer will be looking westwards and the shower is approaching. Reasoning suggests that, with showers already active so early, a changeable day could be in prospect. If it is late afternoon or evening (the more common case) then this shower has passed over and any further shows will tend to die out as the convection effects of the Sun's

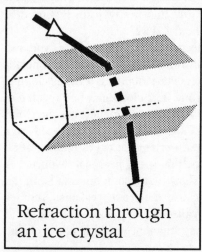

A halo around the Sun or Moon is caused by refraction through millions of tiny ice crystals, usually in a layer of cirrostratus cloud.

Refraction through an ice crystal

heating decline. Hence, an adaptation of the old 'red sky' weather saying is sometimes applied: 'Rainbow in the morning, shepherd's warning, rainbow towards the night, shepherd's delight'. Like so many other attempts at do-it-yourself forecasting, it has a little truth, but is far from totally reliable.

HALOES

A halo around the Sun or Moon is one of the better predictors visible in the sky. It is a much more common sight than might be supposed, but may last for only a few minutes on some occasions. There are many similar optical phenomena including arcs, Sun pillars and mock suns, and indeed, there are at least three sizes of halo. The most common is that of 22° radius, though 8° and 46° haloes have also been seen. The halo is formed by the light from the Sun being bent (refracted) twice as it passes through hexagonal ice prisms. Usually the halo looks whitish but the colours of the rainbow may be faintly seen in the halo case with red on the inside. To give an idea of the diameter of what is usually a perfect total circle around the Sun or Moon, one can hold out a large book or magazine at arm's length. The book will blot out the sun, but the halo will still be completely visible. If you wish to measure or take photographs of the phenomenon, it is far safer for your eyes if you restrict yourself to haloes around the Moon.

Unfortunately for observers there is another phenomenon, the corona, which is similar to the halo. Coronae are usually only distinguishable around the Moon and include a brownish ring. The field inside the ring is coloured a bright bluish-white. The radius varies depending on the size of the water droplets in the atmosphere, but they are typically a good deal smaller, with a 5° radius rather than the usual 22° halo.

The halo is definite evidence of hexagonal ice prisms of a type and horizontal extent commonly associated with cirrostratus cloud at a height of 20,000 ft (6000 m) or so. When seen over Britain cirrostratus cloud is often a sign of an approaching warm front. The cloud may be expected to thicken and lower towards the surface with rain commencing as the cloud thickens and changes its character. Thus the halo may be used as a method of predicting rain (or, in winter, perhaps snow) to follow. Of all the weather-watcher's signs in the sky, this is my personal favourite. A scientific analysis of its reliability will show that it sometimes fails. In the summer particularly, this may be because the front weakens. Another possible reason is that the halo was caused by a patch of cirrus cloud rather than the uniform sheet of cirrostratus that would herald a classic warm front.

When associated with a falling barometer, an increasing southerly wind and a progressive thickening of the cloud from the west, we can be more confident of the approach of rain.

SUNRISE, SUNSET

We know that the Sun rises roughly in the east of the sky because the Earth is rotating from west to east. Someone in Copenhagen can watch the sunrise an hour before a person in Edinburgh. Both are in the same latitude but the Danish observer is in longitude 12° E, whereas Edinburgh is 3° west of the Meridian. The Sun 'travels' 15° westward per hour to achieve 360° in 24 hours – the rotational speed of the Earth. But the Sun does not usually rise exactly in the east. In the British Isles in June the sunrise is seen nearer the northeast, and in December nearer southeast. (Similarly sunset will vary in direction from almost southwest in December to northwest in June.)

The beauty of sunrise is often just as great as that of sunset but fewer people are up and about to appreciate it.

So where is the best area in the world for seeing a glorious sunset? Surely somewhere with an unobstructed view of the western half of the sky, perhaps overlooking the sea or some scattered islands from a slightly elevated position. Preferably not in the tropics because here the Sun sinks more swiftly from its near-overhead position in the middle of the day, cutting downwards like a knife to sink rapidly below the horizon. There may be a magical ten minutes as the sunset glows brightly behind the outline of some palms, but it will all be gone quite quickly. At a more northerly latitude (or in the far south of the southern hemisphere) the sunset will last much longer as the Sun sinks obliquely. In Scotland the glow of the sky is often clearly visible an hour after the time of sunset. Shetland in June and July experiences the 'Simmer dim' with the sky remaining partially lit up throughout the so-called night by the Sun which is only just below the horizon. Add the ever-changing cloud patterns of the Northern Isles or the Hebrides and you must have a candidate for the best sunsets in the world.

The red colour of the Sun as it sinks towards the horizon is caused by scattering. Since the light has a long way to travel through the atmosphere, the molecules and dust particles scatter a good deal of the violet, blue, green and yellow light leaving mainly the red. Another optical process becomes important when the Sun sinks below the horizon. The atmosphere can be considered as a series of layers getting denser towards the Earth's surface. The light from the Sun is now bent (or refracted) as it passes from one layer into another and so we can still just see the Sun when straight line geometry would suggest it had just dipped below the horizon. Just very rarely a green flash of one or two seconds' duration is seen as the uppermost edge of the Sun disappears.

The well-known weather saying 'red sky at night, shepherd's delight, red sky in the morning, shepherd's warning' is of dubious value. Perhaps the best that can be said is when the red after-glow of sunset is lighting up only the sky and there are no clouds, then there is a good chance of a fine day to follow. The implication is an absence of cloud to the west – the usual source of our weather in the British Isles – and therefore we can say that no weather system is imminent. A jet stream could easily prove us wrong during the long nights of winter.

THE BLUE OF THE SKY

Why is the sky blue? This must have puzzled people for centuries. Now we know that the light from the Sun can be split into many different colours. When the atmosphere is cloudless and we look directly upwards from Britain during the day-time, most of the light from the Sun is passing the overhead position without much hindrance. However, some of the blue light is being scattered by the molecules of the atmosphere and reaches the observer. If the atmosphere is very polluted then more of the other colours will reach the observer who may remark on 'how milky white the sky looks today'. Thus the blueness of the cloud-free sky is an indication of a clean airstream.

A visit to the mountains of Scotland or Ireland in a westerly or northerly airflow will provide perhaps the cleanest air possible. Greenland or Iceland are the source of the airstream and obviously non-industrialised.

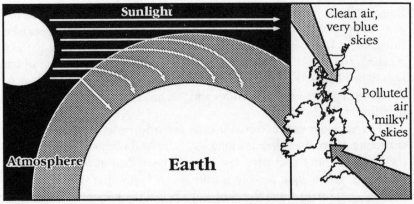

When we look upwards the sky appears blue because some of the sunlight passing overhead is scattered downwards towards the Earth. Blue light is more easily scattered than yellow or red light. In easterly airstreams the air may be so polluted that all colours are scattered downwards and the sky therefore appears milky white.

The sky should look very blue. At high altitudes, especially above 18,000 ft (5500 m) where half the atmosphere (in terms of mass) is below you, the sky may even begin to have a suggestion of purple or black. Photographs from the Himalayas may emphasise this effect, as will those from high-flying aircraft. Mountain skiers can find themselves surprisingly sun-tanned with the absence of pollution and the shorter passage of the Sun through the atmosphere – not to mention the reflection from the snow surface.

One of the lesser-known weather sayings is 'the deeper the blue, the deeper the convection'. This can work quite well in winter and spring. The clean northwesterly airstreams which bring the deep blue skies are also cold throughout a considerable depth, therefore deep convection clouds will develop if enough heat can be found at the surface to start the convection process going. Whilst this may work on a March or April afternoon, it can also fall down in summer when huge convective clouds bring thunderstorms up from the south, preceded by pale blue, hazy skies and light easterly winds.

LIGHTNING AND THUNDER

One of the most impressive displays of atmospheric energy is the lightning discharge. Embarrassingly, despite all the studies by cloud physicists, we do not yet fully understand the mechanism by which the electrostatic potential develops in the atmosphere, though we are some way down the road to an explanation.

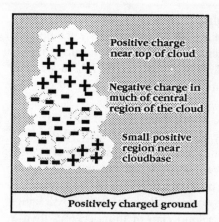

Positive charge near top of cloud

Negative charge in much of central region of the cloud

Small positive region near cloudbase

Positively charged ground

A lightning discharge can occur from cloud to cloud, or from cloud to ground. The distribution of charge within an individual cloud may vary from the typical pattern shown here.

Lightning occurs when static electricity builds up within a cloud. A difference in charge then exists between that region of the cloud and the ground, or between that cloud and a nearby cloud. The electrical charge is thought to build up on ice particles or on water droplets. If the difference in potential becomes sufficiently great an electrical discharge occurs. In simple terms, the spark jumps the gap. Intense heating along the discharge path causes very rapid expansion of the air and this explosive expansion causes thunder.

Sometimes the path of the discharge can be seen and we describe the lightning as 'forked' whereas on other occasions the flash is obscured by a cloud and referred to as 'sheet lightning'. A leader stroke precedes the main, visible discharge.

Light travels at 300,000 km per second (186,000 miles per second) and is therefore seen near enough instantaneously. Sound travels 1 km in 3 seconds (1 mile in 5 seconds) and this gives us a method of measuring the distance away of the lightning discharge. Start counting the seconds as soon as you see the lightning and continue until you hear the thunder, then divide by three to get the storm distance in kilometres, or by five for the distance in miles. Under normal circumstances thunder will be audible within 8 km (5 miles) or so. Lightning, on the other hand, can sometimes be seen at night from 80 km (50 miles) away or more, especially over the sea.

People are fond of describing how a thunderstorm approached them from one direction, circled them twice and departed in another direction. The reality is usually somewhat different. A storm will usually follow a reasonably straight track but may consist of several thunder cells. Thus one cell may travel past to be followed by another heading much the same direction.

In England and south Wales, the great preponderance of thundery days is in the summer half-year, with the winds at medium and high levels bringing the storms up from the English Channel or France on southwesterly or southerly winds. The summers of 1956 to 1958 were notably thundery. Such storms are very memorable when they occur at night, though statistically they are more likely in the afternoon. Inland areas of eastern England tend to be the most prone to storms with 10 to 20 days per year.

In Scotland, Northern Ireland and North Wales thunderstorms are less common and generally occur at any one site on fewer than 10 days per year. Also such storms may well be one flash and a bang and they are gone. Lightning accompanied by snow can occur when big cumulonimbus clouds come racing in from the sea on to our northern coasts in winter.

One unusual and curious feature occasionally witnessed is 'ball lightning'. The usual description is of a loud clap of thunder, and then a glowing ball of light about the size of a tennis ball is seen, often wandering around a room or outside across a lawn. Long dismissed as fictitious, we now know that ball lightning exists, though theories to explain it are far from complete.

TORNADOES

A tornado is a rapidly rotating column of air. It is a violent phenomenon despite its small scale, but is generally short-lived, usually lasting less than an hour. During its brief life a tornado will wreak destruction along its path in a swathe perhaps 100 m (300 ft) across and a few kilometres in length. Despite dramatic pictures of wrecked buildings in the USA, the main damage is usually to crops. Dark clouds and heavy rain are nearby when the tornado is first spotted. It may be visible as a blackish column hanging from a cloud, sometimes narrowing towards the ground, or at a later stage in its life as a rope-like twisted feature apparently connecting the cloud to the surface. Sometimes this connection may be broken temporarily as the vortex lifts away from the ground only to return a few minutes later, but more often this is the sign of decay.

The cause of the tornado is certainly linked with the formation of large, rapidly developing cumulonimbus clouds. Lightning, thunder and hail may well occur simultaneously. Though imprecisely understood, it seems that the huge upcurrent in the storm starts rotating and this induces the funnel cloud at the base of the storm. Pressure is very low in the middle of a tornado, as can be inferred from the damage, which is due to a combination of suction and strong winds. Wind speeds as high as 280 mph (450 kph) were ascribed to a tornado in Texas in April 1958. The fact that 'twisters' rotate anticlockwise in the northern hemisphere is proof that they are large enough systems to be affected by the Earth's rotation (the Coriolis effect again). Descriptions and photographs of tornadoes rotating in the 'wrong' direction are not wholly convincing, because it is so easy to be misled when watching flying debris.

Tornadoes tend to occur in mid-latitudes and since they are restricted to land masses this means mainly in the northern hemisphere over the USA, Europe and Asia. Those over the USA tend to be the most violent, probably because North America has the right combination of warm, moist air moving up from the Gulf of Mexico, and cold air coming down from the northwest. Near the boundary between these two air masses is the breeding-ground of the 'twister'. On some days, 20 or more will be reported in 'tornado alley' – the flat country of the Midwest, stretching from Texas through Oklahoma and Kansas. The worst day ever was 18 March 1925 when 689 people died in Missouri, Illinois and Indiana.

A spotters network keeps a lookout in the USA and tries to warn local communities on high-risk days. March to July can be described as the main season in the USA, and similarly in Europe and Asia, though in the UK really damaging tornadoes are rare. The 'TORRO' scale (from 1 to 10) has been developed to describe their intensity. TORRO Force 3 is rarely exceeded in the UK.

Because heating from the Sun is important in storm formation, they are most likely between midday and 1800 hours, though occasionally a type of tornado will accompany a night-time cold front. Southeast England suffers from such events more often than northwestern Britain, and a notable occurrence was the Leighton Buzzard tornado of 21 May 1950, which ran from Buckinghamshire to Norfolk in four hours but caused its worst damage as it crossed Bedfordshire.

WATERSPOUTS

The waterspout can be considered the cousin of the tornado, but occurring over sea instead of over land. This is a simplification because a waterspout is generally less violent and will not usually move systematically northeastwards as the tornado often does (in the northern hemisphere). However, both are associated with and caused by cumulonimbus clouds and their vigorous upcurrents of air, and both rotate in a cyclonic sense (anticlockwise in the northern hemisphere). A waterspout will usually be seen as a dark grey rotating column of air and water droplets extending from the base of a storm cloud down to the sea. The surface of the sea will be agitated into a foaming state as water droplets are drawn up into the spout. The rotation could be compared in some respects to the

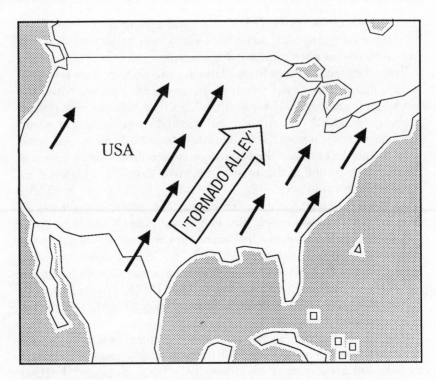

Most tornadoes move roughly northeastwards, with Texas, Kansas and Oklahoma having a high incidence, thus earning this region the nickname 'tornado alley'. The United States recorded more than 300 tornadoes in the month of May 1982 and again during June 1990. Most occur during the afternoon and are associated with thunderstorms.

vortex created as the water flows out of a bath, but in the bath the positions of the air and water are transposed and the movement is downwards due to gravity rather than upwards induced by the vertically rising air current in the cloud above. The diameter of the waterspout is typically 30 m (100 ft) and the distance from the sea surface to the cloud base perhaps 600 m (2000 ft).

As in so many aspects of meteorology there is a strong link between the size and the duration of a phenomenon. The waterspout is a small-scale feature and usually lasts for less than an hour. Contrast that with a depression which may be 1000 km (600 miles) across and lasts for three days.

Because cumulonimbus clouds are normally formed by convection over a relatively warm surface, the high season for waterspouts would logically be August to January (in the northern hemisphere) when the sea surface is warmer than the land. Evidence from reported sightings suggests that they may occur at almost any time of year. The oceans remain at much the same temperature through day and night, and many waterspouts obviously go unreported during the hours of darkness.

Perhaps the most amazing effects occur when waterspouts suck up small fish and crabs as they cross the coast, moving onshore. (Tornadoes too can pick up tiny animals and other objects from the ground and from lakes.) As the waterspout decays over land, fish can 'rain down' to be discovered by the startled inhabitants. Damage to caravans and other property can be caused as the 'spout' reaches land. The English Channel was the scene of several sightings on 18 August 1974 and hardly a summer goes past without at least one report.

LAND DEVILS AND DUST DEVILS

Land devils and dust devils are two examples of small-scale vortices which occur in otherwise fine, sunny weather. They are therefore fundamentally different from tornadoes and waterspouts which are more violent and linked with cumulonimbus cloud.

Land devils, or fair-weather whirlwinds, can form when there are no clouds in the sky. They depend for their formation on vigorous but very localised upcurrents. As the warm air in the thermal lifts away from the ground it starts to rotate. Hay, straw, dust or litter are often carried aloft and these make the phenomenon visible. Some occurrences must take place without any airborne material and therefore go unnoticed, though the effect of the moderate to strong winds may disturb bushes and trees enough to catch the eye. I have also seen a small bird of prey using the rising, rotating air current, though whether to gain height or to catch insects I do not know. Another case was reported to me of fox cubs playing amongst the straw in the 'eye' of the vortex, though perhaps they were there by pure chance. Typical dimensions might be 20 m (60 ft) across and 100 m (300 ft) in height, with duration perhaps running to 5 minutes. Small eddies caused by turbulence around buildings are much less organised and very transient.

Land devils will not form in Britain in winter because of the need for strong heating from the Sun to trigger the thermals. Optimum conditions occur at midday or just after (local Sun time) on a calm June or July day. These are the circumstances when the Sun is at its highest possible elevation, and if it is shining on a south-facing slope, then that would probably help. A strong blustery wind would tend to cool the ground and destroy the parcel of warm air before it could develop into a properly organised rotating thermal.

Rotation can be in either direction depending on the initial random impetus provided by local air currents. Large whirlwinds are more likely to be influenced by the Coriolis effect of the Earth's rotation and are therefore more likely to have a cyclonic direction of rotation (i.e. anti-clockwise in the northern hemisphere).

Dust devils are the desert equivalent of the temperate latitude fair-weather whirlwinds, and they occur in all hot deserts of the world, where the capacity for intense solar heating is obvious. They tend to be more common and more persistent, even moving along tilted forward at an angle like an inverted cone, sometimes with sufficient power to damage buildings.

Stubble burning or even a huge bonfire can generate a fire devil when the hot rising air starts to rotate. The flames themselves may twist into a vortex, and break-away vortices may carry sparks or burning material to extend a forest fire.

Hospitals and other buildings sometimes have a metal chimney with a spiral or helical section of metal running upwards on the outside near the top. This is intended to encourage hot rising air around the flue to start spinning and therefore to carry any smoke or pollutants away upwards from the building, rather than risk a smoky downward eddy.

WEATHER SAYINGS

One view of weather lore is that it is the accumulated wisdom of the ages, and a valuable contribution to forecasting the future. However, a critical look at a wide range of sayings suggests that many of them are useless.

Perhaps easiest to dismiss are the Saints' days which are popularly supposed to herald a long run of wet days, usually 40. If St Swithin's Day on the 15 July is wet, so the saying goes, then the next 40 days will have rain. The saint had died in AD 862 and been buried outside Winchester Cathedral. It was intended in AD 971 to re-bury his remains inside the Cathedral, but this was interrupted by a prolonged spell of wet weather. The rain was taken as a sign of holy intervention and thus the saying was born. Some other saints are less ambitious, only going for a 30-day drought or soaking.

Plants also provide a rich vein of advice. For example, the scarlet pimpernel is said to open its flowers when the weather is going to be good. Observations of the plant indicate that it in fact opens up when the weather is already sunny. Abundant berries on the holly are supposed to foretell a cold winter, since the berries will act as food to sustain the birds. However, a moment's thought will prompt the suggestion that the holly reacts to the weather during the previous summer, and that flowers open or close with sunlight or perhaps humidity. Plants and trees can tell you something about past and present weather, but not about the future.

What about insects, birds and mammals? Spiders are said to spin 'shorter-framed' webs when the weather is about to get windy. Moorhens 'build lower over the water' ahead of a dry summer. Even swallows are said to fly low when cold, unsettled weather is coming, but surely they fly where the insects are to be found – feeding as they do on the wing? In cold, windy weather the airborne insects are less numerous, and nearer to the ground.

Cows are well known for their apparent preference for lying down before it rains. My observations of cows suggests that often one herd will be lying down when in an adjacent field another herd is standing up. One can only assume that very localised showers are expected!

Humans tend to rely on aches in arthritic joints or pains in their corns. My personal view is that these are responding to current weather, though many believe otherwise.

Yet there is some sound advice in other weather sayings, particularly those which describe the sky itself, but none of them work all of the time. Some are based on a subtle logic like 'rain before seven, dry by eleven'. Not many frontal rain bands last more than a few hours, so statistically if the rain has started early there is a good chance that this prediction will come true.

One thing is certain. A set of weather sayings which hold some truth in one location cannot necessarily be used elsewhere on the globe. Even within the British Isles, weather lore may not be transferable from one site to another.

MOON, TIDES AND WEATHER

The tides are caused by the gravitational attraction of the Moon and to a lesser extent the Sun upon the oceans. The Moon, as viewed from the Earth, goes through a cycle of 29.51 days from one full Moon to another. It rises about 50 minutes later each day and as the cycle progresses and the phases of the Moon change, it eventually arrives back at the original situation where the full Moon rises exactly at sunset. Since the Moon appears later each day, it therefore follows that the high tide gets later each day. However, this cannot begin to explain all the complexities of *two* tides per day, the tidal currents and the many worldwide variations. When it is high tide on the side of the Earth closest to the Moon, it will also be high tide on the opposite side of the Earth because of the centrifugal effect of the combined Earth-Moon system.

For those who just wish to understand what goes on at the seaside, it

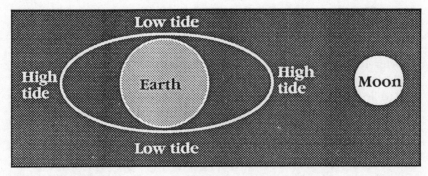

The gravitational attraction of the Moon is the major cause of the tides. When the Sun is also aligned with the Earth and Moon then 'spring tides' occur.

can be explained much more simply. From high water to low water usually takes about 6 hours 13 minutes, and from one high water to the next therefore takes about 12 hours 25 minutes. Thus the following day, after 24 hours 50 minutes, the tidal cycle will be 50 minutes later.

The tidal range from high water to low water varies around the British Isles, generally being around 5 m (16 ft) but at least double that figure in the Bristol Channel where the incoming tide is funnelled between Wales and the southwest peninsula. As the incoming water is concentrated into an ever-decreasing area of the Severn estuary, it creates the Severn Bore, which moves up the river with the incoming tide. Headlands, along the south coast for example, tend to have much smaller tides and at Portland Bill the tidal range is only around 2 m (6 ft).

The largest tides in the world occur in the Bay of Fundy near Nova Scotia. Landlocked seas have no noticeable tide, and even in the Mediterranean it is generally negligible, which is convenient for small-boat operators with jetties and piers, but perhaps a disappointment to children who like to build sandcastles.

At certain times the geometry of the Moon and Sun combines their gravitational pull to give the Earth a bigger tidal range (called 'spring tides'), and these alternate with smaller tidal ranges, called 'neap tides'. From one spring tide to the next takes about a fortnight, and despite their name they can occur all year round, though they are slightly enhanced near the equinoxes.

It has often been claimed that the tides affect the weather, but any such influence seems to be very minor and localised. When fog covers the sea and a large sandy beach is exposed, then the effective coastline is withdrawn perhaps a mile or so. As the tide comes in, so the sea-fog may roll in to shroud the coastal strip. Perhaps some upwelling of cold water occurs, but mainly it is a question of 'moving the coastline'. Apart from this fairly trivial example, there is no convincing evidence that the tides affect the weather. There is the same lack of evidence of any lunar effect, though the idea that the weather changes with the new Moon is persistent. An adaptation of an old saying gives the true version: 'Moon and weather *may* change together, but a change of Moon does not change the weather'. Unfortunately, with the variability of the British weather, it is easy to convince ourselves that the weather pattern has changed when we happen to notice the first thin crescent Moon of a new lunar month.

AURORAE AND HIGH-ALTITUDE CLOUDS

We think of the clouds and weather as originating in the troposphere rather than very high aloft, but aurorae and high-altitude clouds do occur in the mesophere at heights above 80 km (50 miles).

When the Sun is in an active phase, which usually lasts for a couple of years, aurorae become more common, though they can occur at any stage of the solar cycle. The period 1989 to 1990 brought an increased frequency, and we can expect more displays around the year 2001.

The aurora borealis occurs over the northern polar regions and the aurora australis over the Antarctic. We in Britain are well placed to see the northern hemisphere version, though in towns and cities there is usually too much background light. In Shetland it is possible for the northern lights to be seen on about 100 nights a year by someone watching out all through the night, and but for cloud the total would be higher. In the latitude of Edinburgh the chances are reduced to about 20 occasions per year and in Southern England to one or perhaps two.

The cause of the aurorae is particles from the Sun which interact with the atmosphere over the magnetic polar regions at altitudes between 80 and 1000 km (50 and 600 miles). Energy is dissipated in the form of light. When this occurs at great altitude, the display can be seen as far south as Bermuda and Madeira, as on 25 to 26 January 1938. Another tremendous display was on 4 to 5 September 1958, and more recently the aurora of 13 to 14 March 1989 was visible over much of the British Isles.

The displays may be white, blueish, green or a magnificent red. The formation may look like an overall colour-cast or take the form of veils or curtains. Sometimes a great arc appears with rays radiating upwards from the horizon. On other occasions there is a rhythmic pulsing as the light brightens then dims over a period of a second or two. Occasionally the light appears to cascade or 'dance' across the sky. Reports of accompanying whispering noises also occur. As far as we know, the aurora has no direct affect on the weather, although there have been theories to link the two.

Another feature of the mesophere is the noctilucent cloud which occurs about 80 km (50 miles) up and is visible long after sunset due to its altitude. These clouds which somewhat resemble cirrus can be seen on about 30 nights a year from Scotland, mainly around mid-summer, though identification is not easy. They may consist of ice or meteoritic dust, or perhaps both.

ECLIPSES, COMETS AND SOLAR ACTIVITY

Eclipses of the Sun have the temporary result of making the Earth cooler, hidden or partially hidden as it is by the Moon. Apart from a slight reduction or steadying in temperature for an hour or two, and the trivial rise in relative humidity and drop in surface wind speed which might ensue, there are no weather effects.

Comets which follow their usual orbit around the Sun such as Halleys comet of 1910, 1986 and next expected in 2062, do not influence the atmosphere, but when the debris from a 'rogue' comet, or alternatively from meteorites, enters the Earth's gravitational field, it injects particles into the upper atmosphere. Probably there is insufficient material to cool the climate in the way which volcanoes do. There could, however, conceivably be electrical effects of which we are as yet unaware, or the particles could act as nuclei for ice crystal formation. In 1908 the 'Tunguska event' in Siberia flattened millions of coniferous trees and is thought to have been caused by the nucleus of a comet, an explanation which tallies with the lack of meteorite evidence. Neither the Siberian impact nor the regular swarms of meteorites seen each year as 'shooting stars' around 20-24 April (April Lyrids), in the first half of August (Perseids) and 10-15 December (Geminids) have any proven effect on weather.

Changes in solar activity must, logically, affect the climate. The 11-year sunspot cycle is discussed under climatic change in Chapter 11. Other longer-period changes in the Sun's nuclear fusion process that help to account for the ice ages may yet be discovered, but the Milankovitch theory of Earth's orbit variations appears the favourite at present (this is also discussed in Chapter 11).

What, though, about day-to-day weather? We know that despite sun-spots and solar flares, the heat output of the Sun does not vary significantly from day to day or week to week, so it cannot directly cause warm and cold days. Those studying solar flares and the resultant aurora displays on Earth which occur two to four days later have suggested that there could be a link with weather through electromagnetic effects. As yet this is unproven, and it is difficult to imagine what such a link might be. However, it must be admitted that there is a lot of meteorology waiting to be understood, and atmospheric electricity is very much included in this category.

Chapter 7

OBSERVING THE WEATHER

RECORDING VISIBILITY

VISIBILITY IS defined as 'the greatest horizontal distance at which a suitable object can be seen and recognised with the unaided eye'. The word 'horizontal' is important because there may be mist or fog in a small nearby valley but the observer reports the general visibility looking towards distant slopes or hills. Very shallow ground mist of less than human height is also ignored in the visibility estimate, although these phenomena are recorded in the remarks column of the observation book.

The first step is to choose 'a suitable object'. This should be large enough to be clearly visible without being overwhelming, and should subtend an angle of between half a degree and 5° of arc at the observation site. Examples are a nearby bush or small hut, a large tree in the middle distance, a clump of woodland or a small hill at 5 km (3 miles) and a sizeable mountain at 50 km (30 miles). Furthermore, the visibility point should be on the horizon and therefore outlined against the sky to give reasonable contrast. The observer scans the horizon looking at various known objects until, say, a distinctive hill at 8 km is found. If the next more distant reference point, perhaps a rounded hill topped by a tower at 12 km, is not discernible then an intermediate value of 10 km can be reported. Note that if the visibility varies in different directions, which it quite commonly does in fairly calm weather with patchy mist or fog around, then the worst direction is reported.

At night, the same process is repeated with the estimation now based on the brightness of lights or their extinction. An ideal visibility point is perhaps an exterior light on a house at a distance of 3000 m (2 miles) which is always replaced with the same power bulb! Night-time estimations are fraught with difficulty which only experience and full familiarity with the observing site can overcome.

In view of the subjective nature of visibility reports, it is not surprising that they vary somewhat from person to person. An early attempt to overcome the problem was the 'Gold Visibility Meter' which could be used at night, with each observer calibrating it according to their own

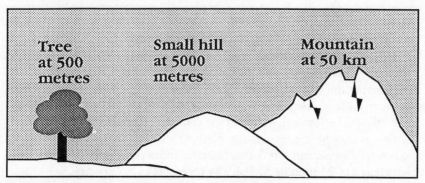

Visibility is estimated by looking at known reference points. The diagram illustrates some suitable 'visibility points'. If the hill is quite clear but the mountain lost in the haze, then the true limit of visibility lies somewhere between the two.

eyesight. More recently the transmissometer has been developed where a beam of light is sent from one piece of equipment to a receiver, say 200 m (600 ft) away. If the air is clean and unsaturated there will be little attenuation, but if there is pollution and moisture a smaller proportion of the emitted light will arrive at the receiver. The 200 m (600 ft) baseline model can suffer if the concrete foundations on which the equipment stands shift in wet soil, so models with very short baselines are now being developed.

WIND DIRECTION AND SPEED

Most basic of all, but not totally obvious, we name the wind by the direction *from* which it blows. 'The north wind doth blow and we shall have snow' reminds us (in the temperate latitudes of the northern hemisphere) that the north wind is blowing from the nearest polar region. An easterly wind is blowing from the Continent towards the British Isles. We can go on to split the compass into 8 points, including for example northeast, or into 16 points to include north-northeast. This suffices for most purposes. Only the most accurate (or pedantic) of sailors will wish to use the complex 32-point compass. The meteorological services of the world measure wind direction in degrees of arc from true north, so a southeasterly is from 135° and a westerly is 270°.

Wind speed is usually measured by 'anemometer' system of rotating cups which are blown around by the wind. Other methods include the wind sock used on airfields. This is a fluorescent orange tube of nylon which flies out horizontally in a strong wind or hangs at an angle in a moderate breeze. The wind sock is especially valuable to pilots because it shows direction as well as speed and is visible from more than a mile away as they approach the runway to land into the wind.

Official measurements of wind strength are made 10 m (33 ft) above ground. This is important because the wind speed decreases as one approaches the ground, becoming almost negligible amongst the blades of grass at our feet. A wind speed measured by a hand-held anemometer at 2 m (6 ft) will be lower than one at the standard 10 m (33 ft) height.

Speed may be expressed in a plethora of units including metres per second, miles per hour, or knots (nautical miles per hour): 20 knots is the equivalent of 23 mph or 37 kph and represents a breezy day.

GUSTS

When the wind is strong, it is frequently pointed out that it is the gusts which do the damage. We are very conscious of these temporary increases in wind speed when a gale is blowing. A gust lasts for only a few seconds. However, the wind is proportionately just as gusty when it is moderate in strength.

A typical ratio of gust speed to average wind speed is approximately 1.7. In other words, a wind of 10 mph (16 kph) will usually be accompanied by occasional gusts of up to 17 mph (27 kph). Note that these are the strongest gusts and many will be rather lighter; also that this ratio only applies over typical rolling countryside with some trees and perhaps an occasional building. Lulls, brief spells of lighter wind, will of course be somewhat below the average speed.

In the middle of a city the average speed will be lower than in the countryside (unless funnelling occurs down a particular street) but the ratio of gusts to average speed will be approximately 2.0.

On the coast or over the sea, the average wind speed will be higher but the gusts less pronounced. This is because the sea surface is relatively smooth; the friction effect is less but more constant in character, so the gust ratio will be about 1.3 times the average speed. A squall is of longer duration than a gust, and must by definition last for at least one minute.

THE BEAUFORT SCALE

The Beaufort scale was devised by Admiral Beaufort in 1805, and was originally meant for use at sea. It is now commonly used on land and there are two versions, including one for 'landlubbers'.

The Beaufort scale is ideal for amateur observers who seeing that 'small trees in leaf begin to sway' will know that the wind has reached Force 5.

A view of the ice-cap Langjokull in central Iceland.
This gives some idea of the British landscape during an ice age.

The sea frozen on the north Kent coast in January 1963.

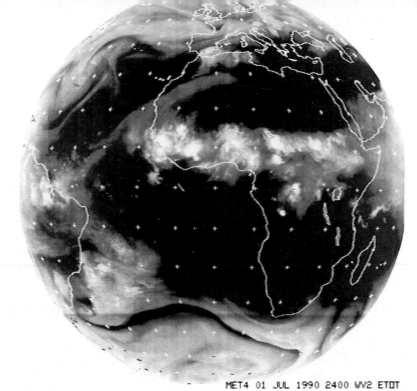

MET4 01 JUL 1990 2400 WV2 ETDT

*A June satellite view shows the tropical rains displaced
to the north of the equator.*

*High pressure with clear skies over Spain and France,
a front lying across Scotland and the eastern Atlantic.*

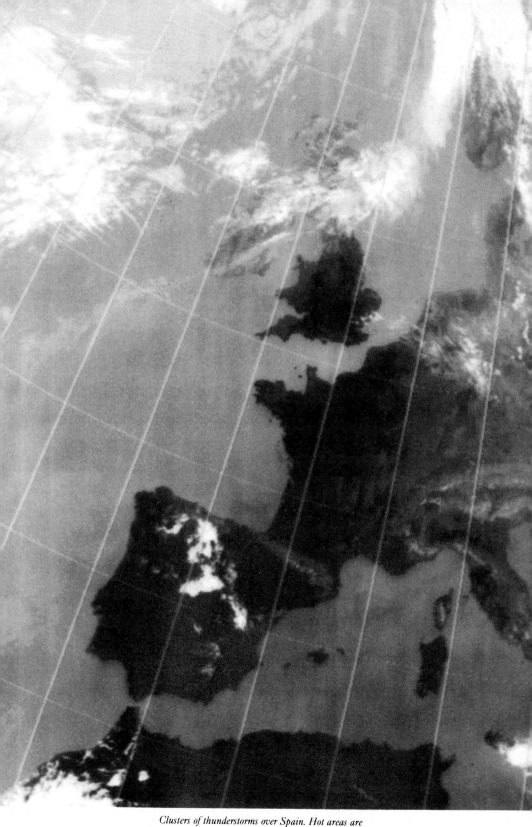

*Clusters of thunderstorms over Spain. Hot areas are
black and cold cloud tops are white on this
infra-red image.*

The dappled pattern in this satellite view is typical of showery weather and convective cloud (cumulus and cumulonimbus).

*Cumulus cloud over the land, but the sea is too cold to
cause convection in this summer scene.*

*Occasionally a tornado will form beneath
cumulonimbus clouds such as this.*

Fairweather cumulus clouds over the land on a summer afternoon.

Shower cloud or 'cumulonimbus' with anvil-shaped top.

Convection is common over the sea in autumn and
winter causing cumulus clouds like these.

A sunshine recorder can focus the sun's rays onto a card.

*The Stevenson screen, with a standard raingauge
visible in the foreground.*

Millions of trees were uprooted in the 1987 gale.

Coastal flooding in Towyn (February 1990) caused by onshore gales.

A child is carried to safety after a hurricane in Puerto Rico.

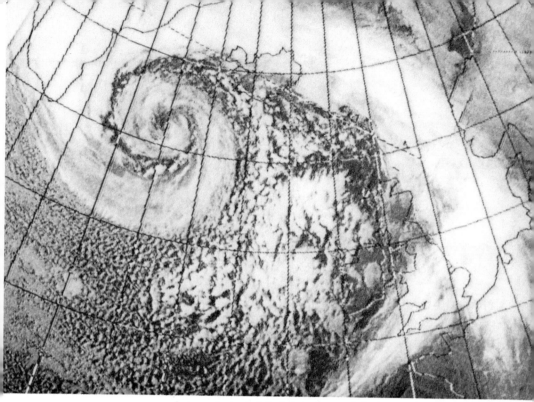

A vigorous temperate latitude depression near Iceland. Its winds are usually less powerful than those in a hurricane.

A halo around the sun is a sign of cirrostratus cloud and usually indicates an approaching warm front.

In anticyclonic weather, high mountains are often sunny when fog fills the valleys, especially in the early morning.

A valley in Cornwall filled with fog after a calm night.

Altocumulus cloud is usually about 10,000 feet (3000 metres) above ground.

Aircraft condensation trails can persist for many hours, but probably have an insignificant effect on climate.

Power stations are a major source of sulphur dioxide
(contributing to acid rain) and of carbon dioxide.

Wind vanes will allow them to estimate the direct to complete their wind observation. Note that the official definition of a gale is Beaufort Force 8, with an average speed of 39 to 46 mph (or 62 to 74 kph). A 40 mph (64 kph) wind at an inland site in rolling country implies gusts of 1.7 times 40 mph, which works out at 68 mph (109 kph) the sort of 'blow' which happens only a couple of times a year at a lowland site in the Midlands or southeast England.

The wave heights given in the 'sea-going' version of the Beaufort scale are typical of the larger waves but the maximum wave height will be higher still. Of course in sheltered waters or with an offshore wind they will be far smaller, and the values quoted here are for the open sea remote from land, or with an onshore wind.

When a steady gale persists at sea, the waves approach their optimum size for that wind speed. Crests are now far apart, and the movement of small ships may become less tortuous. The appearance of the sea will be very different as the gale abates from that which occurred with the rising wind, and all descriptions must therefore be used with some care.

CLOUD AMOUNT

Cloud amount is defined as 'that proportion of the celestial dome which is covered by cloud'. In the past, we used to estimate the amount in tenths but (moving in the opposite direction to decimalisation!) we now do so in eighths or oktas. This change is not as perverse as it sounds because it allows us to use a single figure in our coded report.

The observer must stand in a suitable open space or on a roof to get a good view of the sky. Complete cloud cover will be reported as eight oktas, half cover will be four oktas and a cloudless celestial dome will be reported as zero oktas or 'sky clear'.

It is reasonably easy to estimate, for example, five oktas (five-eighths cover) by mentally splitting the sky into halves and assessing each area separately, then recombining. Another trick is to imagine that all the blue is cloud and all the cloud is blue – would you still get the same answer? Perhaps the major fault of trainee meteorologists is to fail to take into account high cirrus cloud. This may be so thin that the sky still looks pale blue and the Sun is still able to shine, albeit with reduced strength. Nevertheless cirrus is still cloud and must be reported.

Having assessed the total cloud amount we now have the task of reporting the individual layers separately. For example, we might have a total cloud amount of six oktas, composed of two separate layers of cumulus and cirrus. The individual layers overlap each other, but if we watch for a time as the low-level cumulus floats across the sky we can then

BEAUFORT SCALE   *As used on land*

Force	Description	Specifications for use on land	Knots		Miles per hour		Description in forecasts
			Average	*Limits*	*Average*	*Limits*	
0	Calm	Calm; smoke rises vertically	0	< 1	0	< 1	Calm
1	*Light air*	Direction of wind shown by smoke drift, but not by wind vanes	2	1–3	2	1–3	Light
2	*Light breeze*	Wind felt on face; leaves rustle; ordinary vane moved by wind	5	4–6	5	4–7	Light
3	*Gentle breeze*	Leaves and small twigs in constant motion; wind extends light flag	9	7–10	10	8–12	Light
4	*Moderate breeze*	Raises dust and loose paper; small branches are moved	13	11–16	15	13–18	Moderate
5	*Fresh breeze*	Small trees in leaf begin to sway; crested wavelets form on inland waters	19	17–21	21	19–24	Fresh
6	*Strong breeze*	Large branches in motion; whistling heard in telegraph wires; umbrellas used with difficulty	24	22–27	28	25–31	Strong
7	*Near gale*	Whole trees in motion; inconvenience felt when walking against wind	30	28–33	35	32–38	Strong
8	*Gale*	Breaks twigs off trees; generally impedes progress	37	34–40	42	39–46	Gale
9	*Strong gale*	Slight structural damage occurs (chimney pots and slates removed)	44	41–47	50	47–54	Severe gale
10	*Storm*	Seldom experienced inland; trees uprooted; considerable structural damage occurs	52	48–55	59	55–63	Storm
11	*Violent storm*	Very rarely experienced; accompanied by widespread damage	60	56–63	68	64–72	Violent storm
12	*Hurricane*	–	–	> 64	–	> 73	Hurrican force

BEAUFORT SCALE

As used at sea

Force	Description	Specifications for use at sea	Knots Mean	Knots Limits	Description in Forecasts	State of Sea	Typical height of waves in open sea metres (feet)
0	*Calm*	Sea like a mirror	0	< 1	Calm	Calm	0.0
1	*Light air*	Ripples with the appearance of scales are formed, without foam crests	2	1–3	Light	Calm	0.1 (0.3)
2	*Light breeze*	Small wavelets, still short but more pronounced; crests have a glassy appearance and do not break	5	4–6	Light	Smooth	0.2 (0.6)
3	*Gentle breeze*	Large wavelets; crests begin to break; foam of glassy appearance; perhaps scattered white horses	9	7–10	Light	Smooth	0.6 (2)
4	*Moderate breeze*	Small waves, becoming longer; fairly frequent white horses	13	11–16	Moderate	Slight	1.0 (3)
5	*Fresh breeze*	Moderate waves, taking a more pronounced long form; many white horses are formed; chance of some spray	19	17–21	Fresh	Moderate	2.0 (7)
6	*Strong breeze*	Large waves begin to form; the white foam crests are more extensive everywhere; probably some spray	24	22–27	Strong	Rough	3.0 (10)
7	*Near gale*	Sea heaps up and white foam from breaking waves begins to be blown in streaks along the direction of the wind	30	28–33	Strong	Very Rough	4.0 (13)
8	*Gale*	Moderately high waves of greater length; edges of crests begin to break into spindrift; the foam is blown in well-marked streaks along the direction of the wind	37	34–40	Gale	High	5.5 (18)
9	*Strong gale*	High waves; dense streaks of foam along the direction of the wind; crests of waves begin to topple, tumble and roll over; spray may affect visibility	44	41–47	Severe gale	Very high	7.0 (23)
10	*Storm*	Very high waves with long overhanging crests; the resulting foam, in great patches, is blown in dense white streaks along the direction of the wind; the 'tumbling' of the sea becomes heavy and shock-like; visibility affected	52	48–55	Storm	Very high	9.0 (30)
11	*Violent storm*	Exceptionally high waves (small and medium-sized ships might be for a time lost to view behind the waves); everywhere the edges of the wave crests are blown into froth; visibility affected	60	56–63	Violent storm	Phenomenal	11.0 (38)
12	*Hurricane*	The air is filled with foam and spray; sea completely white with driving spray; visibility very seriously affected	–	> 64	Hurricane force	Phenomenal	14.0 (47)

estimate that there is, say, four oktas of cumulus and perhaps five oktas of cirrus. At this stage a bit of common sense and realism is required. We need a sensible snapshot report of the state of the sky.

It may come as no surprise to discover that the most commonly reported cloud amount in the British Isles is eight-eighths, i.e. total cover. A clear blue sky is less common than might be imagined because so often a small wispy patch of thin cirrus is present. A trace of cloud is reported in the observer's coded message as 'one-eighth' rather than 'sky clear', and similarly a cloud sheet with tiny gaps is recorded as 'seven-eighths'.

THE NATURE OF CLOUDS

Why don't clouds fall to the ground? The answer to this question can best be understood by thinking of particles of dust caught in a shaft of sunlight in an otherwise darkened room. The dust particles have such a tiny fall-speed that their rate of fall is insignificant compared with the turbulence and other air motions taking place in the room. Similarly the billions of water droplets which make up a cloud are so small that their fall-speed is usually negligible. A cloud is composed of droplets of very much the same sort of size as is fog at the Earth's surface. If you drive over any mountain road you may well drive up into a cloud and down out of it on the other side of the hill.

Luke Howard (1772-1864) classified clouds into three main groups, and gave each group a Latin name.

Cumulus – a heap or pile
Stratus – a layer
Cirrus – a tuft or filament (e.g. of hair)

The classification has since been expanded to describe ten basic cloud types, but it is still useful to think of cloud as coming either in layers or with large vertical extent. Additional Latin names are nimbus (rain) and alto (high) though the alto species have subsequently been re-classified as medium-level clouds.

The colour of clouds obviously varies, commonly from white to almost black. Sometimes a yellow or brownish tinge to the clouds is a sign of pollution. For layer clouds the colour depends largely on the depth of the layer and the angle of the sunshine falling on the upper surface. These factors, coupled with the size and nature of the cloud water droplets or ice particles, determine how much light gets through to the observer on the ground. A thick layer of cloud viewed from a deep Scottish glen where you are surrounded by mountains and have a restricted sky view is a gloomy sight indeed. When the cloud has a heaped (convective) character, then it tends to be much more variable from place to place, and sometimes changes rapidly in the course of ten minutes. A huge black cloud overhead accompanied by a heavy shower or perhaps thunderstorm may give way quite quickly to a strange, almost eerie, pale yellowish light. The usual cause of strange lighting on changeable days is the reflection of sunlight from a 'wall' of convective cloud down to the Earth through a shallow low-level layer.

CUMULUS

Opening the curtains on a summer Sunday morning, you find there is not a cloud to be seen in the sky. You imagine that after breakfast you will be sitting (or lying, or fishing) in perfect unbroken sunshine. Anticipation turns to disappointment by mid-morning as an army of fluffy white clouds develops in the sky. These are cumulus clouds, which when small look like lumps of cotton wool. With a stiff breeze, they march quite steadily across the sky with their speed of movement giving a clue to their altitude.

Typically the base of cumulus clouds will be about 2000 ft (600 m) above ground in the winter and perhaps 4000 ft (1200 m) or more on a summer afternoon. Individual clouds are usually short-lived. The story is told of an amateur observer who informed the media that he could make clouds disappear just by staring at them! And so it seemed he could, because he pointed out a small cumulus cloud which did disappear before it passed out of sight. A senior member of the Met Office rose to the challenge and did the same – because, as he explained, their lifespan was so short that one had every chance of success providing one avoided a cloud which was just starting to develop strongly.

The cause of small cumulus clouds is convection. After a clear night and a sunny start to the day, the heat from the Sun makes the surface of the ground progressively warmer. By mid-morning, patches of warm ground are overlain by large invisible bubbles or 'parcels' of warm air. Once the bubble of warm air starts to rise it will keep going, carrying some moisture with it. As it rises, so it expands, for the air pressure is less up aloft. As it expands it cools and finally it has cooled sufficiently for its moisture to condense into tiny cloud droplets. A cumulus cloud is born! The air within the cloud will continue to rise until it reaches a warmer ('stable') layer above, or until drier air gets mixed into the warm bubble. The ascending warm bubble or parcel, known as a 'thermal', may have drifted sideways in the wind so that the cumulus cloud does not necess-arily appear above the warm field or the town which caused it.

On some sunny days there is insufficient moisture or instability for cumulus to form. Occasionally a power station, a factory or a stubble fire adds sufficient moisture to the atmosphere to tip the balance and will produce a cumulus cloud of its own. Didcot power station south of Oxford is one example of a favoured location. In hillier regions, little can compete with a high, south-facing slope as a source of thermals and therefore of cumulus. People in Glasgow or Manchester may be able to see distant clouds over the Highlands or the Pennines, respectively. A medium-sized cumulus may hold 1000 tons of liquid water droplets (in addition to gaseous water vapour). This would be sufficient to give a millimetre of rain to a square kilometre of land below!

Among meteorologists a much-favoured saying is 'what goes up must come down'. When air is rising in dry thermals or in cloud, there must be other compensating downdraughts nearby. When cumulus clouds are present the downward motion is in the clear areas between the clouds. Sometimes the first indication of an approaching shower is a bigger-than-usual patch of sunshine. (Large clouds have large downdraughts.) At the end of the day, as the Sun's heat wanes, the convection ceases and the cumulus clouds tend to disappear.

CUMULONIMBUS

Just as cumulus is a heaped cloud, so a cumulonimbus is a heaped rain-cloud (nimbus = rain). In many ways the rain-bearing, or more correctly 'shower-bearing', variety can be considered as a bigger, better-organised version of its little brother, the cumulus. The cumulonimbus may be 10 km (6 miles) across rather than a few hundred metres. Its top may extend to 10 km (6 miles) above the ground rather than a kilometre or two. The air may be racing up the middle of the cloud at 20 metres a second (40 mph) which is perhaps ten times the updraught speed in a small cumulus. Instead of a ball of cotton wool, it will resemble a huge cauliflower. Sometimes it is likened to sprouting towers and bulging turrets – in the words of the song an 'ice-cream castle in the air'. But there is one important structural difference in that the uppermost levels of the cumulonimbus have turned to ice and become fibrous in appearance. This icy section at the top may flatten out into an 'anvil' shape when the cloud is fully developed. The base is usually dark, with rain (or hail or snow) falling from at least some portion of it.

Cumulonimbus clouds may be seen at any time of day but are most common inland in the afternoon in the spring and summer. At these times convection is at its strongest and most organised. Those living on north or northwest facing coasts will be just as likely to see them with onshore

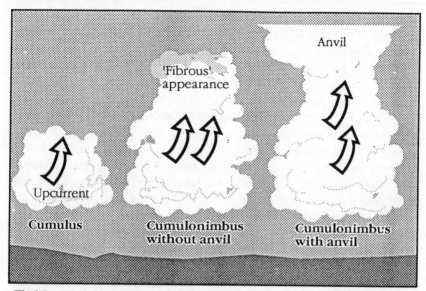

The life cycle of a convective cloud as it grows from a cumulus to a cumulonimbus.
Most small cumulus clouds fail to develop and disperse quite quickly. The air has to be
'deeply unstable' for cumulonimbus development.

winds in autumn and winter, when they develop over the sea and race
inland to blast the coasts and hills with a sudden squally shower.

Whenever you hear the words 'heavy showers' or 'hail' or 'thunder' you
should be aware that the forecaster is predicting cumulonimbus clouds.
Sometimes they will be embedded or half-hidden amongst other clouds.
On other occasions they will be easy to see because they are well separated
by downdraught regions of clear skies. Under these conditions the anvil
cloud may be visible many miles away. This anvil-shaped cloud top is an
almost certain indicator of a shower but it doesn't necessarily mean that
you will get one. Careful study of the cloud over a period of a few minutes
may show whether it is moving towards you. But beware, the lifetime of a
cumulonimbus is usually less than one hour and it may be a spent force by
the time it arrives.

STRATUS

The scourge of both pilots and hill walkers, stratus is the lowest cloud.
The word is Latin for a 'layer' and used alone it signifies a low-level layer
cloud (not to be confused with altostratus and cirrostratus which are high
aloft). Sometimes when a sheet of stratus is affecting an area the cloud
base will be right down on the ground and the visibility will be below fog

limits. The usual stratus base will be between the surface and 1000 ft (300 m), which in undulating country means that many of the hilltops will be obscured by cloud.

In appearance, stratus may often be described as a featureless grey layer. However, careful observation of the cloud as it passes overhead will usually reveal a few minor variations – a slightly darker undulation or a ragged edge. Perhaps the most important indication of its low altitude is the rate of movement across the sky, which is noticeable in anything more than a flat calm. Simple geometry will show that stratus cloud at 800 ft (250 m) moving at say 20 mph (12 kph) will have a greater apparent movement across the sky than altostratus with its base at ten times that height but moving only three times as fast. Thus the changes taking place in the cloud are a valuable indication of its height and a good observer will keep an eye on the cloud between hourly observations.

One sure sign of stratus is when the top of a cathedral spire or TV mast is obscured by cloud. Knowing the height and shape of the building you can easily calculate the height of the cloud base above ground. A local hill can provide much the same opportunity, except that the hill may be *causing* the cloud by forcing the air to rise and there may be no similar cloud directly above the observer. An approximate guide to the height of stratus may be gained from measuring the relative humidity and deducting it from 100. This gives some idea of the height of the low cloud in hundreds of feet. For example, 94% relative humidity would indicate stratus at very roughly 600 ft (180 m) above ground providing that the air is reasonably well mixed by the wind and assuming that low cloud *is* present! Inland, any stratus cloud will tend to lift slightly during the day-time, and in summer will usually disperse completely unless associated with rain. On the coast when a moist southwesterly Tropical Maritime airstream persists, there may be no such respite. Dyfed in Wales is very exposed to southwesterlies so the airfield at RAF Brawdy can get 'thirty-mile-an-hour fog' as stratus sweeps across at ground level.

STRATOCUMULUS

Stratocumulus will often give a sheet of almost total cloud cover, with perhaps a few small breaks. The cloud elements are rounded in shape and almost join up, one with another. Occasionally a stratocumulus sheet is composed of rolls, perhaps lying across the wind.

From a meteorological point of view, one can distinguish between two types. On windy days stratocumulus will often form at 1500 ft (500 m) due to mechanical turbulence as the wind blows across trees, buildings and hills. On quieter days the cloud base may be at 2000 to 7000 ft (600 to

2000 m) and the cloud is due to weak convection currents aloft. In this latter case it is easier to imagine the stratocumulus cloudsheet as a moist layer floating across, largely unrelated to the surface. Such a layer may be only 1000 ft (300 m) or so thick, insufficiently deep to give more than the occasional spot of rain.

Stratocumulus may form huge sheets covering thousands of square kilometres around the flanks of a high-pressure system, especially over the oceans. The weather below such overcast layers tends to be dry, but may be dull if the cloud is quite deep. It can then produce 'anticyclonic gloom' when the sky looks dark, but still no significant rain falls.

ALTOCUMULUS

This cloud, literally 'high cumulus' is found between 8000 and 20,000 ft (2500 and 6000 m). There is no great difference between the properties of stratocumulus and altocumulus since both are usually composed of supercooled water droplets and are normally of limited vertical extent, so the distinction is an arbitrary one. Two professional meteorological observers might well argue over the label to be applied to a particular cloud sheet. A measurement from a laser cloud-base recorder might settle the argument, for height is largely the deciding factor.

The dappled pattern of altocumulus is similar to that of stratocumulus, but with smaller cloud elements on account of the greater altitude. There are several variations on the theme, including altocumulus castellanus, which is like a vigorous medium-level cumulus or cumulonimbus (and sometimes looks like a castle turret, hence the name). Almost any undistinguished patch of medium-level cloud will end up being recorded as altocumulus. Medium-level turbulence, medium-level convection, lee waves or ascending frontal air are all possible causes. This is a cloud usually associated with changeable weather but without imminent rain. The description 'mackerel sky' would fit altocumulus or possibly cirrocumulus.

CIRROSTRATUS

For the professional meteorological observer, the overcast sky seems to present a problem. How can the height of the cloud base be estimated? With much practice and experience, it gradually becomes easier to recognise the tell-tale signs which indicate high cloud: the lack of detail, the relative lack of movement of the cloud sheet, the very slow pace of change of the appearance of the whole sky. An estimation of cloud base is not the result of one snapshot judgement. Rather, it is a matter of continuous monitoring and assessment.

As a textbook warm front approaches, a halo may be seen around the Sun, indicating thin cirrostratus cloud. The sky is still bright at this stage, which was preceded by cirrus and will be followed by altostratus if the front goes according to plan. Cirrostratus is always composed of ice crystals and is caused by widespread but slow ascent of the air ahead of the warm front. The cloud base is usually 20,000 to 25,000 ft (6000 to 8000 m).

ALTOSTRATUS

This is another pale cloud producing overcast conditions, rather thicker and lower than cirrostratus, but the observer can still just see the Sun, which now looks rather as if it is being viewed through ground glass. The usual altostratus cloud base is at 10,000 to 17,000 ft (3000 to 5000 m).

As part of the classic approach of a warm front, the 'cirrostratus and halo' phase suggests rain in about six hours' time, whereas the 'altostratus and ground-glass' phase which follows suggests rain in about two hours' time. This is a rough rule of thumb which works most of the time, especially when pressure is falling. Occasionally the frontal cloud fails to follow right through the full sequence to nimbostratus.

NIMBOSTRATUS

This is the name given to an overall sheet of grey cloud which is producing continuous rain or snow (as befits its name of 'rain-layer'). The cloud base is usually between 2000 and 8000 ft (600 to 2500 m) and the cloud is thick, perhaps solid, right up to cirrus levels.

In appearance, it is rather featureless and sufficiently dense to hide the Sun or Moon – or else we should probably be calling it altostratus. Often, when the rain or snow begins, ragged fragments of much lower stratus cloud will form below the nimbostratus sheet. In midwinter with a southeasterly surface wind, nimbostratus may give an hour or two of continuous moderate snow, perhaps then turning to rain. Even in other seasons, much of the rain which such layers produce will have fallen out of the cloud as snow before melting during descent.

CIRRUS

Hardly a summer day goes past without some sort of cirriform cloud (i.e. member of the cirrus family) being seen in the sky, at least briefly. In winter they are common, though low clouds may obscure them from view rather more frequently.

The cirrus family is found at great altitudes, usually above 20,000 ft (6000 m) though perhaps somewhat lower in the polar regions. They are known as high clouds in contrast to the medium- and low-level families of cloud.

Cirrus itself is very common in the British Isles and throughout most of the world, usually being thin, wispy and white in appearance. The name, coming as it does from a 'tuft of hair', is accurate, and is a reminder of the title 'mare's tail' which is also applied. Cirrus may be hooked or straight, depending on the airflow aloft. Sometimes it comes as a very dense patch with is a left-over from an anvil cloud – the cumulonimbus itself having dissipated and vanished. On other occasions, cirrus may be quite extensive when associated with a jet stream and can then be seen moving across the sky despite its great altitude.

The clouds of the cirrus family are composed of ice crystals, slow to evaporate and usually changing only slowly with time. Aircraft condensation trails ('contrails') are a form of artificial cirrus which can sometimes be seen in 'historical' films for those who enjoy spotting technical inaccuracies. Contrails were obviously impossible before highflying aircraft developed.

CIRROCUMULUS

Cirrocumulus is often present in small amounts along with cirrus, but rarely does it dominate the sky. On those occasions when it is widespread a beautiful spectacle is created, especially at sunset. The individual clouds are very small – often tiny rows of roughly spherical pearl-like cloud elements. Sometimes they occur in undulating patterns like tiny ripples. The important difference from altocumulus is the great height and the small size of the individual clouds which can usually be hidden behind a little fingernail at arm's length.

The cause of the cirrocumulus clouds may be turbulent winds with a layer of unstable air at very high altitude. The base is typically at 25,000 to 32,000 ft (8000 to 10,000 m).

Whilst cirrostratus is suggestive of an approaching warm front, neither cirrus nor cirrocumulus are of much use in forecasting. Sometimes they appear when a high-pressure system is weakening, but they will certainly not tell you whether it is going to collapse or re-establish itself.

The temperature at cirrus levels is commonly around –40 C (-40 F).

CLOUD BASE AND TOPS

Pilots, as they descend from above a cloud layer towards an airfield will want to know the height of the cloud tops and, even more important, the cloud base. Meteorologists will also wish to know the cloud depth, for example to assess the likelihood of rain.

The cloud base is the vertical distance of the cloud above the ground. Observations and forecasts are still given in feet despite the tendency in all other areas of science to change over to metric values. Altimeters and indeed pilots' brains still work in feet!

As I write this, on a summer's day, there are two layers of cloud – cumulus at about 3000 ft (1000 m) and cirrus at 25,000 ft (8000 m). I would be very pleased if my estimates are within 10% of the true values, and they could be a good bit further out. As for the height of the cloud tops, this is even more difficult, especially as they will be less uniform than the cloud bases. Today the cumulus are quite shallow. Looking at a distant cloud it seems to me that the distance from the ground to the base, which I reckon is 3000 ft (1000 m), is about equalled by the height of the cloud itself, so the top is therefore 6000 ft (2000 m) above ground. The cirrus cloud looks thin and nebulous but what I have assumed to be one layer may well be two layers, or a rather random assortment of cloud patches extending up to 35,000 ft (11,000 m). If I had more information, in the form of a vertical profile of temperature and humidity, the estimates could be refined and improved.

Major airfields have a variety of instruments to measure the height of cloud. At night the cloud searchlight shines a vertical beam which produces an illuminated spot on the cloud base. A brass plate with movable pointer (called an alidade) positioned 300 m (1000 ft) from the searchlight allows the angle to be measured and the height of the cloud base to be calculated. Similarly the more sophisticated 'cloud base recorder' can make measurements by day or night using pulsed light or laser beams. But all of these instruments suffer from one problem – they only give a spot value of the cloud over one point. Patches of low cloud approaching will not be measured until they pass overhead. Reports from pilots who have just taken off will help, but a lot of the responsibility falls back on the Meteorological Office observer whose considerable skills are tested to the full when low cloud drifts in.

BAROMETERS

Atmospheric pressure can be thought of as the result of an immensely tall column of air over one point. It is measured by a 'barometer', which gives an instantaneous reading. There are also recording instruments called 'barographs', which give a daily or weekly graph of the changes which have occurred.

Barometers come in two basic types – mercury and aneroid. The mercury barometer is a tall, rather expensive instrument. Because it contains a column of mercury it is difficult to transport and is best left permanently bolted to a wall. The atmosphere presses down on a small reservoir of mercury, rather like an open bowl. As the pressure increases, more mercury is forced up inside a glass column to 29, 30 or even 31 in (74 to 79 cm) above the level of the reservoir. Often some words are added on the dial, traditionally stormy, changeable, fair and very dry, which are intended to give an idea of the expected weather.

Mercury is a very dense liquid. If the barometer was made with a water-filled column, it would need to be almost 30 ft (9 m) tall.

The alternative, more modern, instrument is the aneroid barometer. In the simplest models a small metal capsule or flattish cylinder containing a partial vacuum is connected to a pointer, and as the pressure increases the cylinder is squeezed in and the pointer moves across a dial. Although the atmospheric pressure is now measured directly by the effect on the cylinder or sometimes a series of perhaps 6 cylinders, the result is still often given in inches or millimetres of mercury. The modern meteorological unit of atmospheric pressure is the millibar, which some scientists prefer to call the hecto Pascal.

The world record for high pressure is 1084 mbar in Siberia, and the British record is 1055 mbar at Aberdeen. The lowest pressure ever recorded is 870 mbar in a typhoon, but probably even lower values occur momentarily in tornadoes. The British record low is 925 mbar, measured in Perthshire on 26 January 1884.

All of these values are sea-level pressures, not necessarily those shown on the instrument. Meteorologists read the instrument, then add a correction to convert it to the 'mean sea-level pressure'. This is because we want to make sensible comparisons between the pressure in, say, Edinburgh and that at an upland station such as Aviemore. If we did not correct the Aviemore reading it would always be much lower than that at Edinburgh. The upland barometer would always point to the 'stormy' end of the dial, whatever the weather! An increase of just 8 m (27 ft) in altitude will reduce the pressure by 1 mbar.

You can set your barometer to the sea-level value by adjusting a screw, usually in the back. The best time to do this is when we are in the middle of an anticyclone. The pressure is then fairly uniform across the British Isles and hopefully changing only slowly. A newspaper or TV chart will then give you a sufficiently accurate reading. Older instruments might be best left alone.

CHANGING PRESSURE

When gently tapped, a barometer will often react by moving to a slightly higher or lower reading. (In theory a perfect instrument would not require tapping but in practice the mechanism often sticks slightly.) This change, taken together with the wind direction and the state of sky, will give some idea of what the day holds. Better still, if your barometer has one of those movable gold-coloured pointers it can be set exactly over the barometer needle when you go to bed. In the morning the pressure may well have changed but the gold pointer still shows last night's value and you can therefore deduce the change over, say, a 9-hour period. Professional meteorologists report the change in the last 3 hours – for example, 'falling then steady'. A fall or rise of 10 mbar in 3 hours is exceptional and may happen only a couple of times a year at a weather observing station in the British Isles.

The biggest falls obviously occur when a depression is approaching rapidly. If the low is deepening as it approaches, then the fall is all the more dramatic. Pressure variations are thus due both to movement and to the changes of the system itself.

Perhaps the best home-forecasting signs of approaching rain are a rapidly falling barometer, a southeasterly wind and a thickening cloud sheet. This suggests an oncoming depression which may well pass close to you. (In midwinter the rain could start as snow, so temperature is another factor in the forecasting equation.)

The rising or falling trend of pressure is just as important as whether the reading is at the 'changeable' or 'fair' part of the barometer scale. If the rising trend persists fairly steadily for 2 or 3 days, then the summer fine spell may well last for some time. 'Long told, long last; short told, soon past' is my favourite barometer saying. Another good one is 'First rise after low foretells a stronger blow' but often the gale has set in before you notice that the precipitous fall of pressure has just been reversed and that the rise has already begun.

This illustrates one of the difficulties in forecasting for yourself from a single observation. You are essentially relying on past weather when an upwind weather report would be invaluable.

Quite a reasonable weather chart of the British Isles can be constructed by listening to the radio broadcasts of reports from coastal stations, which consist of statements such as 'Tiree, 1027, rising slowly'. If the Hebridean island of Tiree has a pressure of 1027 mbar and the pressure is rising then this would on its own be an indication of air weather. Taken with a wider range of observations it will supply an overview of the 'synoptic' pattern. ('Synoptic' is from Greek meaning 'seen at one time' because it is a snapshot view of the weather for a fixed time, say 0900 hours GMT.) The easiest way to construct your weather chart is to make a recording of the radio report then transfer the readings to a blank map. You can then draw isobars on the map.

THE STEVENSON SCREEN

Meteorologists measure temperature in the Stevenson Screen, a white painted box which stands 1.2 m (4 ft) above the ground. The screen was designed by Thomas Stevenson (1818-87), the father of the author Robert Louis Stevenson. Its louvred sides allow the air to blow through and its white paint reflects most of the Sun's heat. The roof incorporates an airspace to give further insulation from direct sunlight and the flap or 'door' faces north so that the temperature can be read by the observer without sunlight falling on the thermometers. The screen looks something like a beehive but will usually be inside a small fenced enclosure along with rain-gauges and other equipment.

Sometimes we hear of temperatures being measured 'in the sun'. This can be very misleading because a thermometer lying on a black tarmac path will record a much higher temperature [sometimes over 50 C (122 F), even in the UK] than a thermometer lying on grass. In these examples we are merely recording the temperature reached by the thermometer under the prevailing circumstances. As meteorologists, we wish to standardise the exposure and do so with the Stevenson Screen. And since we measure temperatures 1.2m (4 ft) above ground, this is what we try to forecast. Very often there are four thermometers in a well-equipped screen. One records maximum temperature, one records minimum temperature, and the other two are read each hour. Of the hourly read equipment, the standard mercury-in-glass thermometer gives the straightforward temperature, which is sometimes referred to as the 'dry-bulb temperature'. The fourth instrument is the 'wet bulb', which is used in the calculation of relative humidity. There has been an increasing trend over the last few years to use electrical resistance thermometers with similar characteristics.

The Stevenson Screen is a vital part of the meteorologist's equipment. As interest mounts in climatic change, it is important that we have long series of temperatures measured by a standard, unchanging method. Both the equipment and our procedure must remain fixed if we are to achieve the high standard required to detect a systematic change of, say, 0.5 Celsius (0.9 F) over half a century.

CELSIUS AND FAHRENHEIT

The arguments over which temperature scale is best for any particular purpose will no doubt rumble on, but Celsius is certainly winning within meteorology, apart from in the United States. The Swedish scientist Anders Celsius proposed a scale of one hundred divisions in 1742 though his version ran in the opposite direction. Today's version, formerly known as centigrade, has zero as the freezing point of water and 100 as the boiling point.

The Fahrenheit scale was introduced about 1709 by the German physicist Gabriel Fahrenheit with 32 as the freezing point of water and 212 as the boiling point. There are 180 degrees between the two fixed points compared with 100 on the Celsius scale, a ratio of 9 to 5. To convert Fahrenheit to Celsius you must therefore deduct 32, multiply by 5, then divide by 9. To convert Celsius to Fahrenheit, multiply by 9, divide by 5 and then add 32 (to allow for the different 'starting point').

HUMIDITY

Water vapour is transparent and always present in the atmosphere. We tend to become aware of it when it changes phase and turns to liquid water. Condensation then occurs on our windows, our spectacles 'steam up' or, outdoors, rain falls or dew forms on the grass. We may, however, also notice when there is a high moisture content because the air feels sticky. Sometimes these conditions, when evaporation from our damp skins is slow, are described as sultry. This is mainly a summer problem when our bodies are using the sweating mechanism to cool us. The change of phase from liquid to vapour requires an additional input of energy – this causes evaporational cooling, and it is used in the Stevenson Screen to measure the relative humidity of air.

The 'ordinary' or dry-bulb temperature is measured by a simple mercury-in-glass thermometer. The wet-bulb temperature is measured by an adapted version of the same instrument. The bulb at the lower end of the (vertical) thermometer is covered with a small piece of muslin, rather like a portion of white cotton handkerchief. This is tied on with a piece of string-like 'wick' which sucks up purified water by capillary action from a tiny plastic reservoir. Thus the muslin is kept wet and as the air blows through the louvred screen, evaporation takes place. The supply of latent heat to allow this change of phase comes from the air passing the wet bulb, which therefore reads lower than the dry bulb. On a moist autumn day the dry bulb temperature might be 12.0 C (53.6 F) and the wet bulb 11.5 C (52.7 F), which (after a simple calculation) would indicate

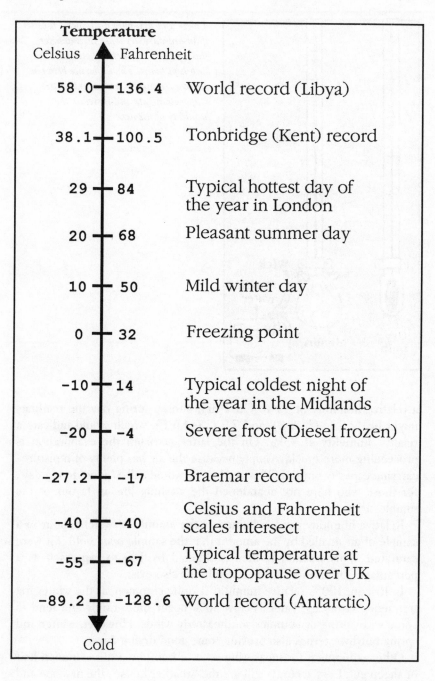

Temperature

Celsius ▲ Fahrenheit

58.0 — 136.4	World record (Libya)
38.1 — 100.5	Tonbridge (Kent) record
29 — 84	Typical hottest day of the year in London
20 — 68	Pleasant summer day
10 — 50	Mild winter day
0 — 32	Freezing point
-10 — 14	Typical coldest night of the year in the Midlands
-20 — -4	Severe frost (Diesel frozen)
-27.2 — -17	Braemar record
-40 — -40	Celsius and Fahrenheit scales intersect
-55 — -67	Typical temperature at the tropopause over UK
-89.2 — -128.6	World record (Antarctic)

Cold

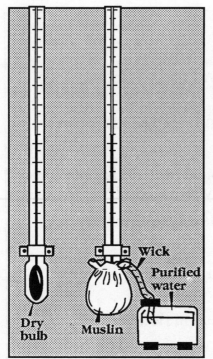

A wet- and dry-bulb hygrometer consists of an ordinary dry-bulb thermometer, plus an identical thermometer with its bulb kept moist. The difference between the two readings is a measure of the evaporation rate and therefore the humidity of the air.

a relative humidity of 93%. On a dry, sunny, spring day the readings might be 12.0 C (53.6 F), and 7.0 C (44.6 F), which would indicate a relative humidity of 43%. On the latter occasion the evaporation is proceeding more quickly simply because the air has plenty of moisture-carrying capacity unused. This is what we would call a 'good drying day', for those who have not abandoned the washing-line in favour of the tumble-drier.

Relative humidity can be defined as the amount of water vapour in a sample of air divided by the amount that the sample *could* hold if it were saturated. This fraction is then multiplied by 100 to express it as a percentage. Other more formal definitions also exist.

In Britain, 100% relative humidity is quite common, as the winter fog frequency shows us. Values below 30% occur quite rarely and tend to come with spring or summer southeasterly winds. However, winter and spring northwesterlies also provide some good drying days.

Other equipment for measuring relative humidity utilises human hair or sheep gut. Less accurate still are the 'weather house', the fir-cone and the piece of seaweed.

These old country methods of examining the air's moisture content provide a spot measurement and not a forecast.

DEW AND HOAR FROST

When we take a stainless-steel jug full of iced drink out of a refrigerator, we may see water droplets condensing on the outside of the container. This is because the jug is at a lower temperature than the dew point of the air. Dew point is defined as the temperature at which the air, when cooled, will just become saturated. On a summer's day when the air temperature reaches 18 C (64 F), the dew point might typically be 8 C (46 F). If the same air remains over the area on a clear, calm evening, its dew point will remain reasonably constant. By sunset the air temperature may have fallen to 12 C (54 F) but the dew point will still be around 8 C (46 F). Incoming solar heat has waned and ceased, so the surface of a lawn continues to cool. By the time it reaches, say, 7 C (45 F), the temperature of the grass is below the dew point (the saturation point) of the air and droplets of moisture start to form. Since the air is now being 'robbed' of some of its water vapour the dew point of the air will actually start to fall very slightly. Next day the dew droplets may be seen sparkling in the early morning sunshine. As the incoming heat gathers strength, the dew will be evaporated back into the air (and the readings in the Stevenson Screen will probably show a slight rise in the wet-bulb temperature and therefore in the dew point). The grass will become reasonably dry and suitable for sitting upon during the day. Dew will rarely re-form until half an hour before sunset, even in very moist airstreams, and often not until well after dark in midsummer. In winter the day-time evaporation is much slower, and in calm weather dew may persist all day.

Hoar frost is composed of tiny ice crystals, feathery in appearance when well-developed, which form by the same process but when ground temperatures are below freezing-point. It should be realised that the temperature in the Stevenson Screen may be reading 2 C (36 F) when the ground temperature is –3 C (27 F), because it is the Earth's surface that cools first and this in turn cools the air. A ground frost may occur even when the air temperature doesn't get down to freezing-point, so when the grass is covered in a white hoar frost at dawn we should not assume that there has been an air frost. Cars also provide a 'radiating surface' and can be 5 C (9 F) below the air temperature. Sometimes dew forms during the evening and subsequently freezes to become hoar frost, and on such occasions a close inspection may show globular lumps of ice on the grass rather than the usual feathery pattern. 'Grass minimum' temperature readings are made by laying a thermometer horizontally with the bulb just touching the blades of grass. On cloudy windy nights it gives much the same value as the air temperature, on clear nights it is several degrees cooler.

There is a weather saying of some value: 'Dew in the night, the day will be bright'. To a certain extent this is self-evident, for dew tends to form on clear, calm nights which occur in anticyclonic (high-pressure) weather. Such conditions also tend to give sunny days. If the high persists, then dew or hoar frost will form on each successive night.

FOG AND FREEZING FOG

The official definition of fog is a visibility below 1000 m (1100 yards). This limit is sensible for aviation purposes but for the general public and the motorist an upper limit of 200 m (say 200 yards) is more realistic. Severe disruption of transport occurs when the visibility falls below 50 m (50 yards or so). Useful labels for these three categories are aviation fog, thick fog and very dense fog.

The reduction in visibility is due to tiny water droplets, usually less than 40 micrometres in diameter. Their fall-speed is small or negligible so they usually remain airborne. Only when deep fog is stirred up by a strengthening wind will they easily grow large enough for some droplet settling or even drizzle to occur.

Thickest fogs tend to occur in industrial areas where there are many pollution particles to form nuclei on which the droplets can grow.

Freezing fog is composed of supercooled water droplets, i.e. those that remain as liquid water even though the temperature is below freezing-point. One of the worst characteristics of true freezing fog is that rime – composed of feathery crystals of ice – is deposited on vertical surfaces such as lamp-posts, masts, fencepoles and on overhead wires. This rime formation occurs when the supercooled water droplets, blowing along in a breeze hit the vertical surface and freeze. The expression freezing fog is also used loosely to describe any fog which occurs at a temperature below freezing point.

A car travelling through a stationary fog at –10 C (14 F) can experience rime accretion on a radio aerial or roof-rack.

For the electricity industry, whose pylons and overhead wires are susceptible, and for the radio and TV industry, whose transmitting masts can become covered in a dangerous build-up of rime, freezing fog is a serious problem. In Scotland and on the Pennines, winter-time low cloud can provide freezing fog conditions. The weight of a mast may increase dramatically as a blast of supercooled water droplets forms fingers of ice on every exposed surface. Under such conditions the Emley Moor transmitting mast on the Pennines collapsed. Hill walkers should beware of falling blocks of ice when near these structures in winter.

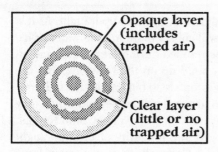

If a hailstone is cut open, it may show layers like an onion which tell us something about its life-cycle.

RAINDROPS

The windscreen of a car is a superb place for the meteorologist to view raindrops, and indeed all precipitation particles. Every second or two the windscreen wipers provide a fresh screen on which to view the next sample. Perhaps the only regret of the professional meteorologist is that there is no camera to record the spectrum of drop sizes. Any water drop larger than 1 mm (0.04 in) in diameter would be classed as rain whereas smaller drops are described as drizzle. Thus the differentiation is based purely on drop size and not on the intensity of precipitation. Heavy drizzle is more wetting than slight rain. The former usually comes from sheets of very low cloud, whereas rain is more likely from deeper clouds which are not necessarily brushing the hilltops. Drizzle with its many small drops will cut down the visibility more than the equivalent amount of water falling as rain. Sometimes the windscreen or windowpane will reveal rain and drizzle falling simultaneously.

HAIL

In the British Isles there are three different phenomena that could loosely be described as hail. In the first, the precipitation particles are beautifully white but easily crushable between the fingers – these are snow pellets, and tend to occur in winter and spring northerly airstreams. The second consists of particles of quite moderate size, composed of clear ice and sometimes conical in shape – these are ice pellets. The third is true hail, which is whitish in appearance and varies greatly in size. If you cut open a hailstone you may be able to see a layered structure showing that the hailstone has grown through a series of stages.

Large hailstones fall from deep cumulonimbus clouds. Much of the cloud will be composed of supercooled water droplets. As the hailstone falls it will collect tiny water droplets which flow around its surface before freezing. If no air is trapped this frozen water will form a layer of clear ice.

Perhaps the hailstone will then be caught in a vigorous updraught. As it is carried back higher into the cloud it will collect more minute water or ice particles but this time some air will be trapped during the process and an opaque layer is formed. Thus layers build up on the hailstone, and the cycle may be repeated until finally the stone is so big that it falls to Earth. Unlike large raindrops which have an upper size limit beyond which they break up under air resistance, there is no such aerodynamic limit for hail. The limiting factor is mainly the speed and longevity of the updraught necessary to keep the hailstone aloft. Certainly they can grow large enough to dent cars, shatter greenhouses and even injure people.

Hail showers are quite common in Britain in westerly and northerly airstreams in spring, but really large hailstones tend to occur in the south rather than the north and are very much a feature of the summer months. Convection reaches a peak of activity in the afternoon and thus hail is most likely at that time of day. Some dramatic temperature falls accompany hailstorms with the transition from sunshine to hail-covered ground taking less than one hour. Strong gusts of wind may also occur, particularly before the storm, and so too may lightning and thunder. (Any melting of the hail by the lightning would be extremely localised within the cloud.)

The record weight of a hailstone in Britain is 141 g (5 oz) from Horsham, Sussex, on 5 September 1958. Certainly anything approaching golf ball size is remarkable in the UK.

The USA, Canada, Central Europe, the southern parts of the USSR, India and China all experience large hail. So too do land areas in the southern hemisphere. The former world record of 758 g (1.67 lb) from Kansas, USA, with a diameter of 190 mm (7.5 in), was beaten on 14 April 1986 by stones of 1020 g (2.25 lb) in Bangladesh in a hailstorm which killed 92 people.

There are also occasional reports of unexplained 'ice meteors', which are blocks of ice said to fall from clear skies, on occasions when no aircraft are flying over.

DRIZZLE AND SNOW GRAINS

A drizzle drop is tiny compared with a raindrop. The mid-winter equivalent is the snow grain, which is also small compared with a snowflake. These diminutive precipitation particles come from low cloud and their formation is quite different from the processes which go on inside shower clouds.

Drizzle drops usually fall from a low-level sheet of stratus or stratocumulus cloud when the moisture content of the air is high.

The mechanism causing the air to rise will be turbulence rather than convection, so generally there will be a good breeze blowing when drizzle or snow grains fall. Thus we arrive at a scenario of moist air, low cloud and probably at least a moderate to fresh breeze. This is drizzle weather. In airmass terminology it may be a Tropical Maritime airstream, in which case the western coasts and hills will be the main recipients. During winter, we occasionally get freezing drizzle with an easterly airstream when the precipitation freezes on impact with the ground at a temperature of –1 C (30 F).

SNOW

Most meteorologists like snow, although they may deny it. It forms inside a cloud typically at a temperature well below freezing-point, say –10 C (14 F) where ice crystals grow at the expense of tiny supercooled water droplets. This is the Bergeron-Findeisen process; the end result is snow. The fall-speed of snow varies enormously but 2 m per second (6 ft per second) is a rough estimate, about a quarter of the fall-speed of rain.

If the snow reaches a level where the air is above freezing-point, then obviously it will start to melt, but at the same time the air will be cooled. In practice, snow will often reach the surface with a temperature of 2 C (36 F). Partly melted snow or sleet is likely at temperatures around 3 C (36 F). The notion that it can be too cold for snow is erroneous, although heaviest falls to tend to occur with temperatures around zero, since the air holds more moisture at zero than at, say, –20 C. When 'snow' is reported in summer it often turns out to be hail.

Individual ice crystals can be in the shape of prisms or plates, or with typical snowfalls, six-pointed stars. The medium to large snowflakes which we normally see in Britain are composed of many ice crystals which have collided and stuck together (aggregated) inside the cloud, and a snowflake can be 3 cm (over an inch) across.

In summer, rain showers can give a rainfall rate of 5 cm (2 in) per hour, though usually only briefly. If the same amount of water were falling as snow, it would equate to 50 cm (20 in) in an hour. We would soon be digging our cars out or perhaps resigning ourselves to a day indoors. Fortunately there are two good reasons why snowfalls of that intensity are almost impossible. First, the necessary massive convective upcurrent is improbable in winter, especially inland. Second, the cold air holds less moisture. However, although we may be spared that kind of snowfall in an hour, that amount can fall over a few hours when the synoptic situation is right. On the Scottish mountains almost any front or depression can give a good snowfall in winter. The lowlands of Britain, though, need perhaps an approaching warm front or occluded front, or a depression passing just to the south of the observer. A showery northerly is another possibility, with snow showers coming in from the sea. Cold fronts which, by their very name, sound as if they should bring snow, tend to be disappointing in this respect, though sometimes rain will turn to snow behind the front before the precipitation ceases.

As we look out of the window at sleet, there are certain factors which favour the transition to pure snow: oncoming night, a cooling airmass, falling pressure, or an increase of precipitation intensity so that the air just cannot provide sufficient melting power.

RAIN, SHOWERS AND FLOODING

To the meteorological observer, rain comes in three intensities: light, moderate and heavy – up to 0.4 mm per hour, 0.5 to 4.0 mm per hour and over 4.0 mm per hour, respectively. (1 inch is about 25 millimetres.) Often the estimate of intensity must be made by eye, looking out of the window at the raindrops landing in a puddle with the addition of a quick check outside in the wet! There are also instruments which measure the rate of rainfall.

The standard 5-in (12.7 cm) diameter rain-gauge could be read each hour, but it is more convenient to use the tilting-syphon rain recorder which provides a chart record, or else the tipping-bucket rain-gauge which can operate a digital readout. With this latter instrument a counter clicks over for every 0.2 mm (0.008 in) of rain.

Another aspect of weather reporting is the continuity of the precipitation. Hourly reports show whether the rain is intermittent (i.e. has started within the last hour) or continuous. Coupled with the three intensities, this gives us six possibilities. It should be noted that 'continuous heavy rain' means that the rain has persisted for at least one hour and was heavy at the time of observation, but it could have been lighter at some stage during the hour. A common fault is to overestimate the rainfall intensity when a strong wind is lashing it against the window panes.

Drizzle is assessed on a different, lower scale of accumulation; showers on a higher scale. Rain and drizzle with their different droplet sizes may fall simultaneously and the reporting code allows for this. Often the mixture of precipitation types suggests that drizzle is falling from one cloud layer and rain from another. Rain and snow may also fall simultaneously.

Assessments are made of the duration of rainfall during each hour. Most of lowland Britain has a total of 500-800 hours of rainfall per year. This total may seem on the low side out of a possible 8000 hours or so in the year, but there are many cases of intermittent precipitation, and hours in which only a 'trace' falls are ignored in both accumulation and duration totals. Typically in the British Isles there is about a 50-50 chance of measurable rain in any 24-hour period.

Statisticians love to argue about what constitutes noteworthy, remarkable or very rare falls. Values for the lowest of these categories suggest that a fall of at least 14 mm in 10 minutes or 25 mm (1 inch) in 1 hour is 'noteworthy'. If you get 22 mm in 10 minutes or 38 mm in an hour then that is 'remarkable'. In the top category, 33 mm in 10 minutes or 57 mm in an hour is 'very rare'.

Statistical analyses of the likelihood of heavy falls of rain are fraught with difficulty. Upland stations are much more prone to high weekly totals than lowland stations, but exceptional short-period falls are common in the lowlands of the south. Adjacent recording stations may differ widely on any one day. As a rough guide in lowland Britain a specified location can expect a fall of 25 mm (1 in) in 24 hours about twice a year, and the same total in an hour about once every 10 years. Whose turn will it be next year?

OBSERVING AT NIGHT

During the night, the meteorological observer is required to send in an hourly report of all aspects of the weather, just the same as during the day. One of the most difficult items to observe is cloud.

Total cloud amount can be estimated by looking up at the stars. If you know the patterns of the constellations, then you can see which stars are missing, i.e. cloud-covered. Cirrus cloud may be too thin to conceal the brighter stars and planets, and the moon should certainly show through any cirriform cloud. A good observer will recognise the presence of cirrus because the stars look indistinct.

BALLOONS AND RADIOSONDES

A weather balloon is used for carrying equipment upwards. In order to be able to rise even when carrying a radar target and a radiosonde transmitter it must be filled with a gas which is substantially lighter than air to give it a reasonably large 'pull' or buoyancy force. Hydrogen is usually preferred to helium as it is cheap and light, although it can cause explosions. Small fairground balloons are filled with a slightly impure version of helium often called 'balloon gas'.

On the way up, the spare carrying capacity of 'free lift' provides the upward force, but air resistance prevents a rapid rise of the balloon, and the usual outcome is a rate of ascent around 6 m per second or 1200 ft per minute.

As the weather balloon ascends, it expands in the decreasing atmospheric pressure aloft. Finally at a height of perhaps 30 km (20 miles) the rubber, latex or other synthetic material is stretched so taut that it ruptures. At this height the pressure is only 10 mbar, which is just one-hundredth of that at the surface, and the balloon is enormously stretched. At this point, a paper parachute should open and both the equipment and the tattered remains of the balloon land safely in a field, wood or, more likely, the sea. Less than one set of equipment in three is recovered, but this does not matter too much since the information has already been collected.

The full 'rig', as it is called, consists of balloon, paper parachute, metallic radar target (rather like two television aerials joined together and covered with a metallic mesh) and a radiosonde or small radio transmitter enclosed in a white polystyrene case.

Radar equipment on the ground automatically follows the radar target. Once we have measured the elevation, azimuth (direction) and slant range, we can work out the height and, more importantly, the horizontal distance travelled by the balloon in each minute. This horizontal distance or 'flat range' enables us to calculate the wind speed and direction at each height up until the balloon bursts. In other words, we can measure how strong the jet steam is.

The radiosonde measures pressure, temperature and humidity, and then transmits this information back to the ground. Thus we get a vertical profile of the atmosphere which we can draw on a temperature/height graph.

Recovery, repair and re-use of the radiosonde is a bonus, but for older types of equipment not cost-effective. A reward label or disposal instructions are fixed to the transmitter and tell the finder what to do with the equipment.

For those taking part in fairground balloon races, it may be useful to know that a balloon with *less* gas inside it will usually drift further horizontally before it bursts. An over-filled balloon will rise more steeply into the rarified upper hemisphere and burst quite quickly, probably to land closer to its point of release.

WEATHER SATELLITES

Among the many pieces of hardware floating around the Earth are a few meteorological satellites. These are classified into two categories, depending on their orbit. Polar-orbitting satellites are fast-moving

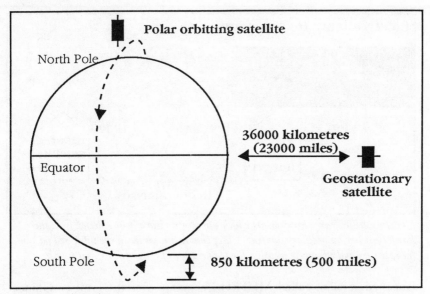

Geostationary satellites can provide pictures or 'images' every 15 to 30 minutes and always look down at the same part of the Earth. Polar orbiters go round in 100 minutes but the Earth rotates beneath their orbit so each 'pass' is further west.

(relative to the Earth) and complete an orbit every 100 minutes. Geostationary satellites are much further away from the Earth and each satellite remains stationary over one fixed point on the Earth's surface according to a pre-determined plan.

The polar orbitters circle at a height of 850 km (530 miles) and make about 14 orbits every 24 hours. As they orbit, the Earth rotates below them, so each passage or 'pass' will be further west. During the 100 minutes between successive orbits the Earth has rotated 25° longitude, so if a pass at 0800 hours crosses eastern Europe, the next pass at 0940 hours will cross the British Isles. Pictures or images are collected by scanning sensors over a reasonably wide swathe below the satellite, so there is some overlap. At the North and South poles, the overlap is total, since every orbit passes over these points. At night, the satellites are still useful since there is an infra-red image as well as a visual image. The current polar orbiters most widely used are NOAA 10 and NOAA 11, which were launched by the USA, but pictures from USSR satellites can also be picked up by those with the right radio-receiving equipment and a timetable of satellite passes. Non-directional helical aerials are used for polar-orbiting satellite reception.

Geostationary satellites are positioned at a height of 36,000 km (22,500 miles) above the Earth. They must be at this height and no other because they orbit the Earth at *exactly* the speed of its rotation. The European

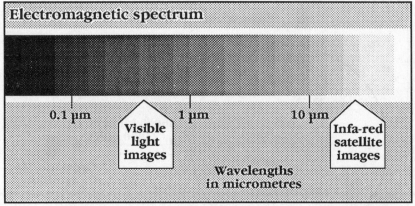

Modern satellites carry instruments which can record visible light reflected from the Earth (just like an ordinary camera). Other channels measure in the infra-red part of the spectrum and effectively measure the temperature of the Earth's surface.

launched version, called METEOSAT, stays over the Gulf of Guinea near West Africa over the intersection of the Greenwich Meridian with the Equator. The centrifugal force encouraging the satellite to fly off into space is exactly matched by the Earth's gravitational pull which keeps the satellite in orbit. The rotational period is once per day so METEOSAT is always over this same location. This is an excellent position for Africa, and quite good for Europe – the location has to be over the Equator for a geostationary satellite to remain in orbit. Reception is via a dish, which from London must point due south at METEOSAT. The USA satellites are near South America and called GOES and the Japanese have HIMAWARI, but information is shared.

VISUAL AND INFRA-RED PICTURES

Having invested huge sums of money in putting meteorological satellites into space, it would be folly not to utilise them to the full. They must carry as much equipment as possible within the limits set by the launch rocket payload, the power available from solar cells and the radio transmission limitations for the collected information. Nowadays, no new meteorological satellite is launched without the ability to collect data in several different 'channels'. At its simplest this can be understood by considering the images from the visual channel and from the infra-red channel.

The human eye is sensitive to electromagnetic radiation in the wavelengths between 0.4 and 0.7 μm (micrometres) which we call 'light'. The so-called visible or visual channels on the current series of NOAA satellites are actually at 0.6 and 0.9 mm, so the latter is marginally outside that which the eye can see, but very similar in character. Thus the visual image is much what we would get if we took a black and white photo out of a satellite window. Bright-looking clouds are deep and dense. Wispy-looking clouds are thin and nebulous – often high-level cirrus formations.

Such images are dependent on reflected light from the Sun and therefore night-time satellite passes produce a totally black picture.

Infra-red images are collected by a heat-sensitive scanner. Warm areas such as day-time land regions are emitting more heat (at around the 12 μm wavelength) than snow-covered regions. Colder still are cloud tops, at perhaps –40 C (-40 F). The picture is displayed using the convention black = hot, white = cold, with grey shades in between as appropriate. Since the infra-red picture depends on *emitted* radiation, night-time pictures are available. The radiometers which 'look down' at the Earth enable very accurate measurements to be made of the cloud-top tempera-ture, and often the height of the cloud tops can be quite precisely estimated.

The two separate pictures provided in the visual and infra-red channels can be evaluated in tandem by the meteorologist. Cloud which is faint and therefore thin on the visual image may be brilliantly white and therefore very cold on the infra-red image. This confirms its identification as thin, high-level cirrus cloud. Conversely, sea-fog will show up quite well on the visual picture but will be very faint on the infra-red because it is at almost the same temperature as the sea.

Thus the visual picture is a measurement of albedo or reflectivity, while the infra-red picture is a measurement of temperature. Together they give us a valuable overview of the atmosphere, and clouds down to about a kilometre in size can be resolved. Over the land areas of the Earth they are highly useful – over the oceans they are indispensable.

The general public tends to imagine that satellites are simply to provide forecasters with 'cloud maps'. In reality their most vital function is to provide upper-air information over the oceans for use in computer forecasting; they collect this information with multi-channel radiometers.

RAINFALL OBSERVED BY RADAR

Since the 1950s a continual problem with air traffic control radars has been interference from areas of rain. While the ability of the radar to detect falling rain is a nuisance for controllers, making it more difficult to locate and track aircraft, this same ability is now being put to a direct use by meteorologists.

England, Wales and Northern Ireland are covered by a network of eight radars, and we are beginning to link up with similar equipment in France, the Netherlands and at Shannon in the Irish Republic. During the 1990s we shall see Scotland included in the coverage, along with much of Western Europe.

The results are presented to the weather forecaster in map format, showing areas which are dry, areas of light rain, moderate rain or heavy rain. The different intensities are colour-coded and relate to the amount of rain falling in units of millimetres per hour. When displayed on a VDU screen the information is in the form of pixels representing 5 km (3 mile) squares. A succession of pictures at quarter-hour time intervals can be animated to show movement of the rain areas and development or dissipation of showers.

Anything technologically so sophisticated has, of course, got some drawbacks. The rainfall intensities are imprecise because the radar echo is very dependent on raindrop size. Also, the dishes cannot scan exactly in the horizontal because of hills and the radar beam has to be slightly elevated, giving a reduction in accuracy at long ranges. Results are dependent on interpretation by the forecaster on the ground, who must decide, for example, whether the precipitation is rain or snow, by looking at human observations and other data. Despite these and other problems the radar rainfall network provides a superb instant display of where rain was falling about 10 minutes ago. It is as near real time as one could wish. Water companies have contributed to the purchase of the system for obvious reasons.

The forecaster can then extrapolate the movement and other trends to predict rainfall for 3 to 6 hours ahead. A couple of examples can illustrate the uses. Heavy rain was predicted for Wimbledon an hour before it interrupted the tennis. A farmer in the West Country was saved money and time on crop spraying when he was warned of an approaching band of heavy showers. Some day in the future these pictures should be available 'on tap' via your television screen.

OCEAN WEATHER SHIPS

There is usually an ocean weather ship in the North Atlantic somewhere just south of Iceland at a position near 57° N 20° W. The ship takes a couple of days to reach this location from Fleetwood, Lancashire, and traditionally stays 'on station' for up to 21 days, so the whole trip is not far short of a month. At one time there were ten weather ships in the North Atlantic, but high costs and the increasing use of satellite data have reduced this to three. Various European nations contribute including the UK, Norway and the Soviet Union. There are also merchant ships doing observations and even releasing balloon-borne equipment.

When a weather ship reaches its nominated position, the engines are turned off and the ship wallows, broadside on to the waves. The engines are occasionally restarted if the ship is drifting 'off station', or to make balloon launching from the stern of the vessel easier.

For the meteorologists on board there are three main tasks: surface observations, balloon measurements and ocean temperature soundings.

Every hour a routine surface observation is completed and sent in by radio. All the usual onshore items are observed plus wave and swell measurements. There is an instrumental wave recorder on board. A previous ship, *Weather Reporter*, recorded a wave of 26.2 m (86 ft) at 59° N, 19° W on 30 December 1972.

Every six hours a balloon is launched and the upper winds, temperatures and humidities are measured, much as at onshore radiosonde stations. However, with strong winds more common at sea, launching the balloon and its equipment is difficult. Roughly speaking, one person releases the balloon whilst another tries to time the release of the radiosonde transmitter to prevent it going in the sea. Meanwhile both try to avoid getting drowned!

The third item to be recorded is the sea temperature profile, starting from the relatively warm surface layers and going down through the 'thermocline' to the cold, deep water below. In normal weather this can be done with a re-usable bathythermograph, which is lowered on a strong wire on the windward side of the ship and then winched back up from the depths. With a strong wind blowing an expendable bathythermograph is used instead. This is fired over the lee side of the ship and the information is automatically sent back up a very fine copper wire, though the instrument itself is lost. As satellites become more sophisticated the main requirement for 'sounding' the upper atmosphere by balloon will become redundant, and the final demise of the ocean weather ship is perhaps now in sight.

WIND WAVES AND SWELL

When a ship ploughs its way across the undulating waters of the Atlantic, the captain may well differentiate between waves of two different types. They may be 'wind waves', caused by the wind blowing in the locality at the time, or 'swell', which is caused by strong winds elsewhere over the preceding few days.

Observers on an ocean weather ship have to learn to distinguish between the two types and make separate reports of wind waves and swell.

A persistent wind of unchanging direction will generate a fairly predictable pattern of wind waves with their crests aligned across the wind. The height of the waves depends on the wind strength, its duration and the distance offshore, known as the fetch. A gale force wind blowing for 24 hours with a long fetch, say more than 800 km (500 miles), will produce waves of 6 m (20 ft). We are for the moment assuming that these are 'deep water waves', with the implication that the sea is sufficiently deep for the ocean floor to have no effect. The shallow waters of the North Sea or a shelving beach will generally produce shorter, steeper waves and a more choppy sea, which is particularly bad news for small vessels.

A tide flowing strongly against the wind will produce a very turbulent water surface with steep breaking waves as can happen in the Pentland Firth near Orkney.

Swell originates as wind waves that are sufficiently large to maintain their identity as they move out of the source region to more distant parts of the ocean. (Similarly, if we throw a stone into a pool the ripples will move for some distance before they finally decay.) A deep depression will produce a wide spectrum of waves, the smallest of which soon decay, but the largest of which may travel thousands of miles into areas of lighter winds. Swell can travel over amazing distances and a study was done of southern hemisphere waves generated in latitudes 40 to 50° S (the 'roaring forties') which approached and even crossed the Equator from the South Pacific to Hawaii in the North Pacific. This occurred in a region where there were no land masses to beak up the wave patterns.

Swell generated in the central North Atlantic can produce good surfing conditions on our western coasts a couple of days later even when the weather here is calm.

Standing high on the bridge of a ship you get a good view of the regular pattern of swell. The observer estimates its height and also its period (the time from crest to crest as it passes a stationary ship or a floating object). Sometimes, there may be two swell systems from different directions which can be separately identified. If wind waves are added to this situation, then a confused sea is likely.

There is a usually unreliable saying that "every seventh wave is bigger". Standing on a western beach, we can imagine the confliction or combination of two different swell systems which might make this true.

LUNCHTIME WEATHER REPORTS

How does the lunchtime weather report from Malaga find its way on to the back page of the *Guardian*?

Much the same sort of procedure is followed at every observing site around the world at each and every hour of the day. All countries use GMT, or Universal Time (UT) as it now seems to be known. This means that when we exchange observations, we all know what time we are talking about.

At lunchtime, say 1300 hours local time (1200 hours UT), the observer at Malaga airport goes out to do the routine hourly observation. He or she looks at the sky to estimate the cloud amount, cloud type and height. Then the visibility is assessed by looking at various known landmarks – in southern Spain probably a nearby mountain. The Stevenson Screen will be similar to ours, and back inside the Met Office will be the barometer and the wind dials, so the observer has all the information needed to fill in the 'observation book' or 'daily register'. This is done in a straightforward manner and then converted into a five-figure numerical code ready for transmission.

Once the 'obs book' is completed, the observer goes to the teleprinter room and types the coded version on a keyboard. This code is used so that all the countries of the World can understand the weather report. Away goes the observation into the Spanish national system. Then it will continue via a communications computer (along with other reports from Madrid, Alicante and Barcelona, etc.) into the global telecommunications system and become available to all the meteorological services of the world.

The global system allows information to flow from Moscow to Offenbach (Germany) to Bracknell (UK) and Washington, etc., with spurs or branchlines running off to connect Nairobi and other places not on the main circuit.

Thus the Malaga report arrives at the UK communications computer (uninspiringly known as Autocom Phase Four). From here it is fed both into the main UK forecasting system (COSMOS) and to smaller weather centres around the country. It arrives in the London Weather Centre data-handling computer (OASYS) and is automatically compiled into a list for the *Guardian*. The fourth group of figures in the Malaga observation might read 10238 which indicates that their temperature was plus 23.8 C. Next comes a bit of human quality control when the supervisor at London Weather Centre checks to see if the 'Around the World' list is complete.

AN OBSERVATION DECODED

A reasonably typical observation can be condensed into eleven groups each, mortly, of five characters. Here is an example of an observation from Heathrow: 03772 41562 63615 10068 20015 40146 53027 78075 86100 333 8682. The decode follows for each group. In many of the groups the first figure is just an indicator so that the communications computers are kept happy.

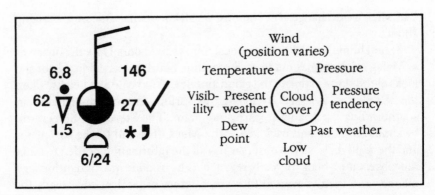

An example of an observation for Heathrow airport is plotted on the left side with the systematic layout of the symbols shown on the right.

03772   Station number of Heathrow airport.

41562   Three indicator numbers, then 62 to indicate (in a rather strange code from which 50 must be subtracted) a visibility of 12 km.

63615   Cloud amount 6 oktas, wind direction 360° (i.e. northerly), wind speed 15 knots (i.e. 17 mph).

10068   Temperature plus 6.8 C.

20015   Dew point plus 1.5 C.

40146   Sea-level pressure 1014.6 mbar.

53027   Pressure tendency 3 indicates falling slightly and then rising, 027 shows that the pressure is 2.7 mbar higher than 3 hours before (the standard period for pressure changes).

78075   Present weather 80 indicates a rain shower which is plotted as a triangle (for a shower) with a raindrop over it. Past weather includes 7 for snow and 5 for drizzle, plotted as snowflake and comma respectively.

86100   6 shows 6 oktas of cloud, 1 shows cumulus, 00 shows nil for medium and high clouds.

333   Indicators (the only three-figure group in the message).

86824   Shows 6 oktas of cumulus at 2400 ft above airfield.

DO-IT-YOURSELF OBSERVING

Without any instruments at all, you can still make a limited weather observation.

Visibility can be estimated provided that you have a reasonable view in at least one direction. If, from an upstairs window, you can see a range of hills then this is a big help. A map will enable you to measure the distance of this visibility point, and with practice you can estimate greater distances by how clear the hills appear. In fog or mist there are plenty of 'vis' points and you can pace out the distance.

Wind speed can be estimated using the Beaufort scale, but remember that you should be in a reasonably open, unsheltered location, or at least make an allowance for sheltering effects.

Wind direction can be estimated once you know the orientation of your home. (The Sun is near enough due south at 1200 hours GMT (UT) i.e. 1300 hours clock time during summer.) If you use low cloud to estimate wind direction, face directly towards the oncoming cloud and then allow for the fact that the surface wind will be blowing from a point fractionally to the left (by about 20° of arc). You can record wind by a 16-point compass (e.g. WNW) or as a bearing (e.g. 290°). Usually *true* north is used as the reference point, rather than magnetic north, though the error is only 7° of arc.

Cloud amount can be estimated in oktas. For the more ambitious, cloud type can also be recorded, and, for the real expert, cloud base can be estimated.

Present weather is fairly straightforward. This should distinguish between showers, rain, drizzle, hail and snow, and include fog, thunder heard, lightning seen, plus any of these which have happened in the previous hour.

Finally, the 'state of the ground' is the record of the typical appearance of open, flat ground – in practice often a grass-covered playingfield or park. This may be dry, moist with dew, moist with rain, wet, flooded, frozen, or covered in hoar frost or snow. With lying snow, the average depth should be recorded.

For a site with instruments, one would hope to add temperature, including a 'max and min' thermometer, and also readings of rainfall and atmospheric pressure (usually reduced to sea-level at, say, 1 mbar per 8 m (0.1 in of mercury per 90 ft).

Usual rain-gauges are 5 in (12.7 cm) across but a 2-litre lemonade bottle can be sawn-off as an alternative. Small quantities need to be measured carefully by tipping them into a tall narrow container and making some sort of calibration. Ideally the thermometer should be in a Stevenson Screen but a north-facing aspect may suffice providing it is shaded from early-morning and late-evening summer sun.

Chapter 8

FORECASTING

HUMAN FORECASTING

IF WEATHER systems were not continually changing, forecasting would be a straightforward task of timing the arrival of fronts or troughs at a particular place. However, the forecaster has three influences to balance: movement, diurnal changes and development. The speed of movement of a rain-band is rarely constant; the variation from day to night is vital; systems do intensify, change their character or dissipate. Traditionally, when faced with this task, the meteorologist has relied on hard work and experience. Now there is another string to the bow – computer guidance – but there are still quite a few tasks which the human does better than a computer. These are explored in the next few sections, with the help of examples, before we move on to computer forecasts.

WILL THERE BE SHOWERS?

On arrival at work, the forecaster will start by drawing isobars on a chart on which there are observations from all around the British Isles, and looking at the overall situation. He or she will look at their completed, analysed chart and at the computer-based forecast chart, scan the satellite pictures and consider the type of airmass which the weather centre is going to experience during the day. If this quick assimilation of the general situation suggests the possibility of showers, then the next step is to reach for a 'tephigram' or vertical profile of the atmosphere. A forecaster at Birmingham in a northwesterly airstream will be looking upwind and will want to study the vertical profiles measured at Liverpool and even as far away as Stornoway in the Outer Hebrides. This information will have been collected by balloon-borne equipment released at midnight.

Put at its simplest, the conditions necessary for showers to occur are plenty of heat and moisture at the bottom of the atmosphere and really cold air aloft. On the tephigram this will be represented as an unstable profile, approaching absolute instability. A forecaster can calculate the temperature required for convection to commence, the height of the cloud base and indeed the height of the cloud tops, and must then assess whether there is sufficient depth for cumulonimbus clouds, or at least large cumulus. Moisture content will be a guide to the shower frequency and many other plus and minus factors may colour the forecaster's judgement before he or she writes in the radio script '. . . and the showers will be fairly heavy and frequent, especially in the east of the region'.

FORECASTING THE MAXIMUM TEMPERATURE

If clear skies exist, then we know fairly precisely the amount of heat which a particular square kilometre of Earth will receive at say 1000 hours on an April morning. We can also calculate the total energy expected to fall on that area during a particular day. If we have a vertical profile of temperature measured at dawn, we can calculate the maximum temperature which will be reached by 1400 hours that day – providing the airmass does not change. Diurnal changes are therefore potentially one of the most satisfying aspects of meteorology for the individual forecaster who can make these calculations on charts and graphs. But it is rarely that easy. Skies are rarely totally clear; the vertical balloon measurement was probably made 100 km (60 miles) away at midnight; the airmass probably *has* been subtly changing.

Let us consider a difficult day with a northwesterly airstream bringing colder air as the day goes on. Also, let us suppose that a cloud sheet exists which only allows a proportion of the Sun's energy to reach the Earth's surface. Now the forecaster has a real task. How can the incoming solar energy be balanced against the progressive cooling of the airstream?

Let us complete the picture by introducing a 'development' term into the equation. We can now imagine that the cloud sheet is dissipating as high pressure builds over the region. As the thickness of the cloud decreases and the sheet begins to break up, so a higher percentage of solar energy will get through to the ground.

Our scientist has to make a judgement, based on a mixture of calculations and experience, of the likely maximum temperature. He or she weighs up the cooling airstream, the reduction of incoming solar energy due to cloud, and the likely dissipation of cloud due to anticyclonic development, and makes a forecast: 'the maximum temperature in London will be 14 degrees Celsius'.

FORECASTING THE MINIMUM TEMPERATURE

We can illustrate a forecast of minimum temperatures by examining two rather simplistic extreme cases. Let us assume a starting-point on a spring

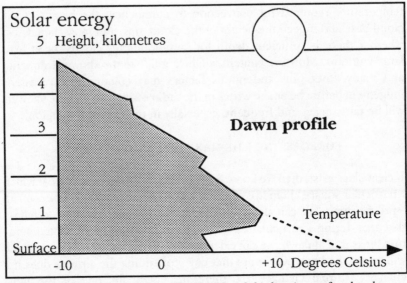

During the daytime, the Sun warms the ground and this heat is transferred to the lowest part of the atmosphere. In this example the lowest kilometre will be warmed and the temperature in the Stevenson Screen will rise from perhaps 5 Celsius to 14 Celsius. The expected midday profile is shown by a dashed line.

afternoon around *maximum* temperature time with 12 C (54 F). If it is going to be a very windy, cloudy, moist night then the temperature will probably only fall by a degree or so to, say, 10 C (50 F). On the other hand, if the forecaster expects a clear, calm night then the temperature will fall quite quickly during the evening period, and continue decreasing until dawn or just after. A rough empirical calculation working in Celsius is to add the maximum temperature and coincident dew point, divide by two, then subtract 8. Starting with a temperature of 12 C and a dew point of 6 C, we end up with a forecast minimum of 1 Celsius for a typical site. A frost hollow will be colder still, whilst an urban site will be warmer.

But what if the night is not going to be absolutely clear and calm? That's where the skill and judgement come in! If the forecaster can get the overnight cloud and wind forecasts correct, an accurate minimum temperature forecast will result.

LOW CLOUD

A light aircraft is about to take off from Cardiff in good weather in order to fly to a small airfield in Cornwall. One of the thoughts uppermost in the pilot's mind is what weather he will encounter at his destination. He

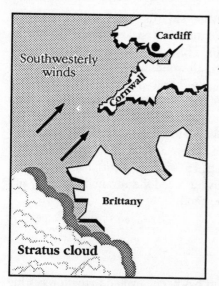

Forecasters in Wales and southwest England watch out for moistening airstreams and low cloud when Tropical Maritime airstreams occur.

knows that the airstream is a southwesterly which often brings low stratus cloud, although at the moment reports from Cornwall show that the visibility is good and only high cloud is present. Since he is aware of the potential deterioration he checks the latest 'AIRMET' (telephone weather information system for aviators) before leaving Cardiff. The meteorologists have been studying the latest observations in Brittany and the Isles of Scilly to see what is coming.

One of the difficulties for the forecaster is that the cloud leaving the coast of Brittany is not exactly what will arrive at an airfield, say, 300 ft (90 m) up in Cornwall. There will be additional moisture added as it crosses the sea, so the dew point (a measure of the moisture content) will be higher. Also, if the sea is relatively cold, the air temperature may be lowered on its passage across the English Channel, which will raise the relative humidity even further. Thirdly, the air will be forced to rise the 300 ft (90 m) to pass over the airfield and this upslope motion may well be the final straw which causes stratus to form. Then there are the diurnal considerations to be taken into account. During the evening, the land surface in Cornwall will be cooling and this is another factor favouring the formation of very low cloud. As all the factors are combining to produce a deterioration, the forecaster can be fairly confident. Calculations show that a temperature of 10 C and a dew point of 9 C can be expected at the airfield by 1800 hours and the forecast is for cloud at 400 ft (120 m) above ground. With the airstream continuing to moisten and the loss of incoming warmth from the sun, the forecaster is going for cloud right down to the surface by 2100 hours. Cloud on the ground implies fog and will preclude a landing.

The pilot's expectation, as he heads westwards from Cardiff in what are still quite good conditions, is that he may just make it home before the cloud gets down below 200 ft (60 m). This is his 'decision height', below which he should not land. Large aircraft would have far more equipment but he relies on seeing the airfield lights. Three-quarters of his return leg has been covered when he glimpses the first wispy patches of low cloud below him. Soon he can see a continuous grey blanket of stratus stretching ahead. A radio call to his destination confirms the worst – cloud already down to 100 ft (30 m) above airfield. There are old pilots and bold pilots but there aren't many old, bold pilots. He decides to turn back immediately to Cardiff, knowing he can easily outspeed the advancing stratus, and landing conditions there will still be good.

VISIBILITY FORECASTS

Throughout this century much effort has been devoted to the forecasting of fog, but far less work has been put into the forecasting of visibility once it gets to 1000 m or more.

Traditionally we refer to 'mist' when the partial obscuration of distant objects is primarily due to water droplets and to 'haze' when the visibility reduction is primarily due to solid particles. With mist the relative humidity will usually be 90-99%, whereas with haze it will be below 90%. But why should water vapour make any difference if the air is unsaturated? The answer lies in the nature of the minute particles present in the atmosphere which come from both natural sources (sea salt, volcanoes, dust-storms, forest fires, meteorites) and from human pollution (power stations, oil refineries, factories, vehicles). Particles, perhaps less than a micrometre across, are often hygroscopic – that is they attract water. They can therefore act as nuclei which will swell in size as they absorb moisture. Their size is dependent on the relative humidity, and so rising humidity is linked to decreasing visibility.

Moisture and pollution are thus the two keys to a forecast of visibility. If the air is both heavily polluted and very moist, murky weather can be predicted. Such conditions tend to affect southern England when there is a slow-moving depression over the near Continent. The trajectory of the air is then from Poland, Germany or Czechoslovakia (laden with pollutants) out across the North Sea (where moisture is added) and reaches us on a northeasterly wind.

For Scotland the worst airstream will usually be a southeasterly from the industrial areas of England or Europe.

Trajectories are an important part of visibility forecasting but we must also remember the part played by diurnal changes, for example in a

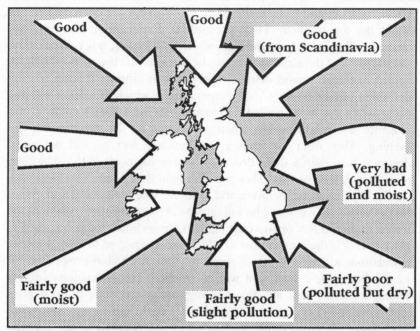

Visibility associated with different wind directions. Northwesterlies are clean and nearly always bring good visibility, whilst continental airstreams bring haze. However, wind speed and the moisture content of the air are also very important. The worst visibilities come with light winds and moist, polluted air.

stagnant, home-polluted high-pressure area. As evening progresses the temperature falls and this raises the relative humidity so the visibility is steadily reduced. Both pollution and high humidity near the ground tend to be maximised in light wind regimes at night. A strong northwesterly wind will bring good visibility to the British Isles. Scotland, Ireland and Wales quite often enjoy visibilities up to 80 km (50 miles) or more, but such clean air is less frequent in southeast England and rarer still in lowland parts of central Europe.

FORECASTING FOG

Will there be fog tonight? Motorists and aviators, themselves perhaps amateur forecasters, will start by studying the sky. A good breeze or persistent cloud cover will prevent fog formation but there are many marginal nights, especially in winter, when the answer is less clear-cut.

Let us consider an autumn day when the mid-afternoon temperature is 14 C (57 F) and the dew point of the air is 7 C (45 F). The visibility is good. At an inland airfield the forecaster surveys his chart and thinks about the fog problem. High pressure is dominant, not moving, not changing. Winds are light and skies are clear. The first task is to calculate the fog point of the airmass. It might be thought that the air need only be cooled to the afternoon dew point in order to saturate it (after all, the definition of dew point is 'that temperature at which saturation will just occur when the air is cooled'). However, we must take account of the moisture which will be lost when dew forms on the grass during the evening. Also, drier air from a few hundred feet up will be mixed downwards in even a slight breeze. The true fog point of the air will be perhaps a degree or two below the afternoon dew point. The forecaster studies a graph of temperature and moisture (the tephigram) and makes his calculations. In essence he will find the *average* moisture content in the lowest thousand feet or so which he will convert into a fog point, say 5 C (41 F). This is the temperature at which fog is expected to form. Further calculations will allow him to forecast the time at which the fog point will be reached and, indeed, *if* it will be reached. His estimations suggest midnight on this occasion. Fog warnings are issued to air traffic control and other interested parties around the airfield during the afternoon. Each hour the temperature and humidity are checked to see that the forecast is still on course. Just after sunset there may be a bit of a scare as shallow ground fog can be seen in a nearby water-meadow but happily the general visibility remains quite good and is reducing only slowly. Things are going according to plan. By the time the relative humidity has risen to 95% the observer, standing out in the darkness watching the last aircraft returning, is estimating the visibility at 2000 m. He is fairly sure that fog is already forming in the favoured site down near the river to the south. A few minutes later and the airfield is in fog. The forecaster makes a note in his diary – this will be a success he (or she) will want to remember.

DISPERSAL OF FOG

The normal cause of the dispersal of inland ('radiation') fog which has formed overnight is incoming heat from the sun. We say that the fog will be 'burnt off' which is a rough approximation to the truth.

Much of the Sun's radiation is reflected from the top of the fog and lost back to space, but a good proportion – roughly half – penetrates the fog and reaches the ground. So it is the Earth's surface which is heated and this in turn heats the air. As the lowest part of the atmosphere is warmed up, it will eventually reach the temperature when all the minute fog droplets have been evaporated and the visibility will improve – this is the

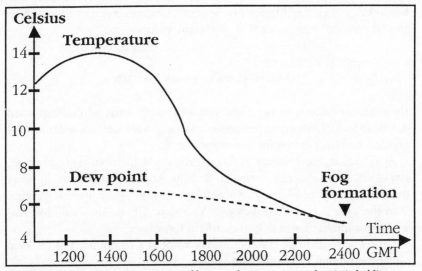

The dew point is an accurate measure of how much water vapour the air is holding, and is therefore the key to fog prediction. The temperature falls quickly during the evening in this example and the air becomes saturated by midnight.

fog clearance temperature. If the fog is shallow and conditions are calm, then the improvement will be from fog to perhaps clear skies, but if a breeze has sprung up, then fog may lift into low cloud.

Even in a flat calm situation there are clearly some problems in predicting what time the fog will clear. There are three main variables that the forecaster needs to estimate: first, the amount of incoming solar heat available in each successive hour of the day (if skies are clear aloft then this is fixed by the time of year – a known amount of energy dependent on the solar elevation); second, the fog clearance temperature, which will usually be a degree or two higher than the temperature at which fog formed on the previous evening; third, the depth of the fog, which will often be 300 to 800 ft (100 to 240 m) after a winter's night.

Given these three estimates and a few more assumptions, the forecaster can make scientific calculations of the time of the clearance. In summer and autumn a rather bizarre rule of thumb gives a guide to the time of clearance. There is some logic in that it is loosely related to the time of sunrise: June is the sixth month and fog will clear at 0600 hours GMT, in July at 0700, in August at 0800, in September 0900 and in October 1000 GMT. Since the Sun's heat is crucial to the process the most delayed clearances (inland) occur in November, December and January, when fog can persist all day, particularly after a cold spell. February, March and April and May equate to October, September, August and July, respectively. No broad-brush rules can really work in winter, when the forecaster has to keep alert, watching out for synoptic changes, such as approaching frontal systems, which can ruin all the calculations.

MESOSCALE RULES OF THUMB

Because computers do not cope very well with some of the important details of local weather, forecasters continue to use local rules of thumb to predict the onset of certain important events.

At Gibraltar, the 'levanter' is an easterly wind which can bring moist air, low cloud and turbulent airflow around the Rock. It usually sets in when the atmospheric pressure at Alicante in eastern Spain becomes higher than the pressure in Casablanca in Morocco. Obviously a rule like this whilst not infallible will help the airfield forecaster.

On a global scale we cannot manage without a computer, but for local detail the human still holds some of the cards.

MOVEMENT OF RAIN AREAS

Lying on your back on the grass in Regent's Park watching the clouds, it is obvious to an aspiring meteorologist that the wind high aloft can be very different in direction to that near the ground. So which way will a deep and complex weather system move? The simple answer is that individual cloud elements will move with the wind at their appropriate level, but the system as a whole will move with the overall *pattern* of the upper wind flow. A strong westerly jet stream of 120 mph (180 kph) lying across the British isles will not extend eastwards across Europe at this speed. Its rate of propagation downwind may be more like 40 mph (60 kph). A comparison could be drawn with the rapids in a river which accelerate the water: but the acceleration of the water is due to the downward slope of the land, *which has not moved*; similarly, the temperature contrasts which create a jet stream may not move, or may shift only slowly.

In trying to anticipate the movement of individual small showers, forecasters will rely on the low-level pressure gradient and move them with the winds at, say, 3000 ft (900 m). Deeper rain areas, for example associated with frontal systems, are effectively forecast by using the wind at 10,000 ft (3000 m). Really deep, well-developed thunderstorms are best handled by using the 14,000 ft (4000 m) wind, but here there are extra difficulties. Often one thunder cell will start to die, only to be replaced by another cell triggered nearby. This system of 'daughter cell' formation may slightly change the apparent direction of movement of the storm.

Watching the rainfall movement on radar during a summer afternoon, it is often possible to see individual rain cells running northwards while the main band of rain which contains them moves slowly east. A forecast on radio for the public must anticipate this general movement.

CONDENSATION PROBLEMS

On the last weekend of June 1987, cool weather was followed by a sudden transition to a moisture-laden southwesterly airflow. The results were interesting. Cars were difficult to start, squash-court walls ran with moisture and steel objects in some places were subject to flash-rusting. Perhaps most peculiar was the story of a plumber in Norfolk who was inundated with telephone calls from people who thought they had leaking cisterns and pipes. On examination, these apparent leaks were in reality condensation problems.

What was the cause? Rather cloudy weather had kept many objects cool over the preceding day or two, particularly larger items whose temperature was slow to change and which were protected from any sunshine. The change of airflow brought moisture and, in forecasting parlance, rising dew points. The rapidity of the change meant that for a few hours the dew point of the air was higher than the temperature of large objects like car engines, and so moisture from the air condensed on the cold surfaces. Pipes and cisterns are particularly vulnerable to this kind of event in spring and summer when the water coming out of the mains pipes in the ground is cool. Windows may run with moisture, but here the equation is complicated by the difference between the warm air inside the room and the cold window which is constantly losing heat by conduction. Perhaps the classic example is that of the car engine (and the sparking plugs which are attached to it). The results are frustrating when the moisture, conspiring perhaps with poor maintenance, prevents the vehicle from starting. Such problems are rare in summer, but in autumn and winter become quite common, with the car battery also now less efficient. The forecaster will be watching for a cold anticyclonic spell of weather breaking down into a mild, moist (Tropical Maritime) southwesterly airstream. If this occurs around dawn in December, one can be fairly sure that somebody will be having car-starting difficulties.

AIRCRAFT AND ICING

Flying in large jets with recognised airlines is a pretty safe method of transport, but it is interesting to look at some of the potential hazards which today's airliners overcome. Aircraft take off facing into the wind as this gives them extra lift and allows them to use a shorter stretch of runway to gain the necessary air-speed required to fly. If it is very hot, then air density is reduced from normal, which used to create considerable take-off problems in hot countries for the aircraft of the 1960s. Today an airfield must be both at high altitude and very hot to cause take-off to be a significant hurdle. Quito and La Paz could sometimes qualify.

Whilst in flight, icing and turbulence are just about the only kinds of significant weather. Icing is the build-up of ice on the aircraft which sometimes occurs when flying in cloud, rather like the ice that can form on a car windscreen when driving in freezing fog.

In the atmosphere, water droplets often exist at a temperature of –10 C (14 F). They do not necessarily turn to ice at the so-called freezing-point on account of their small size. When the aircraft hits the supercooled water droplet at 500 mph (800 kph), the water will often freeze around the leading edge of the wing. This may be clear ice or, if air is trapped within it, rime ice. It can very subtly change the shape of the wing or interfere with flaps or other controls if not combated by heating or other prevention devices.

Other bad places for ice to form are on the cockpit windows, in the engine intake (where the reduction of pressure can enhance the problem) or on helicopter rotor blades. Helicopters are perhaps more prone to serious problems of engine icing than are normal jet aircraft because they tend to be flying in the critical height bands below 13,000 ft (4000 m), whereas jet airliners are above the problem at their cruising level.

TURBULENCE

'Have a smooth flight' is an appropriate variation on '*bon voyage*' for those departing on holiday by air. Of course a smooth flight implies no hold-ups at the airport but also, quite literally, a turbulence-free flight.

Turbulence can be described by the practising forecaster as being mechanical, thermal or clear air turbulence.

Simple mechanical turbulence occurs when strong low-level winds blow over rough countryside. They are like the rapids in a shallow river where the water flows over a rocky bed. This kind of turbulence is most likely to be felt in a small aircraft, perhaps a two or four seater, flying at low altitude in strong winds over an undulating countryside. A large passenger jet would experience this low-level turbulence when coming in to land on a windy day but it is rarely a serious matter.

The second type of turbulence is associated with thermal activity. On a summer day, some pockets of air get hotter than others and therefore rise as 'thermals'. Between the rising thermals are regions of descending air.

What goes up must come down! When an aircraft flies across a hot summer landscape, it will fly through alternate pockets of rising and descending air. Passengers will feel these variations as turbulence.

When the thermals are small and relatively weak, as they usually are when associated with fairweather cumulus clouds, then they will not make much difference to your holiday flight. However, when they build up into huge thunder clouds they can make things uncomfortable. Over the British Isles, the tallest thunder clouds usually won't reach much above 30,000 ft (9000 m) so a jet airliner cruising at 35,000 ft (11,000 m) will usually be just above them. Over southern Europe or central United States, the cumulonimbus tops can reach to 45,000 ft (13,000 m) or more, and even a jumbo jet can be thrown around by the massive upcurrents. A light aircraft can even be bodily torn apart by the most extreme cases of turbulence, but jet airliners are made of sterner stuff. Also, pilots in modern jets can take avoiding action much more easily than a lower-flying light aircraft.

A third method by which you can be buffeted around the skies is clear air turbulence (known to meteorologists as CAT). This is a form of high-level mechanical turbulence, which often occurs near jet streams, particularly where they have just crossed mountain ranges. Sometimes an airliner can hit a patch of CAT unexpectedly, and yet at other times one aircraft will report CAT while a following aircraft on the same route may get no turbulence at all (and the passengers will be left wondering why the pilot asked them to fasten their seat belts).

DOWNBURSTS

This is the American name given to severe downdraughts which occur near cumulonimbus clouds. As air rises within the thundercloud itself there has to be some compensating downward motion. Often the downburst includes heavy rain or hail, and the evaporation of rain plays a part in keeping the descending air cool. As it hits the ground the downburst spreads out as a horizontal wind. Downbursts, or 'microbursts' as they are also known, are dangerous for aircraft coming in to land. As the aircraft approaches the airport it may be flying along quite happily when there is a sudden change in horizontal wind speed accompanied by a downward 'push' of heavy rain. Past calculations of the downward force have used the normal fall speed of 9 m (30 ft) per second for the rain, but of course the precipitation is falling much faster than this, embedded as it is within descending air.

Aircraft crashes have sometimes resulted, for example in the southern USA, and this has heightened awareness of severe cumulonimbus activity

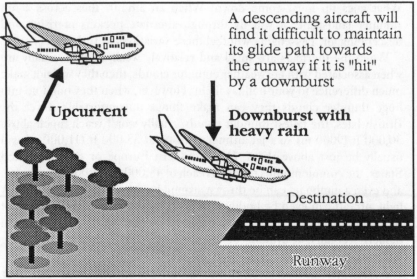

Violent thunderstorms, for example over southern USA, may be accompanied by downbursts and sudden changes in wind speed.

and downbursts. Pilots today know that a strong *upcurrent* on approach to an airfield is a danger signal, for somewhere nearby will be a strong downdraught.

WIND SHEAR

When the wind velocity changes with height, we describe this as 'wind shear'. Since wind has both speed and direction, the change may be in either – or more commonly in both. A certain amount of low-level wind shear is common on breezy days due to the friction of the Earth's surface. Extreme cases are dangerous for aircraft, which may experience a sudden change of air-speed.

High aloft, wind shear often creates turbulence and can be a factor in forming clouds such as cirrus.

SHIPPING FORECASTS

'Humber, Thames, Dover, Wight . . . ' the names roll off the tongue of the radio announcer. The shipping forecast areas are part of British life. They proceed in a roughly clockwise sequence around our islands, covering the region between Iceland, Norway and Portugal.

Some are named after islands, such as Rockall, Lundy or Utsire (which is just off the Norwegian coast near Stavanger); others, for example Bailey and Dogger, are named after banks or shallows in the sea, and there are also river estuaries, such as Cromarty, Forth and Tyne. Trafalgar is the most southerly area and outside the area of the map, adjoining the Portuguese coast.

'Forties, southerly five veering westerly and increasing gale Force eight, showers, good.' This indicates to fishermen and the oil industry that in shipping area Forties the wind is expected to change in a clockwise sense from south to west and to increase from Beaufort Force five to Force eight. The weather will be showery and the visibility will be good. Hopefully this will help those who earn their living offshore and might otherwise be 'in peril on the sea'. The forecasts are updated by gale warnings.

Over the sea, wind speed and direction are very closely related to the isobar pattern – the highs and lows. Forecasters measure the distance between the isobars and thus can calculate the present wind speed. Predicted isobaric patterns enable them to complete the shipping forecast. This is one of the few specialist forecasts which is heard by the general public, but people seem to take an interest when they hear 'Southeast Iceland: westerly gale Force eight increasing severe gale Force nine and veering northwesterly, storm Force ten.'

A SHORT HISTORY OF FORECASTING

Whilst the Ancient Greeks initiated the principles of scientific thought, there was a long wait until the Renaissance before things got moving again. Milestones in meteorology must include the invention of the thermoscope (an early type of thermometer) by Galileo in 1600 and the barometer by Toricelli in 1643. Later in the same century Isaac Newton's laws of motion provided the basic scientific rules for all moving systems. Robert Boyle and others added their contributions on the behaviour of gases. Progress continued through the eighteenth century, and there were various attempts to construct maps of wind, pressure and weather. However, useful weather charts depicting one instant in time were not feasible without rapid communications. Samuel Morse and the invention of the electric telegraph made them possible in the middle of the nineteenth century. The new science was spurred on by balloon flights, experiments with lightning by Benjamin Franklin and the demand for weather information which stemmed first from shipping and then from early aviators.

In the first two decades of this century, there assembled a remarkable

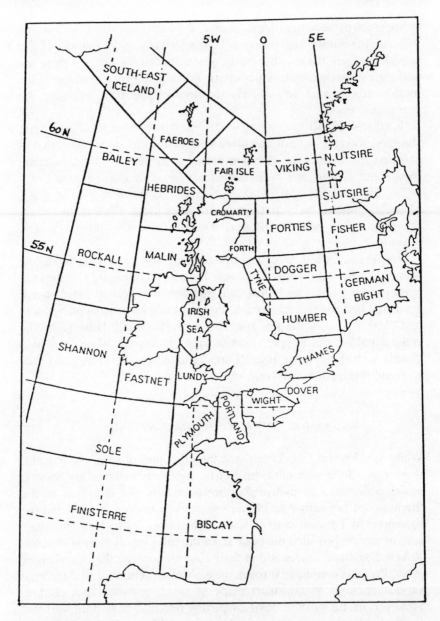

*The sea areas used in shipping forecasts. Trafalgar is just outside the map area,
adjoining Portugal.*

group of meteorologists in Norway, under the guidance of Vilhelm Bjerknes. Their first important contribution was the concept of weather fronts, which took their name from the battlefield terminology of the First World War. The group included Carl-Gustav Rossby, Tor Bergeron and Bjerknes' son Jakob, who between them went on to develop the meteorological groundwork for much of our science today.

During the First World War and just after, a noted British scientist (and pacifist) L.F. Richardson proposed the theory of numerical modelling of the atmosphere. In other words, he suggested that a team of mathematicians could predict the future weather simply by solving equations. He even worked out an example which took many months and produced a disastrously wrong forecast, but as a pointer to the future it was brilliant. To produce an accurate forecast Richardson would have needed an estimated 64,000 mathematicians working flat out, but with the development of electronic computers in the 1950s and 1960s his dream eventually became a reality.

From 1930 until 1960 meteorologists employed what might be described as traditional methods, or by analogy with the railways 'steam forecasting'. They received reports from all around their country and to a lesser extent their continent, plus a few ship, aircraft and balloon reports. An assistant would plot all these observations on a map by hand in an agreed format (because presented like that the reports made more sense and the information could be readily assimilated). The forecaster then, as now, drew fronts and isobars on the synoptic chart. Given a good map of the weather situation now, a human can forecast where the lows and highs will move to and thus the future wind pattern. If the future wind speed and direction at a given place are known, the temperature, cloud, etc., can be estimated.

This type of traditional forecasting is largely a matter of 'moving around' the existing lows, highs and airmasses. Some of the real experts have a feel or intuition for future developments. (Perhaps the word 'intuition' is just a label for some mental process which we cannot fully explain.)

In the past, using the limited information from a ship or two in the Atlantic, the forecaster could make some sort estimate of how much rain a warm front would produce over the British Isles. If the pressure was particularly low and still falling then the front would be active, and especially so if the moisture content was high.

Then in the early 1960s came satellites, which gave a far better picture of the present weather, and early computers, which gave a second opinion on future developments. Instead of assuming that the warm front would be a typical, textbook affair, the forecaster could now estimate how active it was from the satellite image, and see whether the computer forecast

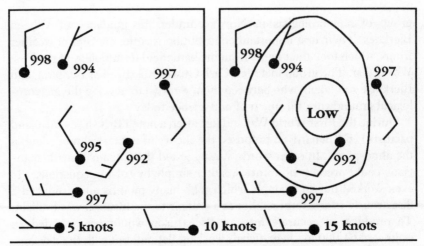

A forecaster faced with the left-hand chart will soon be able to draw isobars, for example for 996 and 992 millibars as on the right-hand chart. The key shows how different wind speeds are plotted.

confirmed the continued deepening of the depression or predicted that the low would start to fill. Now the human can still 'argue' with the computer out to about 24 hours ahead, but for a longer forecast there is no way to compete with the numerical model. Back in the days of 'steam forecasting', two or three days was the limit.

Now we will proceed to look at computer models, the human–machine mix and the different problems of forecasting for an hour ahead or a week ahead.

COMPUTER MODELS OF THE ATMOSPHERE

With the increasing demand for worldwide forecasts out to a week ahead, even a team of humans is confronted by a task of such complexity that a computer becomes necessary – and not just any old computer. Hence the Met Office has acquired a machine which can make literally billions of calculations per second. This replaces the previous version which was capable of 'only' 400 million calculations a second. Speed of production is not the real object of this multi-million pound outlay. Rather, it is the greater accuracy and increased detail which arithmetical speed makes possible.

How then does the computer forecast the weather? The first task is to gather information from all over the world for, say, midday today. Reports from human observers, automatic weather stations, ships, buoys, satellites and balloon-borne equipment are processed and fed into the mighty computer.

The computer 'assimilates' or 'digests' this information with various checking and smoothing procedures. Obviously the computer program has to have some sort of map of the Earth. This is in the form of thousands of 'grid points' running around the lines of latitude and longitude, in a systematic array. Calculations are made of temperature, etc., at each and every grid point.

All the information from around the Earth is collected and the values are then assigned to the nearest 'grid point' though with suitable adjustments. Where there is no data for a particular grid point, then the best estimate available is a previous short-period forecast. Perhaps the assimilation process is best regarded as 'taking an average' between the computer's own first-guess value and a newly received observation.

This process is carried out not just at the Earth's surface but at about 20 levels up through the atmosphere. Then the machine begins to carry out the calculations, doing a very short-period forecast for each grid point. The equations and constants which describe atmospheric processes would cover a page of newspaper and more, but can be reduced to a simple example. If the wind at a grid point at Birmingham is northwesterly and the air there is cold, then the computer will 'move' that cold air down to the London grid point. (Oh, that it were really that simple!) When you consider the thousands of grid points, the many levels of atmosphere, the shortness of the time steps (currently around 10 minutes), etc., then you start to get an idea of the task required to produce a forecast for the whole Earth for, say, five days ahead. This will be printed out via another computer as a forecast pressure pattern.

Now the human re-enters the process, for we must interpret this pressure pattern in terms of weather, and express the forecast in a suitable format for the user: text for the general public, maps for the press and tabulated temperatures for the electricity and gas industries.

DIFFERENT COMPUTER MODELS

A computer model which covers the Earth in a series of grid points is reasonably easy to visualise and can be described as a 'grid-point model'. Another version using a similar super-computer but in a different way is the 'spectral model', which produces complex equations to describe the shape of the flow around, say, the North Pole. If we look down on the Pole, we can imagine a jet stream meandering around the northern hemisphere until its head catches up with its tail. The shape described by this jet stream could be represented by an equation. Thousands of equations can represent the wind flows over the Earth up and down through the atmosphere.

When someone with a spectral model meets someone with a grid-point model they will compare notes upon how many vertical levels or layers they have, but especially they want to know the effective resolution. With a grid-point model, the resolution simply means how far apart the grid points are. A good quality global (i.e. world-wide) model today might have a resolution of about 100 km (60 miles) and perhaps 20 vertical levels. In other words, a vertical profile (as with a balloon) which measured the temperature, humidity and wind about 20 times between the surface and a height of 25 km (15 miles) would be as much vertical detail as it could cope with.

The vertical layers are not equally spaced because we need extra detail near the ground, and again up around the jet-stream level.

If a global model covers the whole world at a resolution of 100 km (60 miles), this means that it can keep track of any depression, bar the very smallest, but of course individual clouds or thunderstorms are totally lost. A regional or limited-area model might cover just Europe and the North Atlantic, with a resolution of 50 km (30 miles). A mesoscale model would cover just the British Isles and a little surrounding area with its grid points only perhaps 10 km (6 miles) apart.

Usually all three models would be run, one after another, on one computer. Here comes one of the problems. The local information comes in first and the fine local detail is wanted as quickly as possible. There is a temptation therefore to run the mesoscale model first. However, if the winds aloft are 100 mph (160 kph) then the air will travel across the Atlantic in 24 hours. The mesoscale model needs some of the results from the regional model to know what is happening over eastern USA and the Atlantic, and that in turn requires the starting information from the whole hemisphere (but perhaps not the whole globe). Ideally, all the information from the whole Earth would be received very quickly, and the global model would run first, then the regional, followed by the mesoscale prediction.

Superb detail over the British Isles can sometimes be generated by the mesoscale model, which will produce sea-breezes and even localised bands of rain in fairly calm conditions. On the other hand, there are many occasions when the weather over us in 18 hours' time depends on the fine detail of what is happening far to the west of Ireland. Unless satellites can deliver good information through the whole depth of the atmosphere the mesoscale will have a poor-quality start and be based upon old forecasts from a previous regional model run. Yes, forecast accuracy still depends on good quality information. If you do not know where you are starting from, then you are unlikely to end up in the right place at the right times. 'Rubbish in, rubbish out' say the computer buffs.

Just as the mesoscale model moves with, say, 1-minute steps out to 18 hours ahead in great detail, the regional model can use 5-minute steps to get out to perhaps 48 hours in moderate detail and the global model makes 10-minute jumps to look forward 6 or 8 days in coarse detail. If you try to use longer time-steps, then the model may become 'unstable' and give erratic results when the upper winds are very strong.

The vertical resolution or number of layers will not vary much between models, and 20 or 30 levels might be considered sufficient in any of these computer simulations or numerical models.

The errors in, say, a weather chart of highs and lows for 72 hours ahead will depend upon two things. First of all, errors in the starting position or 'initial field' caused by inaccurate observations or even areas with no information at all. (There will always be some 'guess' at what is going on, even if it is simply the computer's own prediction from 12 to 24 hours before – which could in turn be based on the prediction from the day before that, etc!)

Secondly, the equations and so-called 'constants' used in the calculations may be slightly inaccurate. For example, the model will have estimates of the amount of the Sun's heat reflected by the Earth, the clouds and the oceans. The real values will vary from day to day and place to place, so the average values used by the computer system will never be quite correct. Worse still, there are well-known omissions. We imitate the atmosphere, but not the oceans (except in some very specific climate models). Only a model which could include every feedback and predict every raindrop would ever be totally correct.

THE HUMAN–MACHINE MIX

Once the computer has completed its work and produced a forecast chart then humans set to work with the pattern of isobars, along with some supplementary charts of forecast rainfall, wind velocities and temperatures. They must use all the available information to turn out a forecast which will make sense to ordinary people. Here the human–machine mix comes into action. Humans know some of the foibles of the computers, they will ignore some details and give others more emphasis. By the time the forecast from the midnight computer run is being used at 6 a.m. they will already know, perhaps, that an approaching rain-band is moving more slowly than the computer has predicted. Computer and humans together produce a better final result than either could on their own. Also we in the

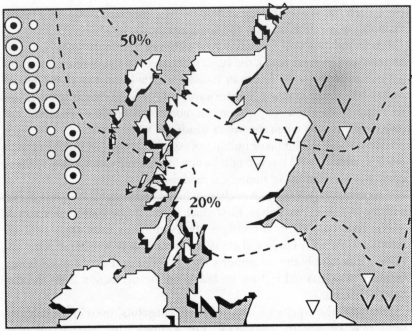

An example of computer forecast chart of precipitation, which could help the professional forecaster to write a radio script. The Vs and triangles represent light and heavy showers respectively whilst the small and large circles represent light and heavy dynamic (i.e. frontal) rain. The 20 and 50 per cent dashed lines indicate the probability of the precipitation falling as snow at sea level. The forecaster will be wary of placing too much credence on the predicted values at individual grid points.

British Isles have not yet entered the time when our weather computer actually produces a written script. Although it is entirely possible even now, and has the dubious advantage of providing the excuse that 'the computer got it wrong', for the moment at least the human forecaster still has a lot to offer.

THE MISSING CUMULUS CLOUDS

It is difficult to relate what we can see happening in the sky to what is going on in a computer model. Let us consider the example of a cumulus cloud. Its time scale is short – an individual cloud sometimes lasting only a few minutes. Its horizontal scale is small – often only a kilometre or so. Thus it is quite beyond the scope of a global computer model, which has its grid points around 100 km apart.

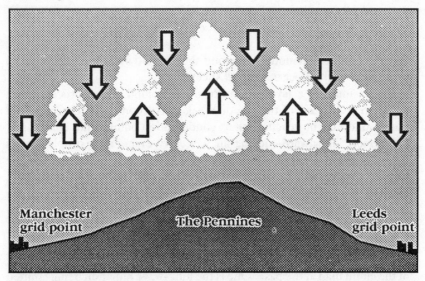

The grid points in a modern computer model of the atmosphere may be 100 kilometres apart. There is a lot of meteorology going on between the grid points, and some details are too small for the model to handle directly, for example convection clouds and their updraughts and downdraughts. Such small-scale processes are included in the computer model by using area averages.

The computer describes the state of the atmosphere at a Manchester grid point, including the temperature, the moisture content, the wind, the vertical air motion. It does the same at Leeds. But between the two grid points there could be a hundred cumulus clouds with rising air, and a hundred patches of clear sky with a downward component of air motion. The computer cannot show every cloud. Does this deficiency matter? Unfortunately the answer is yes. The thermals are not just creating cumulus clouds, there are lots of knock-on effects. The rising air carries moisture and energy with it from the surface to the middle levels of the atmosphere. Also, however transient the cumulus may be, when considered *en masse* they reduce the amount of the Sun's heat reaching the ground. For some regions of the Earth, particularly in the tropics, the cumulus and cumulonimbus clouds are just about the most important thing happening, so to leave them out of our computer models is a major omission.

The solution to the problem is a scheme called 'parameterisation' where the results of convection are included without modelling individual clouds. This is achieved by introducing what the unkind critic would call 'fudge factors' to simulate the vertical flow of heat, moisture, etc. Not a perfect solution but certainly the best we can do given the current state of the art.

MODELLING A CLOUD LAYER

A perfect numerical model of a cloud sheet would include all the physical processes which affect that cloud sheet.

Let us imagine a layer of stratocumulus cloud. What processes are going on at the base of the cloud? Weak convection currents rising from the ground may be reaching their condensation point at the cloud base. Conversely, downward-moving air will carry evaporating droplets, thus naturally maintaining a reasonably level base. Heat radiated from the Earth's surface will be absorbed at or near the bottom of the cloud, keeping it relatively warm. Within the cloud layer itself, vertical air currents will be carrying minute droplets up and down. (The micro-processes around a cloud droplet cannot be modelled on the same scale and will have to be allowed for by 'fudge factors'.)

Two processes help maintain a lower temperature at the upper surface of the cloud than at the base. One is the long-wave radiation being emitted from the cloud top into space; the other is the natural decrease of pressure upwards, which means that rising air parcels are, *de facto*, expanding and therefore cooling.

All these processes are well known to scientists but to assign accurate values to them is another matter. How fast are the vertical air motions? How much dry air is being mixed downwards from above the cloud? What proportion of the sunshine is reflected from the cloud top? What differences occur at night?

A relatively simple (perhaps one-dimensional) computer simulation helps us to answer these questions, and the lessons learnt can be fed back into our main computer which is used for world-wide weather prediction.

FORECASTING RESEARCH

Some of the current research will produce small step-by-step improvements in the next few years, generally imperceptible to the public and even to the forecaster. First of all we need to experiment with how we take in and use the observations. If there are two ships in the Atlantic only a couple of miles apart giving different observations, then the computer has to decide which one to believe. This assimilation of data is no simple matter.

Another chance to improve comes from some of the average values used in the calculations, which are perhaps just estimates based upon a few readings collected from a research aircraft. A further example comes from the mountain heights stored in the computer. A simple average altitude for the Alps does not produce good results in our computer models. It is the level of the higher peaks and ridges which are the

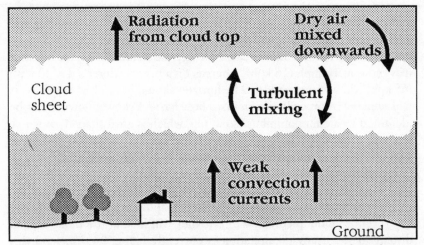

There are more than 20 important processes taking place in a cloud sheet but only a selection are shown here. If we are to accurately predict future climates then all of the vital processes must be represented in our computer models.

deciding factors, and many models now use something called 'envelope topography' to simulate mountain ranges. After all, we want the computer to produce a rain-shadow to the lee of the mountains because we can be confident that it will exist. Another way of improving models is to look at occasions when they go badly wrong. If a depression deepens unexpectedly then we need to know why. We can go back and look at the computer's analysis or starting-point and run the whole forecast again, adding in extra ship reports which were received too late for the original run. We can perhaps try an adjustment to the model to see if that would have given a better answer.

In the longer term computers will be quicker and models will become more detailed. We shall need fine-detailed observations over the whole Earth to feed into them. The area of the Earth is 500 million square kilometres (190 million square miles), so obviously the ultimate cover of observations must come from satellites. They will carry a whole host of equipment to look down at various different levels of the atmosphere, with some that can look right down to Earth to measure accurately the surface pressure, sea state, surface wind and temperature.

We will now return to the present and examine forecasts from very short periods through to months and seasons.

AN HOUR AHEAD

When we, as individuals, need to forecast an hour ahead, perhaps if we want to walk into town or intend putting the washing out to dry, then we look out of the window. Ideally we would go to the top of the building and look directly upwind at where the clouds are coming from. The wind speed must be taken into account because on a gentle summer's day the weather may move at 10 mph (16 kph), whereas on a breezy winter's day 40 mph (65 kph) will be more typical. The horizon should be studied carefully. Is it blotted out by precipitation or just a little hazy? A shower upwind may be identified by a cumulonimbus cloud top, which is anvil shaped, or worse still just about to become so. Thus we forecast for ourselves, and those who live in the country sometimes become especially good at it.

A professional forecaster will do the same thing but will add perhaps four other bits of information. They will mentally check to see whether the regional or mesoscale models are predicting showers. They will glance at any recent satellite pictures. Thirdly, they will look at the radar rainfall display to see if any precipitation is currently falling upwind (and this means allowing for the winds aloft). Finally, and most important, they will check the observation of the next airfield or other reporting station upwind. The weather which that station has now, they can expect in one hour's time – but still with a couple of provisos. The cloud base will usually remain at the same height with respect to sea-level, so the forecaster must adjust for any altitude difference. Secondly, the forecaster must allow for changes about to take place – the airmass is not just coming along in a lorry. A developing low will mean a deterioration. Diurnal changes may produce an improvement in the morning or a deterioration in the evening. There are a hundred and one factors to consider, but on most occasions the simple advection (blowing along) of weather which already exists is the easiest form of short-period forecasting.

AN AFTERNOON AHEAD

Much the same principles apply to a forecast for an afternoon as are used for one hour, except that we can only look at the upwind sky for about one hour's run of wind, so a bit more thought is required. Now we should consider the changes over the previous few hours. Has the cloud base been systematically lifting? Has the barometer been steadily rising? These are good signs.

For the professional forecaster it is the mixture as before but with rather more emphasis on distant observations, tephigrams, computer models, scientific reasoning and experience.

A DAY AHEAD

The general public will now rely heavily on the professional forecasts and less upon the barometer, though if this has been rising for a couple of days, it bodes well.

The professional forecaster, answering an enquiry about the next day, will have looked at tephigrams, satellite pictures, a plotted weather chart of the eastern Atlantic and Europe, as well as the computer prediction frames for 12, 18, 24, 30 and 36 hours ahead. They will already have evaluated the computer run to see if it looks reasonable in terms of rainfall. The main job is to turn a series of computer forecast maps of pressure and rainfall into a couple of brief phrases: 'Dry and sunny again, a fraction warmer than today, a light southerly wind, rather a pleasant day'. This does of course assume that the forecaster knows when, where and why the forecast is required. It is no good giving a forecast for gardening in Norwich when the customer will be flying a helicopter in Snowdonia. Given a forecast pressure pattern from the computer any forecaster worth their salt can give a prediction for a chosen location anywhere in Europe. They will not know all the local peculiarities, but with a reasonable knowledge of the topography of Europe should be able to produce a forecast for, say, Berlin, Bucharest or Barcelona. The tropics are much more difficult because the pressure pattern is little guide to the weather. Here they would look at satellite pictures, use their knowledge of climatology, or better still seek expert local help. An airfield forecast for, say, Nairobi which has been produced by the Kenyan airfield forecaster will be available automatically in UK via a communications system.

A WEEK AHEAD

Just as the computer can produce forecast pressure patterns for 18 and 24 hours ahead, so it will produce charts predicting 5, 6 or 7 days ahead. A major question is whether those charts will be correct. Usually the answer is 'no, not in detail'. However, they will give a general idea. A large anticyclone can usually be relied upon. On the other hand, a forecaster using the chart to give detailed timing of rain from a fast-moving low is asking for trouble. 'Unsettled and very mild' would be justified five days ahead, but 'dry in the morning and wet in the afternoon' would not. An error of 10% in timing will amount to a 10-hour error over a period of 100 hours. There is, if anything, a tendency for fronts to move more slowly than computers predict – but not always.

Over the last 20 years, the improvement in forecasts for five days ahead has been remarkable. The charts for five days ahead are now as good as those for two days produced in the early 1970s. The forecast given on television at Sunday lunchtime is generally considered to be of a high standard. Sometimes it goes wrong, but anyone watching it for 52 weeks in the year would get far more good advice than bad.

A MONTH AHEAD

The computer, if left to carry on crunching numbers, will do so for ever. Charts can be produced for 28, 29 and 30 days ahead. These charts will look very plausible with lows moving around just as we know they do. Unfortunately, when day 30 comes around, they will be shown to be a load of rubbish. (Well, nearly always. Occasionally they might look about right by chance. Just very, very rarely the whole sequence for a month might be broadly correct.) Forecast charts for individual days are currently of some value out to 6 to 10 days ahead. Beyond that, detailed synoptic forecasting is impracticable, but this does not mean that the forecast ends here. Let us examine three ways to go further ahead.

THE MONTE CARLO METHOD

First of all we can run the computer model for, say, 20 days. We then change the starting conditions very slightly and run it again. A slight further random change to our starting position and we produce a third attempt. Now we look at the three different versions of the future. If they all give the same result then we can have confidence in it. If the patterns diverge, then we have to try to understand why. This 'ensemble' forecast may allow us to increase the range of numerical forecasting to perhaps a month or more. Also, if we know the type of situations when the computer gets it right then that is of value. Conversely, if we know that the results are wrong, then that is of some value in itself. Statistical methods to predict above-average rainfall or below-average temperatures can be developed in conjunction with the ensemble forecast. It is hard to make progress, but the potential economic benefits are enormous. In practice, the ensemble may consist of up to 100 computer runs from the same basic starting position. The title 'Monte Carlo method' is quite appropriate in that it emphasises the underlying random nature of the atmosphere which we are trying to imitate in our computer model.

SEA TEMPERATURE ANOMALIES

It is known that regions of unusually warm or cool ocean water often persist for months. A persistent patch of warm water in the Atlantic (known as a positive sea temperature anomaly) may produce systematically higher pressures over western Europe and therefore below-average rainfall. This type of forecast is generalised but still of use. The Met Office has used this method to produce forecasts for rainfall in the Sahel (the southern fringe of the Sahara) for a season ahead. In the temperate latitudes it tends to be of less value, but the extent of sea-ice near Greenland obviously has some effect on Europe's coming weather. (The El Niño phenomenon in the Pacific is the classic case of fluctuation in sea temperatures, and is currently receiving worldwide attention, see Chapter 11.)

THE PAST MONTH – FUTURE MONTH METHOD

One of the first attempts at monthly forecasting which is still in use today looks at the past month as a guide for what will happen in the future. Let us suppose it is the last day of November. The computer hunts through its archive of past weather looking for Novembers similar to that just experienced. By similar, we mean over the whole of the northern hemisphere and in the upper air, not just at the surface. Perhaps the computer produces the Novembers of 1894, 1912, 1937 and 1957 as roughly comparable. The Decembers which followed in those years should be a guide to December of this year. It works, but not all that well. An oil company relying on the forecast of temperature will perhaps save itself three million pounds one month on a good forecast, but lose two million next month on a bad one. Over the year as a whole they will save money. However, someone who decides to bet upon a white Christmas on the strength of that type of forecast is taking a decided chance. Such forecasts say nothing about individual days and are not intended for detailed planning.

Anyone who thinks they can forecast the future by finding a similar weather chart from one day in the past just does not realise how complex the atmosphere is. The charts would need to be similar over the whole of the northern hemisphere to work reliably for even a week.

A YEAR AHEAD

One of the commonest questions asked of meteorologists is 'will it be a nice summer?' or alternatively 'will it be a severe winter?' Unfortunately, we do not know. If you want some sort of estimate for the weather a year ahead, then climatological statistics are the best guide. In some ways it is best to look at statistics for the past 30 years, but with the greenhouse effect, it may be that the past 10 years is a more appropriate period. Furthermore, if planning a wedding or a special day out, do not assume that 16 April is in any meteorological sense different from 14 April or 18. Ideas such as 'Buchan spells' do not work. Just because there have been ten successive dry 16 Aprils does not mean that next year this day will be dry. The average number of dry days in the whole month of April is a better guide to your chances.

The idea that weather 'evens itself out' is misleading. If we have had four successive months with above-average temperatures then the following month may be warm or cool. Indeed the odds will probably be shaded slightly in favour of a further warm month because the sea temperatures around the British Isles will be running a degree or so above average for the time of year. High soil temperatures can be obliterated in a week of cold or wet weather but a sea temperature anomaly takes longer to extinguish.

A week is a long time in meteorology and any sort of forecast for a year ahead must be looked at with scepticism. Perhaps the odd-year summers have been better over the last century including 1959 and 1975 (but then came 1976). Perhaps the irregular cycle of El Niño which is often around 3 to 6 years does have an influence in Europe, but it is a tenuous one. Perhaps the greenhouse effect is gradually leading to milder winters in Britain and a dearth of snow in the Alps. Having said all that, the best guide to the first half of February next year is the long-term averages for the first half of February.

CHAOS THEORY

Why are we not able to forecast in detail for a month ahead with every depression and every front correctly predicted?

As we have seen, one problem is the patchy nature of the observing network, for both surface and upper atmosphere. If this were the only problem then it could be overcome by having saturation coverage just once, and letting the computers carry on from there. Another problem has been the lack of computing power, but that will gradually become less of a factor as computational speeds continue to increase. Gradually all the constants such as albedo, conduction, the exchanges of turbulent energy and moisture, will become better known. Even then, chaos theory shows us that further progress will be slow.

Put simply, the theory says that tiny components of the system can eventually become important. We can express it as the 'butterfly effect'; it means that a small gust of wind or turbulent eddy on the far side of the world will eventually effect the weather in Britain – so a butterfly can change the course of climatic history. Normally meteorologists think of an energy cascade among atmospheric processes. This describes large weather features causing smaller and smaller features, going down the scale. For example, a major depression gives rise to a small trough which in turn causes a shower cloud which delivers a gust of wind. The energy cascades down from a huge system which lasts for a week to a mesoscale system lasting a day, to a large cloud lasting an hour, to a gust which lasts for only seconds.

On the other hand, chaos theory starts with the tiny gust of wind which provides the initial impulse for a new depression to form, and thereby changes the large-scale evolution.

If we release a marble or small ball to run down a sloping road, then it will not always take the same course down the hill. However many times we release it from the same point, it will probably not follow the same track. A minute change in some apparently trivial detail (the way we release it, an imperfection in the marble, even a change in temperature) will cause a new evolution. So with weather forecasting there will always be tiny, unmeasureable details which alter the future.

Chaos theory does not mean that we have now reached the limit of weather forecasting – merely that we have made sufficient progress to see that there is going to be a limit. When we looked at the problem of prediction for the next month, the concept of 'ensemble forecasts' was described. These forecasts recognise the importance of chaos theory and attempt to overcome it with a series of computations, each starting from almost the same initial conditions. Such batches of computations could be used to identify crucial points in the evolution of the weather during the next month, when the pattern is so finely balanced that it could 'go either way'. This raises the spectre of intervening with some action such as cloud-seeding at the critical points where the weather could be intentionally diverted down a more 'beneficial' path. (But beneficial to whom?) Fortunately that spectre is a long way off.

PROBABILITIES

All predictions of the future carry obvious uncertainties. We are not surprised when political or economic forecasters get it wrong, and in the science of meteorology we must also expect predictive errors. On some occasions though, it is useful to give an idea of the confidence in the forecast by using *probabilities*.

Perhaps the easiest example to understand is that of a showery day. We are a very long way off being able to predict individual showers, say 8 hours ahead (though we can follow their progress on radar and predict their track for 2 or 3 hours). However, we can identify some areas where showers are more probable on a particular day.

We usually express this probability in a local forecast by using a phrase like 'and the showers especially frequent near western coasts, whilst in the Severn Valley they will be few and far between'. The terms isolated, scattered, quite a few, indicate an increasing chance of getting wet.

In the United States, some weather people go one stage further by allocating probabilities to these expressions, such as 20, 40, 60 and 80%. They are useful for comparing one area with another but what do these numbers actually mean? A strict definition of a 20% shower risk in Worcester might indicate that there is a 20% chance of getting at least one shower in the city during the period from 8 a.m. to 6 p.m., or in other words a 1 in 5 chance of getting wet during the working day. Over a flat county like Cambridgeshire it will be almost impossible to distinguish between the risk at one end of the county and that at the other until the showers are actually being followed on radar.

On days with 'isolated showers' it is difficult to please everybody, because those who catch a shower are disappointed, and those who remain dry think that none have developed. Generally a car driver will see more of the weather, perhaps crossing a few miles of wet road, and they therefore have a different perspective from the stationary observer.

Some other aspects of forecasting do not lend themselves to probability forecasts. A depression may be heading towards Shetland and be expected to pass just to the north of the islands. To say that there is a 10% chance of it passing to the south is rather unhelpful to the general public if the forecast is rain in either case, and television broadcasts would get more and more complex. Better by far to go for our best shot and be judged on the results.

ACCURACY

Accuracy is obviously the goal of meteorologists in their forecasts, but how can it be measured? If we predict a maximum temperature of 23 C and it reaches 25.2 C, then we must assign a mark. But is it right, wrong, or half marks?

Forecast which can be assessed by precise instruments like thermometers are relatively easy to verify and assess. We can devise a system giving, say, full marks for within 2 degrees, half marks for an error of 2 to 4 degrees, and nil for anything more than 4 degrees out. Similarly, wind speed and direction are easily checked, since they can be accurately measured by an anemometer.

Even for these relatively simple parameters, we have to choose a representative site at which to verify the forecast. Heathrow Airport might be chosen as a location to mark a forecast for southeast England, but sometimes an alternative verification site nearby, say Gatwick Airport, would have given a different mark. This is all the more true in hilly areas of Scotland and Wales, where the weather often varies over a distance of a few miles.

Attempts are made to mark yes/no forecasts of rain in London within certain periods of time. The story goes that a forecaster who predicted rain, was stuck in floods on his way home from work, yet scored nil because no rain fell at the verification site.

When we get to the more esoteric descriptions of the sky and general weather, then assessing the forecast becomes more subjective. How do we mark a prediction of 'rather cloudy, mainly dry but just the odd spot of rain overnight' if the weather is totally dry? Showery days are also a big problem. Very often it is not a matter of right or wrong. The simplistic view of a 40% correct forecast being 'worse than taking the opposite to what was said' just doesn't stand up to scrutiny. Meteorology is not a yes/no science. We are dealing with a many-sided dice.

One of the more common scientific methods used to assess computer output is to record the error in mean sea-level pressure at various grid points which are forecast by the numerical model (i.e. the Bracknell supercomputer). These assessments show the improvement of computer models over the last 20 years and are a valuable bench-mark of progress.

Although, as we have seen, the percentage accuracy itself is of limited value, the marking of forecasts does have many uses. We can measure our progress from year to year. We can also compare one prediction method with another, one computer system with another, a human against a computer or even one forecaster with another. As long as we run the checks for a good period of time, in other words months rather than days, then the comparison should be valid. System A scoring 80% is better than system B scoring 70% just so long as we don't take the numbers themselves too seriously.

Forecast verification is time consuming but vital. Many radio forecasts are marked. Computer errors are continually logged. The increasing tendency to mark and evaluate is a sign of professionalism. It also helps to put the occasional 'bad day' into perspective.

For events like thunderstorms, which may occur only ten times per year at any one location, we need a special marking system – otherwise we would forecast 'no thunder' and be correct 355 times out of 365. Our marks must amply reward correct forecasts of thunder, but sufficiently penalise a person who cries wolf too often.

By and large, the further ahead we try to forecast then the less accurate we will be. The fall-off in accuracy is fairly steady from one day ahead out to seven days – though of course there is the odd occasion when the original effort was better than the subsequent 'change of story'.

Chapter 9

HOLIDAY WEATHER

FAVOURED AREAS OF BRITAIN IN WINTER

THOSE LOOKING for a weekend away within the British Isles in winter will not have high expectations of the weather. Obviously the best policy is to leave the decision on where to go as late as possible and use the weather forecast. Favoured areas will then depend on the wind direction.

A cold northerly or northeasterly should send you heading to South Wales or the south coast of England, but Central Scotland also gets a good deal of shelter and so too does the southwestern corner of Ireland.

The bitterest cold in winter often comes with easterlies, and in midwinter southeasterlies are not much better. The Welsh mountains provide shelter to the western and northwestern coasts of Wales, and the same applies in Scotland where Oban, Mallaig and Ullapool can be quite pleasant – though daylight hours are very short and even a hill can be sufficient to keep the low-angle sun hidden.

Any airstream from the southwest will tend to be mild but very moist. Inverness and Aberdeen are two of the most sheltered places, but the Clwyd coast, Shropshire and York also do quite well.

A northwesterly will tend to be showery but the southeastern corner of Wales may escape along with the Severn Valley and perhaps Torbay.

For those who like to pre-plan or who need to pre-book, there is certainly a large element of pot luck. Westerlies are statistically the most probable airstream, but not so common as to be reliable. One could plan a week on the Northumberland coast in March in the hope of a westerly or southwesterly which is likely to bring a good week, and find that you end up with a northeasterly and its accompanying raw cold. The east coast of Scotland or England is no place to be with an onshore wind in so-called spring-time.

Over the winter half-year it is Cornwall, the Isles of Scilly and South-western Ireland which are consistently milder than elsewhere due to the proximity of the Atlantic, but the risk of drizzle or strong winds is appreciable. The eastern side of the country is drier but often cooler in winter. The Thames Valley is relatively gale-free but quite fog-prone, and the same could be said of the Vale of York and also of much of the low ground in the English Midlands.

Nowhere in the British Isles can carry anything like an unqualified recommendation in winter but Perth, Bath and Salisbury at least have sheltered valley locations.

THE BRITISH ISLES IN SUMMER

A quick résumé of the summer climate shows that we have the highest sunshine totals in June (partly because the days are then at their longest), the highest temperatures in July and August, and the highest sea temperatures in late August.

If one was considering three possible holidays, then the time of year might be the deciding factor. Inland places like York, Stratford or Oxford warm up quickly in the spring and are usually suitable for sightseeing in April and May. The mountains of Scotland benefit from long hours of sunshine in June and July. Coastal resorts are favoured by the higher sea and air temperatures in August and September.

For those who can wait until a day or two before departure, then the same sort of logic which applies in winter can be used. An easterly or anticyclonic situation suggests the Lake District, western Scotland or western Wales; a westerly synoptic pattern suggests Inverness, Northumbria, Yorkshire, Shropshire, the Severn Valley and the east coasts of England, Ireland and Scotland.

On average, the coasts of the British Isles are sunnier but cooler than inland. Annual sunshine totals are highest in the Channel Isles followed by the Isle of Wight and then the remainder of the coastal strip of southern England. However, the enhanced sunshine compared with inland stretches right around the coasts of the British Isles up to Tiree and the Hebrides in the west, and up the east coast to St Andrews and beyond. The same pattern of longer hours of coastal sunshine is repeated around Ireland. If you are going on holiday by car, then peninsula locations are particularly good because you can always find a sheltered beach. If sea-fog afflicts one coast, then an assessment of wind direction and the shelter afforded by high ground should lead you to the best weather. Cornwall is the classic example, but the idea is also valid in Dyfed, the Lleyn Peninsula of North Wales, Kent, North Norfolk, southwest Ireland and some of the larger Scottish islands. Those who have heard special advice such as 'the Lake District is always good in the last week of August' may face disappointment. No such rules exist. I would never dissuade anyone from a chosen location in Britain between May and September inclusive. (Last-minute choices with a series of depressions imminent are

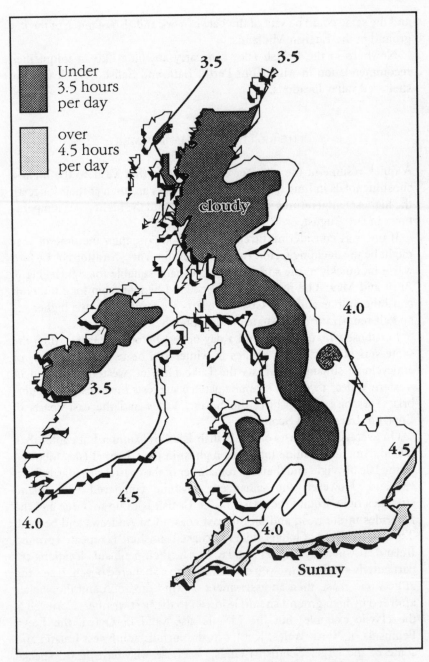

Average sunshine duration in hours per day. The south coast of England has about 5 hours per day, whereas in the mountains the average is around 3 hours per day. Whilst there is more sunshine in summer, the general pattern shown here holds true throughout the year (but not necessarily in any one week!).

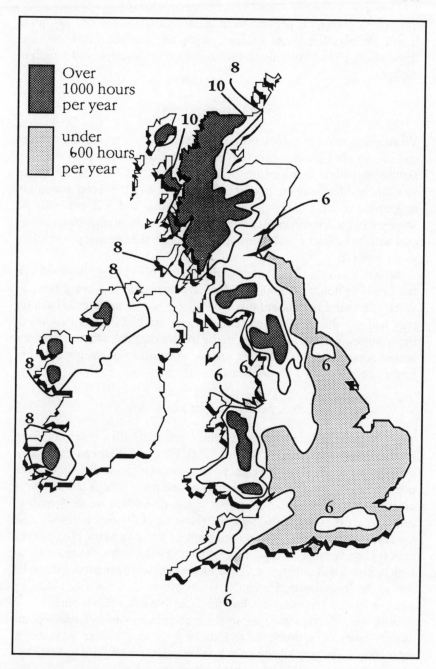

The duration of rainfall in hundreds of hours per year. Lowland areas of eastern Britain have 500 to 600 hours of rain per year whilst the Highlands of Scotland have roughly twice that duration.

a different matter.) If pressed to nominate a month, I would say 'go in June'. The weather is not guaranteed but the daylight hours are. The Appendices include various tables of climate information and length of daylight.

OVERSEAS HOLIDAYS

Weather can make or mar an overseas holiday, but when studying weather statistics in a holiday brochure only you can decide whether you want to go sightseeing, ideal temperature perhaps 15 to 25 C (59 to 77 F), or sunbathing, ideal temperature 20 to 30 C (68 to 86 F). Average maximum temperatures are usually quoted in brochures, and will generally be achieved in the afternoon. At a Mediterranean resort in high summer you may wish to sunbathe mid morning and again in the afternoon and take a siesta between.

Rainfall totals should not necessarily put you off a foreign destination if the sunshine hours are good. In the Caribbean, July can bring twice as much rain as in London, but this is because it rains four times as hard for only half the duration. When temperatures are high, rainfall comes in heavy bursts. Very often, though, in the tropics the rainy season is also the humid season and this will be a real factor against sightseeing trips but might not matter on a breezy beach.

SUNTANNING AND SUNBURN

This brings us to the subject of sunburn, caused by ultra-violet rays from the Sun. Both ultra-violet 'A' and 'B' (UVA and UVB) can cause skin damage, especially if you have not built up your tan gradually. Contrary to popular belief, the wind will not burn you and nor will high temperatures on their own. Suntanning or sunburning is dependent on the length of time you are exposed to the Sun, the elevation of the Sun in the sky and the nature of your skin. To a minor extent we should add the clarity of the atmosphere, because a polluted sky will reduce the Sun's strength, just as high altitudes will enhance it. The quickest tan will be achieved if you lie flat on the ground with the Sun vertically overhead. Do not be fooled by wind or modest temperatures into thinking that you will not burn.

With the reduction in ozone in the stratosphere, sunburn has become slightly more of a problem, and the risk of skin cancer is probably increasing very, very slowly year by year. Skin creams which filter out ultra-violet rays seem certain to help reduce the risk of burning, and so too will a gradual build up of your tan. Reflection from snow and to a lesser extent sand or water will add to the amount of ultra-violet light falling on your skin. Swimming with your back just under water will not prevent sunburn as a substantial amount of energy penetrates the top metre (3 ft) or so of water. Suntan lotions which are waterproof will avoid the need for frequent reapplications.

For those who are sightseeing, the same skin-care rules apply for exposed areas such as face, neck, arms, etc.

The Sun is highest in the sky, and therefore most powerful at midday GMT (i.e. 1 p.m. clock time in summer) in Britain. Because many countries have their clocks biased towards daylight saving, the general rule of the sun being at its most potent from 11 a.m. to 3 p.m. is about right.

WHEN AND WHERE TO GO

If you know *when* you want to go, but not yet *where*, then the following month-by-month section may guide you. If you have chosen your *destination* then the brief summaries of best months may help you.

Remember the saying, 'you book your holiday depending on the climate, but when you arrive, there's only weather'. This is a tactful way of saying 'don't blame me'. Also these lists include personal bias and assumptions on my part. If you want to see snow in Moscow, then you will go in midwinter; for autumn colours ('the fall') in North America, then late October is best, but depending somewhat on the location and the current weather. Flowers and trees often look their best in spring, so the Mediterranean countries, for example, usually look dried out in September despite the pleasant weather and warm seas at that time. Also, every now and then, parts of the Mediterranean get a very wet spell with floods, even in September. You could be unlucky.

The Mediterranean is difficult to summarise. April, May, September and October can be good. Midsummer will suit those who simply want to stay on the beach. Winter has some days suitable for sunbathing, though January is usually too cool. The Costa Brava has a shorter summer season than Spanish resorts further south, and the same north-south rule applies in the Greek Islands and Turkish coasts. For southern Spain and the eastern Mediterranean, April and October are essentially summer months. For simply baking in hot sun, then Southeast Asia around January, or the Mediterranean islands in June and July come close to cast-iron guarantees, but a desert is the safest bet of all. The eastern Mediterranean experiences a persistent northerly wind from about June to September, known as the 'meltemi'. This is caused by the circulation around the huge Asian summer low pressure system, and brings relief from the potentially oppressive heat of midsummer to the Aegean region in particular. Whilst it provides a cooling breeze on the Greek Islands it can sometimes be strong enough to prevent windsurfing, sailing or swimming on north-facing coasts.

MONTH BY MONTH

This list is not comprehensive – just a selection. The main bias is towards sunbathing at obvious coastal resorts. Remember though that few places have *guaranteed* weather, so these are only suggestions. Usually a month either side of the suggested dates would not be disastrous.

January Thailand, Penang, Goa, Acapulco, Gambia, southern Florida, southern California, northern India, Egypt, southwest coasts of Canaries, Red Sea, Caribbean.

February Thailand, Penang, Acapulco, Gambia, southern Florida, southern California, northern India, Egypt, Red Sea, Marrakesh, Agadir, southwest coast of Canaries, southern Tunisia, Caribbean.

March Florida, California, New Orleans, southern Morocco, southeastern Spain, eastern Sicily, eastern and southern Tunisia, Cyprus, Canaries, Madeira, Caribbean.

April Florida, Southern USA, Madeira, most of the Mediterranean (swimming pools will be warming up but the sea is still cool), Soviet Central Asia, inland Turkey, Canaries, Caribbean.

May New York, Washington, Richmond, Chicago, Canada, Japan, inland areas of Europe, most of the Mediterranean, Venice, Yugoslavia, Italy, Athens, Istanbul, Portugal, Rio de Janeiro.

June New York, Canada, northwestern USA, northern Europe, Scandinavia, Moscow, Leningrad, Mediterranean islands, British Isles, Rio de Janeiro.

July Canada, Northwestern USA, Scandinavia, Moscow, Leningrad, British Isles, small Mediterranean islands, Rio de Janeiro.

August Canada, northwestern USA, northern Europe, British Isles, Moscow, Leningrad, small Mediterranean islands, Rio de Janeiro.

September Mediterranean, inland central Europe, Switzerland, Austria, Soviet Central Asia, California, central and northern USA, Canada, Portugal, Madeira, Madrid.

October Madeira, Canaries, southern Mediterranean, southeastern Spain, Tunisia, Malta, Cyprus, Crete, Rhodes, sightseeing in central and northern USA, New York, New England and Canada, Mediterranean (mainly sightseeing).

November Hong Kong, southeastern Spain, eastern and southern Tunisia, southern Morocco, eastern Sicily, southwestern Canaries, Florida, southern USA, southern Mediterranean (sightseeing).

December Hong Kong (sightseeing), Thailand, Goa, Acapulco, southern

California, northern India, Egypt, southwestern coasts of Canaries, southern Florida.

EUROPE AND AFRICA

Athens   Apr, May, Sep to Nov
Cairo   Nov to Mar
Cyprus   Apr to Oct (sightseeing Apr, Oct)
Dubrovnik   May to early Oct
Gambia   Nov to Feb
Istanbul   Apr to Jun, Sep, Oct
Jerusalem   Feb, Mar, Oct, Nov
Madrid   Apr, May, Sep, Oct
Malta   Apr to Oct (sightseeing Apr, May, Oct)
Marrakesh   Oct to Apr
Moscow May to Sep (midwinter for snow)
Nairobi   Jun to Sep, Jan, Feb
Paris   May to Sep
Rome   Apr, May, Sep, Oct
Scandinavia   May to early Sep
Seville and Cordoba   Mar to early May, Oct
Sousse (Tunisia)   Apr, May, Sep, Oct (sightseeing in winter)
Tangier   Apr to Jun, Sep, Oct
Tunis   May to Sep
Upper Egypt   Nov to Feb
Venice   Apr to Jun, Sep, Oct
Vienna   May to Sep
Zimbabwe   Apr to Oct

ASIA AND AUSTRALASIA

Auckland (NZ) Nov to Apr
Bahrain   Nov, Dec, Feb to Apr
Bangkok   Dec to Feb
Beijing   Apr to Jun, Sep, Oct
Brisbane   Apr to Dec
Colombo (Sri Lanka)   Dec to Mar
Delhi   Nov to early Mar
Hong Kong   Nov, Dec, Mar
Melbourne   Dec to Mar
Penang   Dec to Mar

Perth   Oct to Apr
Singapore   All year (but always humid and showery)
Sydney   Oct to Apr
Tokyo   Apr to Jun, Sep, Oct
Wellington (NZ)   Dec to Mar

THE AMERICAS

Acapulco Nov to Mar
Caribbean   Dec to Apr
Hawaii   All year
Las Vegas   Sep to Nov, Mar to May
Los Angeles   All year/especially Apr to Nov
Mexico City   Oct to May (can be cool in midwinter)
New Orleans   Oct, Nov, Mar, Apr
New York   May to Oct
Northern Florida   Nov, Feb to May
Oregon   May to Oct
Rio de Janeiro   All year/especially May to Sep
San Diego   All year/especially Apr to Nov
San Francisco   Apr to Oct
Southern Canada   May to Sep (late Oct: autumn colours)
Southern Florida   Nov to Apr
Washington   Apr to Jun, Sep, Oct

SKIING WEATHER

For those planning a skiing holiday, there seems to be an ever-increasing choice of resorts, and a wide variety of factors to consider in making that choice.

Snow is obviously the first priority. For nearly all northern hemisphere destinations February and March will tend to be more reliable than December or even early January in most years. Higher resorts will be more likely to have snow than lower sites, especially early and late in the season. On north or northeast facing slopes, the snow will probably lie longer, being sheltered from early afternoon melting by the Sun. The direction of the slopes is given in some tour operators brochures.

Since even the most logical approach has brought some failures in the last couple of years, you may wish to consider resorts with snow-making machines or with permanent glacier skiing (which will inevitably get crowded should you need to use it).

Another disadvantage to the 'aim high' approach comes in breezy weather, when the high altitude runs will be colder and the wind much more difficult to cope with, thus calling for warm clothing and good ski technique. It also takes longer to reach the higher runs.

Scotland's skiing has traditionally been centred on Aviemore, a town at about 700 ft (200 m) which serves the Cairngorm mountains just a few miles away. There is also skiing at Glencoe, Glenshee (on the A93 north of Braemar), Lecht (on the A939, southeast of Tomintoul) and a new development at Aonach Mor near Fort William. Most of the towns cater for skiing at altitudes between 2000 and 3300 ft (600 and 1000 m) and centres would hope in an ideal season to be active from December to April. There is no reason why November and even May should not provide a few suitable days, but of course it is all subject to our variable British weather.

Length of daylight is an important factor in ski-holiday enjoyment. In the northern hemisphere it reaches a minimum in late December but lengthens through the new year at a rate which depends on latitude. Times can be quoted from sunrise to sunset but you may also be able to make cautious use of the after-glow. The average day-lengths at latitude 57°N in Scotland for the months November to April are 8, 7, 7, 9, 12 and 14 respectively. In the Alps the same months give 9, 9, 9, 10, 12 and 14 hours.

Your choice of resort should certainly take account of other non-meteorological considerations. Is there alternative entertainment in the resort? Are all of your party going to ski? Is the resort suitable for beginners or experts? How long is the journey from the airport? These are questions which must be asked alongside the snow prospects.

SAILING AND WINDSURFING

These are two of the most popular totally weather-dependent sports. Rather than repeat information given elsewhere in the book, I would refer enthusiasts to the section on geostrophic wind in Chapter 2. Coastal sailors will also need an understanding of the sea breeze from Chapter 5, and those going further offshore can look at airmasses, front and depressions in Chapter 2.

An interesting point arises for northern hemisphere yachtsmen going off to sail in Australia and other venues south of the Equator. In our hemisphere, the wind increases and veers during the morning, but down there, it backs. When the wind gusts more strongly near a shower it usually veers slightly here, but down there it backs – and all because the Coriolis effect acts in the opposite direction.

Chapter 10

WEATHER FOR BUSINESS

FARMING WEATHER

WE THINK of arable farmers ploughing, sowing, and then harvesting their crops, but these are not necessarily their most weather-sensitive activities. Some of the key decisions come in the spring and early summer, and are connected with the application of fertiliser and sprays. Anti-fungal spray may cost £1000 for a large field. If rain falls within about four hours of application (depending on the spray) then the benefit can be lost and the money wasted. Farmers can arrange a contract with the local weather centre to ask about rainfall risk. The forecaster sitting in front of a radar display can see where the rain is at that particular time and also the direction of movement, and can therefore predict for a specific location.

Agricultural advice is obviously not restricted to yes/no decisions about rainfall. Various pests and diseases will only thrive under certain meteoro-logical conditions. Potato blight occurs when the weather is warm and moist. A simple warning system can be based on what has already occurred as well as on forecasts.

Cattle and sheep, hens, and even fish farming are all weather sensitive. Hill farmers try to get their sheep to lower ground before bitterly cold spells. In the spring, lambs are very susceptible to windchill if it is both cold and wet. The vulnerable youngsters then are rather like a wet-bulb thermometer with the evaporation of moisture causing extra cooling, so a standard warning service exists for windchill effects on lambs.

Farmers generally turn out to be amateur forecasters themselves, and experts in their own locality. If it is 'looking a bit dark over Will's mother's house', then that will help them to forecast for an hour or two ahead. The very best ones, however, use every aid available including the barometer, an estimation of wind direction, a regular listen to Radio 4 in the morning, a study of the weather maps in the newspaper and an update on TV in the evening A true expert will use this information but, tongue in cheek, he may still like to pretend that his expertise comes from feeling seaweed or watching the cows.

Farmers with two different crops maturing may need rain for one field and sunshine in another. Just very rarely, nature may even oblige.

BUILDING WEATHER

Every building should be designed and constructed with the local weather in mind.

At the design stage the need for structural soundness will be paramount. Usually a major building will be designed to withstand a fairly extreme gale, for example a 'once in two hundred years gust' of 95 mph (150 kph). This 'return period' can easily be misunderstood, but means that for this given location a gust of 95 mph will, on average, occur once every two hundred years. Chance being the random beast that it is, such a gust could occur the week after the building is finished and again a year later, but then not for a few hundred years. To build a cricket pavilion or garden shed to this standard would be excessive, so it depends what you are designing. Also, we have to admit that often a return period of a hundred years has to be estimated from only twenty years of local wind records, so some extra statistical calculations are needed. Fortunately the design engineer will add on a bit for safety.

Another factor they will consider is the arrangement of adjacent buildings and topography. Ideally one needs a wind-tunnel test complete with models of the surrounding buildings (built or planned).

Another design problem with modern glass-sided office blocks is the amount of heat absorbed on a sunny day. Such offices can be highly dependent on cooling systems, especially when windows have to be kept shut to maintain a low-humidity environment for computers.

Once the construction phase is reached, the day-to-day weather becomes important. Earth-moving is difficult in wet weather. Concreting is adversely affected by sharp frost, though damage can be prevented by covering up the work or by adding a form of antifreeze to the mixture. Drying winds can lead to cracking of large areas of concrete due to shrinkage of the surface layer as it dries out.

Tower cranes are often 40 m (130 ft) high and cannot be used in winds gusting beyond about 38 mph (60 kph) – though it depends on the location and the task in hand. If a large sheet of metal cladding has to be raised, then it could act like a sail in the wind. A delicate positioning job such as the lowering of a concrete section into place might also call for a calm period.

Finally, as the building nears completion, high humidity days must be avoided for the sealing of concrete joints and for painting.

GOOD WEATHER FOR SELLING

Everyone knows that ice-cream sales go up in hot weather. What is less obvious is the exact breakdown of different types of ice-cream. For example in moderate warmth a soft ice-cream in a cornet will sell rapidly, but when it gets exceptionally hot, people will be looking for something thirst-quenching which is effectively a drink on a stick, and the orange ice-lolly may become the best-seller.

Other products such as lager have a threshold value, around 23 C (73 F), above which sales start to soar. Food which does well in hot weather includes yoghurt, lettuce, and tomatoes. Rather a surprise though are sausages, until you think of barbecues. Ready to cook meals such as pizza appeal to those not wishing to spend all day in the kitchen on a glorious Saturday in summer. By contrast, meat and potato sales are generally enhanced in cold weather along with soups and hot chocolate.

There are plenty of examples of weather dependence from outside the food industry, quite apart from umbrellas in wet weather and T-shirts or swimwear in the heat.

For many purposes sunshine is just as important as warmth. April 1990 was a terrific month for the sale of garden furniture. Because of the record April sunshine totals, retailers sold more of this range of goods in the month than in the whole of the summer of 1988. Lawnmowers, however, generally do better in wet summers when the grass keeps growing.

Cars are always in demand but even so they are subject to a weather effect – no one wants to go browsing around an outdoor sales area in a biting cold January wind. Three or four bad Saturdays in a row will depress second-hand car sales for a time, though purchases will eventually be made when a warmer weekend comes along in February.

NATIONAL AND INTERNATIONAL COMMITMENTS

As the state meteorological service, the Met Office is asked to provide all sorts of information. The Department of Social Security runs a cold weather payment scheme to help offset high heating bills during severe weather. Whilst the Met Office does not decide policy, the actual temperature readings over the past week at various sites around the country are issued to the DSS.

From time to time the police need to know the weather conditions prevailing at a particular place and time. This could be connected with a traffic accident, or more rarely with a criminal case. The story is told of a criminal who plunged across a river in a vain attempt to avoid capture. When subsequently caught he denied being involved. Finally, asked why he was soaking wet, he replied that he had been caught in a shower. The police of course had to produce evidence to show that the weather had been dry. Here, as with many enquiries about past weather, the difficulty for the meteorologist is interpolating between two or three professional observing sites and between observation times. Incidents never occur right outside an observation station at the time of an observation, though there is always a wealth of other information available from radar, satellite and human judgement.

The Met Office warns the military if severe weather is expected which could require them to give assistance to the civil community, for example due to gales, floods or severe drifting snow.

Internationally, the UK contributes to the European Centre for Medium-range Weather Forecasting (ECMWF) based at Reading, and the Met Office plays a role in the World Meteorological Organisation (WMO). The WMO decides upon the international codes and agreements by which information is shared all around the World. Now we also have the Hadley Centre for Climate Research located at the Met Office HQ at Bracknell, opened in spring 1990.

EDUCATION

It has gradually been realised that meteorology is an avenue par excellence for teaching children about science. The children can look upon the atmosphere as a huge scientific experiment going on outside the classroom window. All the ingredients are there: measurements, scientific reasoning and the occasional unexpected result. Better still, teacher has no control over it! Meteorology ties together the Sun, Earth and seasons, the transfer of heat by radiation, conduction and convection and changes in phase from water to vapour or ice.

Perhaps the best feature of all is that the students can take readings which are meaningful. If it has rained in the night and there are puddles, they can estimate how much rain has fallen, then go and look at the rain-gauge total for the past 24 hours.

WEATHER FOR THE GAS INDUSTRY

The gas industry supplies both domestic and industrial users with a hydrocarbon which is burnt to give heat. Natural gas is composed of methane, along with an added smell to make it detectable by the human nose, plus a few minor impurities. It replaced town gas, which was formed from coal, during the 1960s. These days, the main domestic use of gas is in central heating boilers which means that demand is highly weather-sensitive.

When the temperature falls outdoors, the houses lose heat more quickly by conduction through their walls, windows and roofs. Warm air also physically escapes through doors and windows, when they are opened and because of draughts. Although we have to have at least a minimum rate of ventilation to avoid the air becoming stale, this is likely to be well exceeded when a gale is blowing outside. Only a thoroughly draught-proofed room in calm weather is greatly at risk from stagnant air.

As the temperature plummets on a winter evening, literally millions of thermostats click on all over the country. Some people will even turn their thermostat up as the temperature decreases. The logic of this action might seem dubious because if 18 C (64 F) is a comfortable temperature for indoors, then it should remain so whatever the weather outside. Another school of thought is that we should turn the thermostat down a little in cold weather to minimise the huge temperature differential when we go out of doors. This latter course of action will also reduce fuel usage.

If the weather outside is sunny, then some heat will be gained through south-facing windows, but human perception and therefore perhaps the thermostat setting may also be altered. On a really dull, grey, winter day, demand will rise due to the 'misery factor': if we feel miserable, then we turn the heating up.

The industry has to order its supplies from the North Sea and elsewhere to meet tomorrow's demand. When the decision-makers try to forecast the amount of gas needed for the next day, they are dealing primarily with meteorology but also with human psychological aspects such as the misery factor.

Weather centres supply detailed temperature predictions to the gas industry, together with forecasts of wind speed and general weather. On the basis of this forecast, along with the recent history of gas demand, for example on the same day in the previous week, the required amount of gas is ordered.

The decision-makers just cannot afford to run out of gas, and they take their responsibilities very seriously and include a safety margin. In this respect they are at a disadvantage compared with electricity, which can, *in extremis*, be turned off. On the other hand the gas distribution system is more forgiving. Gas can be stored by raising the pressure in pipes and using the old gas-holders. It can also be moved around the country (though at about 30 mph (50 kph), it is a lot slower than electricity). This means that as long as meteorological estimates are not uniformly wrong throughout Britain, then one region can help out another. An error in temperature forecast of 1 C (2 F) can induce roughly a 5% error in gas demand. Fortunately, some industrial users have a contract whereby their supply can be interrupted when domestic demand is very high. By this means, the huge fluctuations of our central heating are smoothed out.

WEATHER AND ELECTRICITY

Domestic electricity is used for heating and illumination, which are strongly weather-sensitive, as well as for cooking, hot water and electrical appliances, which are only loosely related to weather. Electricity demand in UK usually rises between 7 and 8 a.m., runs at a fairly high level during the day and goes up to a peak at around 5 or 6 p.m., before dwindling during the late evening. Superimposed upon this routine pattern are all sorts of social and weather-related quirks of human behaviour.

A dark cloud passing over London or another major city during the day will cause a surge in demand as electric lights are turned on; cold weather inevitably heightens demand for heating; and a dull, cool, wet evening will mean more people indoors watching television, cooking substantial meals and making cups of tea. The timing of major television programmes and of television adverts is of course a separate problem for the electricity supply industry, but one can imagine the electrical response at half-time in the cup final if everybody turns on the kettle for tea. (Although, of course, on a hot day, they may have a beer instead.)

Fortunately, this is an industry which is able to respond quickly to fluctuations. With the weather forecast in one hand and the TV papers in the other, they are well prepared. Power stations are already on stream and can be turned up or down. Additionally, there are installations like the Dinorwic pumped storage scheme in North Wales, where water is pumped uphill at night and can be released downhill to generate hydro-electric power at the incredibly short notice of only a few seconds. The trouble with electricity is that you cannot save it for later, so surplus generation is wasted. Accurate forecasting is paramount for efficiency.

OIL DEMAND

Whereas gas and electricity demand is immediate, oil is more easily stored and response times can be slower, though ultimately the oil tankers must keep pace with the customers' calls for re-supply. A cold spell in the major affluent regions of the northern hemisphere in winter will trigger an increase in the spot price of oil on the Rotterdam market. When the USA had severe weather in the winter of 1989/90, the price rose strongly – despite the mild conditions in Europe at the time.

For the private customers with their own oil tank, the order for more fuel takes the form of a refill after the cold weather has depleted reserves, and is therefore largely retrospective. Conversely, those dealing on the commodity market or in shipping or distribution will obviously wish to be ahead of the game by using temperature forecasts.

OFFSHORE OIL

Much of the activity on an offshore oil rig goes on 60 m (200 ft) up at deck level and is therefore only heavily influenced by gales or perhaps fog. If, after three weeks on a rig, the helicopter coming to take you home is delayed, then it is a serious matter.

More commonly though, the business of the rig is affected by the state of the sea which in turn depends mainly on the wind speed. Rough seas or a large swell will prevent routine maintenance or repairs down at sea-level or below water. Divers cannot operate safely and supply ships will have difficulty in bringing in equipment or consumables. Major maintenance may have to wait perhaps for a three-day 'weather window' of quiet conditions. The same might apply to the towing of a rig from Scotland or Norway out to its permanent position in the North Sea, or even to a tow across the Mediterranean from, say, Port Said to Tunisia.

PROFESSIONAL AND LEGAL WEATHER

This is one of those market sectors which tends to have only an occasional need for weather information, and then it is rather a random assortment of information which is required. Sometimes an advertising agency will wish to maximise the impact of a pre-prepared campaign by launching it to coincide with a certain sort of weather. The first hot week during May is a good time to be selling a new suncream; if it is a cloudy week then some of the punch is lost.

Commodity brokers need to keep abreast of the weather. Just as low temperatures in Europe can raise oil prices, coffee in Brazil is vulnerable to frost when an outbreak of cold air (originally from the Antarctic) pushes northwards across South America.

Large insurance firms like to have all the data at their fingertips when disaster strikes, and therefore need a wide range of after-the-event weather summaries. The October 1987 storm and the February 1990 gale in the UK each cost over £1 billion. Hurricane Hugo in the eastern USA was even worse.

LEISURE AND TOURISM

Here there can be various conflicting interests. Even at the long-term planning stage, a tour operator will want to research the climate of the country where the tour is to run, and the potential visitor will want to do the same – preferably from independent information, though the holiday companies' information is generally honest as far as it goes, despite the occasional mistake. Perhaps the underlying error is for the holiday-maker to imagine that the foreign destination has definite, fixed weather when in reality it is variable, as in Britain. For advice, see Chapter 9.

At the British end, there are a lot more off-the-cuff decisions about going away for a day, weekend or week. Now the weather *forecast* comes into the equation rather than the climate. The owner of an amusement arcade wants a forecast of good weather to get the 'punters' to the seaside, then rain to drive them in from the beach. The hotel industry wants a forecast of sunshine to attract the customers and the actuality of good weather to keep them happy and bring them back next year. Organisers of fêtes, pop concerts and sports events are generally hoping for good weather but will be alert to the need for a wet weather alternative plan – with or without insurance.

To those tourist boards who think that the forecasters are biased, then all one can say is that we try to be honest and that any bias is unintentional.

Weather forecasts are very important for many types of organised sport: skiing and sailing are obvious examples; for horseracing, rain will make the going soft or heavy; cricket can be suspended due to bad light, rain or even, as at Buxton in Derbyshire on 2 June 1975, lying snow; and tennis also suffers its interruptions – not all Wimbledon's stoppages are for strawberries and cream. Of the more unusual sports, pigeon racing is notably weather sensitive. Pigeons like 'Sun on the basket', which is the expression used for the Sun being visible when they are released. This helps them to set off in the correct direction and to navigate. Fog and thick low cloud are bad news, and so too are strong headwinds. The birds seem to cope quite well with crosswinds, being able to allow for their sideways drift. And no, the birds do not know what the forecast is, but their release can be delayed awaiting suitable conditions!

TELEVISION FORECASTS

Most of the television weather presenters are professional meteorologists (including all of those currently doing BBC national broadcasts), but this is not true on every TV station. Of the non-meteorologists, some have a scientific background whilst others do not.

The professionals must have some say in their forecasts or there would be no point in being there, but equally they need computer output and guidance from a large central forecast office. The compromise reached is that the broadcast which the public sees is entirely in the presenter's own words using graphic map displays which they have chosen. However, they must stay within the general guidelines which the central forecast office has laid down. Normally this is no problem and they will have a chat by telephone an hour or so before they go 'on air' just to talk through the forecast. Perhaps the television presenter is reminded by the senior forecaster to 'play down the showers' compared with what the computer has suggested, or perhaps they may discuss the threat of sea-fog to the resorts on the east coast of England. Most TV forecasts are live and unscripted, and the allotted slot may be suddenly shrunk to 90 seconds just before the presenter appears. If the weather is generally good, he or she may throw in a joke, whereas in winter they will usually be concentrating on getting over the message about frost in Wales or snow in Scotland. They must remember that they are speaking to farmers, windsurfers and hill walkers as well as the ordinary general public, whoever they may be. One difficulty for the presenter is in deciding how far to stray away from meteorology into the effects of the weather. Heavy rain could mean river flooding or delayed trains, but these effects also depend on other people's actions. The presenter's job is to inform, educate and entertain – but information, whether verbal or displayed on the map behind them, comes top of the list.

There will always be some dissatisfied customers even when the forecast has turned out well. The irate farmer in Devon who did not get a shower when all those around did, the hotel owner in Skegness who is up in arms over the forecast of cool sea breezes, the tourist officer in Fort William who is annoyed that rain in the Highlands has been mentioned yet again. One can only do one's best.

Our television presenters are the public faces of meteorology, and as such they sometimes carry the can for mistakes which are not their own. Fortunately, good humour and professionalism usually see them through.

RADIO FORECASTS

The radio is a natural avenue for local weather information but national programmes provide the weather-people with a challenge.

Scripts are often provided for newsreaders or continuity announcers to read out, and sometimes these scripts are edited. It is difficult enough for the forecaster to write a script for the whole country in 30 to 40 words. If they then hear it edited down to one inappropriate phrase, life seems a little unfair.

A great problem for the forecasters who make live radio broadcasts is how to 'divide up' the British Isles. The listener is in one place and probably just wants to hear about the local weather. How to signpost the different weather zones for that day is an ongoing problem in a national forecast. Regional forecasts are easier and can be more chatty.

Some radio broadcasters write a complete script beforehand, but with two alternative different-length outlooks. If time is running out, then they use the shorter one. Others write notes on each area and speak from those. One or two 'old hands' can produce an excellent unscripted broadcast just talking off the weather chart and into the microphone.

Informal local radio stations tend to prefer a 'chatty' question and answer format. This is nerve-racking for the beginner but perhaps more fun for the experienced broadcaster.

THE PRESS

Newspapers have two great advantages over radio and television for weather coverage. They can show weather maps to which the reader can refer at any time of the day; secondly, they can provide lists of information around Britain and around the world which would make little sense on radio or TV.

On the negative side, in a rapidly changing weather situation they cannot be updated after their deadline in late afternoon or early evening, though with improving technology, deadlines are gradually getting later.

At present, some newspapers are supplied by their weather centre using Fax, some by Telex and some by on-line computer links. And, of course, when severe weather makes the headlines, then journalists descend upon the nearest professional meteorologists, either in person or more commonly by phone.

ON THE ROADS

The direct influence of weather is an obvious one: increased traffic on hot, sunny bank holidays, slow-moving vehicles on wet or foggy days, near-chaos perhaps when a heavy fall of snow occurs just around dawn in winter. These weather effects can be seen against a social pattern of Monday to Friday work, with some extra long-distance commuters at the beginning and end of the week. There are also the patterns of heavy transport, social driving in the evenings, cars at 9 a.m. and 4 p.m., running children to and from school (which are more numerous in wet weather). Many of the jams or slow-downs are inevitable and due simply to demand for car space on the road, with the weather an exacerbating factor.

On the other hand, for those whose job it is to maintain our roads, the weather is crucial. In summer they need dry conditions to repair or 'top-dress' the road with chippings. Rain or extreme heat can prevent the chippings from binding properly. Very cold weather may call for a special mix of asphalt on a major re-laying job.

In winter, the county council (or Scottish regional council) road maintenance engineer has a decision to make each afternoon on 'whether to salt'. This is an operation which can cost the county £20,000 for one night. After studying the forecast supplied under contract from a local weather centre, the engineer may decide to stand-down staff if a mild night is expected, to do a 'pre-salt' or precautionary salting if frost is expected, or to initiate a major effort to get as much salt down on the road as possible if snow is coming.

There are sometimes more subtle choices such as delaying the decision until 11 p.m. or calling for an early morning salt run before the traffic increases next day. Alternatively, if the roads have been treated the night before and the weather has continued dry then much salt will remain on the surface and the gritting lorries need not go out again despite a forecast of frost.

Rock salt comes from Cheshire and East Germany at a bulk price of around £25 per ton. A low spread-rate is used (except for snow) to minimise corrosion of bridges and damage to the environment. Alternative de-icing agents are more costly.

During the 1980s, many county councils and Scottish regions started installing road sensors (a special kind of thermometer which is about the size of small book) into the surface of major routes to measure the road surface temperature. Along with routine meteorological readings from a roadside weather station, this information is relayed in real time both to their headquarters and to the local weather centre. Using the road temperature readings, the salting decisions can be updated.

The road sensors enable the forecasters to check on the accuracy of their work day by day. An error of 1.5 C (2.7 F) is typical for a forecast issued 18 hours ahead of road surface temperature, but even a small error like this can be important when temperatures are close to freezing-point. Sometimes one stretch of road in a frost hollow may develop ice when other areas are clear, so every winter night a decision has to be made which balances caution against wasted money. Many people will be ready to criticise road engineer and weather forecaster alike.

RAILWAY WEATHER

Railways are usually less affected by the weather than road users, but there is still a wide range of impacts from various weather parameters.

In summer, high temperatures can cause the rails themselves to expand and perhaps to buckle, though engineers are gradually overcoming this problem. The little gaps left between sections of rail allow for some expansion and many of our lines now have a different system of continuous welded rails, but the problem can still occur. The new continuous rails are first laid and then subsequently stretched so that they are under tension, which will allow for a certain amount of heating by the Sun. They are particularly susceptible during the period of up to a few days between being laid and being put under tension. During this time, if weather forecasts indicate that high temperatures are likely, the track will be inspected regularly to make sure that no buckling is occurring.

Another possible summer hazard for the railway engineer is heavy rain, which apart from causing flooding can affect the electrical wires of the signalling system. Lightning too can disrupt the power supplies to electrical lines.

Winter is more of a problem time with gales, snow and ice. Gales affect the overhead electric lines, especially on our upland moorlands where the wind blows unabated. Here too, snow or rime ice can build up on gantries and wires. Gales may also blow down trees, fences and garden sheds, all of which can end up across the track causing delays. This happened after the 16 October 1987 gale and disrupted diesel-hauled lines which would otherwise have been all right. The electrified lines were, of course, unavoidably put out of action for a time by power cuts.

Snow, when it drifts, can cover low-lying sections of track and in bad cases can completely fill a cutting. This may sound like an exaggeration but for upland routes across Shap Fell, the Settle to Carlisle railway and various Scottish lines this is a real hazard. Ploughing the snow clear is possible for moderate cases, but if the worst comes to the worst, then it is better to be stuck in a train than a car.

Ice is a major nuisance to those electrified lines around London which use the 'third rail' system of electrical pick-up. A good contact must be maintained between the electrified rail which is several inches off the ground and the metal of the pick-up shoe on the train. Ice on the conductor rail can prevent this proper contact and cause jerky running, damage or even a total standstill. Freezing rain or freezing drizzle which solidify on impact are much worse than the more common hoar frost. Even our underground railway trains come out in the open to face this hazard on winter mornings. De-icing trains can be run to prevent or disperse ice build-up, but like so many remedies this is not cheap.

The final weather problems thrown at the railway system are those which affect the passengers who slip on the pavement, arrive late at the station and leave their umbrellas on the train. Next day they leave their season ticket behind at home in their raincoat and then complain that the train is too cold!

SEA TRANSPORT

A sea journey of a week across the Atlantic, or of a month via the Cape of Good Hope to Japan, will usually commence whenever the vessel is ready to sail. Any savings come from routeing the ship slightly to one side or the other of the usual 'great circle' route in order to avoid storms. A vessel sailing from Europe to Canada which would intercept a major low can be diverted slightly further north to make use of the easterly winds around the depression's northern flank. Tropical cyclones are well worth avoiding! Occasionally there may be a benefit from reduced insurance premiums in using· a ship-routeing service. After initial guidance before sailing, further messages are relayed by radio during passage.

One cannot mention sea transport without acknowledging the tremendous contribution which coastguards, lighthouse keepers and seafarers make towards day-to-day meteorology by sending in their weather observations.

AIR TRANSPORT

Modern commercial jet aircraft designs are very slowly making progress towards the ultimate goal of being weather-immune. Already there are systems which enable them to land in moderate fog (though they may not be able to taxi around the airport, and their potential passengers may be stranded on the motorway). They can land in snow and with a moderate crosswind – even on a wet runway. For scheduled services a 'problem with low cloud' suggests a very low cloud-base of 100 ft (30 m) rather than anything run-of-the-mill. Airline pilots will brief themselves with TAFs (i.e. Terminal Airfield Forecasts) for their destination and a nearby alternative airfield before taking off. During the climb and descent phases, icing is less of a problem than it used to be, turbulence is rarely anything more than a nuisance which requires the passengers to be strapped in, or spills their coffee. (Many of these subjects are covered in greater detail in the forecasting section of the book.)

Headwinds and tailwinds are of particular interest to the Civil Aviation Authority and to the airlines, since they determine the amount of fuel required. Upper air temperatures are also needed since they affect the efficiency of the engines. The world's airlines save hundreds of millions of pounds per annum by using forecast upper winds and temperatures for the entire globe which are supplied by high-speed computer-to-computer links from Bracknell (known for this purpose as 'London') and from Washington. These two world centres act as emergency relief for each other in the event of computer or communications failure. They also have a 12-hour-old back-up forecast available from previous calculations, so this is a belt-and-braces operation.

THE WATER INDUSTRY

Now split into the National Rivers Authority and the water companies, these industries are ultimately dependent on rainfall.

Whilst the NRA is interested in avoiding flooding, it also hopes for sufficient rain to avoid low water levels and the exacerbation of pollution. Forecasts of rainfall out to five days ahead can help it fulfil its duties.

The water supply companies get their water from rivers, reservoirs and boreholes. Their domestic customers expect a continuous stream of good-quality water, and consume far more during hot, sunny weather in the summer half-year. Forecasts therefore mainly relate to the consumption requirements rather than to the source of the water. Only rivers react really quickly (typically 12 to 24 hours) to rainfall. Reservoirs may take weeks to be recharged and ground water held in porous rocks such as chalk will take months to recharge. If rain should fall during a hot, dry August, then the water companies breathe a sigh of relief. However, in the main, it is not because of the replenishment of their sources, but because demand drops. Hardly anyone will water the garden or wash the car during rain.

THE GENERAL PUBLIC

Here is a huge section of weather forecast users who are, quite reasonably, non-paying customers. (In Europe, we are not attuned to the idea of paying for information; the United States is slightly different in this respect.) Many people get the information they require from the newspapers, radio or television. For those occasions when someone wants an immediate answer for any region of the country, there are also the premium-rated telephone services such as Weathercall. This type of forecast has improved over the years, and now the technology enables the recording always to start at the beginning of the forecast, regardless of where the previous caller finished. One potential problem though is that the forecaster who writes the script does not know who the end user will be – photographers, dinghy sailors, those wondering about a barbecue or a day at the coast. Certain basic information, such as wind strength, is therefore always included apart from the obvious wet, showery or dry prediction.

Chapter 11

CLIMATE CHANGE

INTRODUCTION TO CLIMATE CHANGE

CLIMATE CHANGES may be natural or the result of human activities. These activities can be divided into those which deliberately change the weather, for instance using aircraft to spray clouds to induce rain, and those whose effect on the climate is unintentional, such as the release of gases into the atmosphere. It is ironic that this latter category has the greatest effect, whilst our attempts to induce rain are virtually fruitless.

We shall start by looking at natural causes. After all, as we saw in Chapter 1, it was only 15,000 years ago that much of Northern Europe was covered in ice, and the melting that followed had a natural cause. Until scientists understand the natural causes of the ice ages and other climate changes they cannot predict the future.

OUR 'CONSTANT' SUN

Since it is the Sun which drives the 'heat engine' of the atmosphere, then this must be the first place to look for the cause of climate changes. If your car engine is speeding up and then slowing down, do you not enquire whether there are fluctuations in the fuel supply? Is the Sun burning just as brightly now as it was 15,000 years ago? There is no way of being certain, but measurements made during this century do not suggest any significant change in the Sun. Minor differences between this year's readings and last year's may be put down to tiny instrumental errors.

The average amount of heat reaching the outside of the Earth's atmosphere is known as the Solar Constant. The very title implies that it is not changing! Amusingly, every few years the official Solar Constant does change when a new and more accurate series of measurements is completed. The value is around 1360 watts per square metre. This is the amount of heat which would be received on the Earth with the Sun vertically overhead if the atmosphere was totally transparent and cloud-free.

If the Sun does vary significantly over a period of, say, 100,000 years, then that would have tremendous significance for the Earth's climate, and could totally explain the ice ages. However, astronomers in general do not believe that such variations have occurred.

SUNSPOTS

Every 9 to 13 years, say 11 years on average, there is an increased frequency of sunspots which lasts for a year or two. The next sunspot peak is expected around the year AD 2000 or just after.

Sunspots are irregular dark blotches on the surface of the Sun which are occasionally visible with the naked eye when the Sun's disc is seen through low cloud or early morning fog. (It is not advisable to look directly at the Sun as it is potentially damaging to the eyes.) Astronomers project the image of the Sun onto a card or screen which is then photographed so that the number of sunspots and their total area can be measured. Individual spots last for a few days or even weeks. These dark areas are cooler, but perversely they occur when the Sun is in an active phase with solar flares more common. The net result is of remarkably little change in the Solar Constant. Though the proportions of infra-red and ultra-violet energy may change slightly, the total amount of heat reaching the Earth does not appear to alter significantly (i.e. by more than about one part in 1000). Therefore, logically, if we are still receiving the same amount of heat as usual then the sunspots presumably do not affect our weather. Researchers have hunted high and low through past records to try to discover increases or decreases in rainfall or temperature every 11 years, but without any totally convincing evidence. What seems to work in one tiny corner of the Earth proves to be irrelevant in many other places, and could therefore be written off as chance. Certainly, every 11 years or so, aurorae and radio interferences become more common as the Sun becomes more active, but we don't know if these effects in the high atmosphere feed down into the weather-making zone of the atmosphere.

A further complication is that the Sun's magnetic field reverses every sunspot cycle, so some researchers claim that we should be looking for a 22-year cycle, but again the evidence for any regular weather fluctuation is weak. However, before we abandon the sunspot theory altogether, we must look further back in history.

The Chinese have been recording sunspots for over 2000 years and this has provided a marvellously long record. Sunspots seem to have been less common around AD 1400–1700, which is roughly the period of the Little Ice Age, so perhaps there is something in the theory after all.

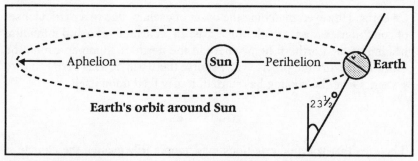

Some of the variable features of our orbit around the Sun which Milankovitch calculated might be important for causing climatic changes. The date of perihelion (closest approach to the Sun) currently occurs in January. Our angle of tilt is currently 23.5 degrees.

THE MILANKOVITCH THEORY

The Yugoslavian scientist Milankovitch did not originate this idea, but it was he who did many of the calculations which brought it to prominence. The Earth's orbit is not the simple, permanently repeating journey around the Sun which we might imagine, and there are three changing components. First of all the angle at which the Earth is tilted on its axis (currently 23.5°) is not fixed. This present arrangement means that the Sun reaches the overhead position on the Tropic of Cancer at 23.5°N (21 June) and the Tropic of Capricorn at 23.5°S (21 December). In the past the Sun has reached beyond 24° or fallen short of 23°. This makes the seasons more pronounced or less pronounced as the cycle progresses.

Another change concerns the orbit. We do not carve out a circular path around the Sun but an oval ellipse. But this is not always the same shape, at some stages being more elongated and at other times more circular.

Thirdly, since the Earth is not a constant distance from the Sun, it follows that there must be a particular date at which we are closest. This date is currently 3 January which happens to be during the northern hemisphere's winter, but over thousands of years this will change, so eventually it will fall in our summer. At the moment, therefore, the great landmasses of Eurasia and North America get slightly more warmth from the Sun in winter than is 'usual'.

Each of these three variations in the Earth's relationship to the Sun is small, but together they seem to be significant. But why should scientists be prepared to accept this theory of ice ages without solid proof? These three variations – tilt, stretch and roll – have a great attraction as the explanation for ice ages in that they produce a complex but regular series of changes which can explain a *series* of ice ages rather than just one ice age. Also, they seem to be at least partially supported by the evidence from ice cores. However, matching the onset of each ice age to a particular set of conditions, say a large tilt of the axis, an elongated orbit and minimum heating of the northern hemisphere in the northern summer, cannot be expected to work out precisely. Of course there will be a lag in the climate system. Once the cooling has started, it may feed upon itself.

VOLCANOES

The idea that volcanic eruptions may temporarily change the climate is well established. It would be wrong, however, simply to link famous eruptions with cooler spells without examining the process involved. The Vesuvius eruption in 79 BC, which overwhelmed Pompeii with lava, or the Mount St Helens eruption in western USA in AD 1980 are famous, but by no means the worst climatically speaking. What is significant is the amount of fine volcanic dust blown into the stratosphere, i.e. reaching 15 to 30 km (10 to 20 miles). Lava, pumice and coarse ash can devastate the area around the volcano but it will not last long in the air. Dust in the lowest part of the atmosphere will be deposited or washed out by rain quite readily. We are talking about particles roughly 1 micrometre (a millionth of a metre) across and thus invisible to the naked eye, which have such a tiny fall-speed that they can persist in the stratosphere. Tambora in Indonesia (1815). Coseguina in Nicaragua (1835) and El Chichon in Mexico (1982) are little-known eruptions but produced notable dust veils. Coseguina, for example, produced 20 cubic kilometres of dust (about 5 cubic miles) which was ten times as much as Mount St Helens.

In 1883, the island of Krakatoa exploded, with its dust producing at least two years of vivid sunsets. For a time the Moon even looked blue to some observers in the northern hemisphere. Attempts have been made to produce an ongoing dust-veil index for each eruption. A typical drop in temperature after some major eruptions seems to be 0.5 C (almost 1 F) world-wide for a year or so. However El Chichon, and maybe some other eruptions, were not followed by cooling. Possibly the climate effect differs according to the type of material ejected into the stratosphere as well as depending upon the location of the volcano. For the first few months the main effect would be in the hemisphere where the eruptions happened. The dust would spread around the globe, intercepting a small proportion of the Sun's heat, and gradually extending into the other hemisphere. An Iceland eruption, like those of 1783, would be less effective, since a large proportion of the dust would have been deposited before reaching the tropics where the climatic damage is more readily done.

One eruption, however vast, would not seem able to cause a prolonged cooling sufficient to extinguish the dinosaurs or cause an ice age. The

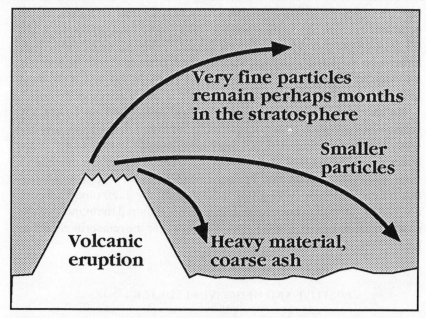

Volcanic eruptions can make the Earth slightly cooler, particularly after explosive eruptions where very fine dust is ejected into the stratosphere.

question is whether a few really cold years could produce an increase in lying snow which reflected more of the Sun's summer heat and therefore started off a cooling process which fed upon itself. In other words, we need a positive feedback loop – something which builds a small initial change into a lasting shift of climate. Volcanoes are a possible but by no means the most likely cause of climate change.

Thin volcanic dust layers have been found in ice cores from Greenland and in sediments elsewhere on Earth which help to date the strata (of ice or of rock). Whether volcanic dust plays a significant role in climate change or not, the dust layers are very useful for dating other evidence.

'Nuclear winter' is the name given to the sort of climatic shift which could happen if a major war involving many nuclear weapons occurred. Assuming that the nuclear explosions were ground bursts, which cause dust and also ensuing fire (which themselves add smoke to the atmosphere), then the final result could be a far greater cooling than volcanoes could cause.

METEORITES AND OTHER SPACE PHENOMENA

Perhaps the variation in the amount of heat reaching the Earth is not due to changes in the Sun itself, but to another space phenomenon. Meteorites are lumps of stone, sometimes very rich in iron or nickel, which occasionally reach the Earth's surface. Many more burn up on entry into the atmosphere thereby contributing to minute dust particles aloft. Huge hollows on the Earth's surface, such as the Barringer Crater in Arizona, are evidence of large meteorites hitting the earth. In the past, there must have been explosive impacts which resulted in much atmospheric dust.

On the Moon, with no atmosphere, no erosion and no longer any volcanic activity, such craters last virtually for ever. On the Earth they are eroded away and obliterated, but there is evidence of an even larger, older crater near Hudson Bay, so the Earth has been struck by sizeable bodies from space in the distant past. Perhaps one of these threw up so much dust that it caused a major cooling which finished off the dinosaurs. However, it would be difficult to imagine an impact every hundred thousand years or so which caused a series of ice ages. This is where the meteorite theory of ice ages tends to stumble.

POSITIVE AND NEGATIVE FEEDBACK LOOPS

Many of the proposed mechanisms for climate change have a short-term effect but cannot explain a cooling process which continues for a thousand years and starts an ice age. Many of the theories require that once the event has happened, be it volcanic eruption, meteorite or solar fluctuation, the process continues on its own.

A notable feedback loop is the one where a really cold winter leaves lying snow much further south than usual over North America and Eurasia. Snow has a high albedo, that is a high reflectivity, and during the following summer much of the Sun's heat is reflected so that some of the snow survives on uplands and in the more northern latitudes. One more snowy winter and the process is under way. Cold produces cold, and this is a positive feedback, since it enhances the original climatic shift.

Similarly, an initial warming which allowed ice to melt in the Arctic margins could allow further warming of the seas so that it did not re-form in the following winter, thus resulting in another example of a positive feedback loop.

By contrast, negative feedback extinguishes or reduces the change which started it, like the thermostat in a centrally heated house which turns off the boiler. A simple example of negative feedback in the atmosphere is the suggestion that if the Earth started getting warmer, more evaporation would occur from the oceans, causing more cloud, which would arrest the warming process. Many of the proposed loops are only 'kite-flying' suggestions and in reality just would not work, but they are difficult to prove or disprove. Computer simulations of these loops rely on so many estimates. For example: How much sunlight would be reflected from a typical six-month-old snow surface at latitude 50°N in summer-time? How much of the Sun's heat would be intercepted by the stratosphere if it were carrying an extra cubic kilometre of dust? Who knows? It depends on the size of the dust particles, amongst many other things.

One can come up with some quite surprising suggestions by apparently sound scientific arguments. A case can be made by which a warming of the Earth causes the world's sea level to *fall*. If it becomes slightly warmer then the atmosphere can hold more moisture. In the Antarctic, where most of the precipitation is of snow, the increased snowfall will add to the all-important Antarctic icecap and the result of global warming will therefore be a net accumulation of ice and a fall in sea level. This is a perverse argument, contradicting both the obvious logic and the evidence of the last 15,000 years, when rising sea levels coincided with increasing warmth. Nevertheless, it is a warning that we should not always jump to the obvious conclusion. In reality some of the interactions might be very complicated, for example with melting land-ice causing a drop in salinity at the ocean surface around the ice caps and thereby allowing earlier autumn ice formation. The relationship between the atmosphere, the oceans and the ice or land surface of the Earth is almost infinitely complex. Not until we have computer models which accurately simulate every important process will we understand all the feedback loops. That time is a long way off. A more complex example relates to a 'conveyor belt' discovered in the oceans. This brings warm water from the Pacific and Indian oceans to the Atlantic. It has been suggested that climate changes might cut off this flow of warm water and possibly slow down the greenhouse warming in the North Atlantic regions.

Oceans and atmosphere are inextricably linked. You cannot study one without the other. The 'cryosphere' or realm of ice should also be added as a third element in the scientific threesome.

CONDENSATION TRAILS AND CHANGES IN CLOUDINESS

Even the effect of cloud amounts on climate is not clear. You might think that cloudier weather would be cooler, but it is not that simple. Cloud is a cooling influence during the day-time, but a warming influence at night when it acts like a blanket. A cloudy winter in northern latitudes will probably be a mild one, but a sunny summer will be a hot one, so it also depends on the time of year. An increase in high cloud certainly has a net warming effect on the Earth, but suggestions that high cloud has in-creased during this century are dubious. Observations from professional meteorological observers do show more high cloud in recent years, but this increase could just be a reflection of increased training: on a sunny summer day very thin wispy cirrus cloud may be present in the sky, so the observer will report perhaps 6 oktas (i.e. three-quarters of the sky covered) when a member of the general public would have said it was a cloudless sky. Observers half a century ago with less training might have sent in a different report and the apparent increase in high cloud could be a total myth. On the other hand, there is undeniably an increase in aircraft condensation trails, some of which persist for many hours and effectively form high cloud. After an hour or two it is difficult to tell whether or not the cloud is natural, and either way, it can affect the weather.

The truth is that we do not know if the increasing warmth during this century has caused more cloud or has been caused by it. We do not know whether human activity is responsible. We cannot even be sure if cloud amounts have increased.

Those who are trying to model the greenhouse effect have got a major problem in simulating clouds. Many more measurements are needed from the ground and from satellites. These will gradually help us to understand what is going on. Good measurements and observations are usually the first step towards scientific understanding.

EL NIÑO EVENTS

Over the centuries scientists, phenologists (those who study plant life and keep records of the flowering dates of plants, etc.) and others who try to predict the future have searched for cycles in the weather. An 11-year cycle linked to sunspots was an obvious starting-point, though with disappointing results. Cases exist of four- or five-year cycles in nature, for example in Scandinavian lemmings and in the snowy owls which feed on them, but these increases in population have not been linked to climate. They appear to be a natural population growth followed by a lack of food and then a population crash. In nature some broad-leafed trees are claimed to have an ill defined two-year cycle with more fruit or nuts in alternate years. In the 1960s there was considerable interest in a theory of a two-year cycle in British weather, which appeared to give us better summers in the odd-numbered years than in even years. However, 1976 and other recent examples have tended to undermine this idea. If we do claim to discover climatic cycles, we cannot be happy until we have found an external cause (e.g. changes in the Sun's output) or an internal feedback system which operates on the appropriate time scale.

Areas of unusually warm air will perhaps last for only a few days and are easily dispersed by the winds, but the surface temperature of the ocean is much slower to change and anomalies can persist over huge areas for months and even years. Such an anomaly occurs irregularly on a two- to seven-year cycle in the Pacific, just west of South America.

Peruvian fishermen have long known that around Christmas a weak warm coastal current affects their catches, and they called this phenomenon 'El Niño' (pronounced 'el neenyo' and Spanish for 'the boy child'). Every few years however, on an irregular basis, the water is *much* warmer than usual, the fish are scarce and scientists now describe this as an 'El Niño event'. Sea surface temperatures are sometimes 4 C (7 F) above average. This encourages low-pressure systems and rising air, which flows westward at high altitude and then descends near Southeast Asia, returning in a loop towards the Peruvian coast at lower levels. This 'reversed Walker cell' is operating in the opposite direction to the normal flow. Winds, though, affect ocean currents and this wind regime can maintain a supply of warm water to the Peruvian coast and thus maintain the El Niño. Eventually however a combination of currents deep in the ocean and maybe winds far afield provide a negative feedback whereby the process, once started, will destroy itself within a few years. The oceans affect the atmosphere; and the atmosphere, mainly via the winds, affects the oceans.

The influence of El Niño is spread far and wide, with variations in rainfall in Australia and other tropical areas, and some effects in temperate latitudes especially America. The warmer-than-usual ocean covers such a large area that it shows up in global temperature averages. The opposite case of cold seas near Peru is sometimes known as 'La Niña' (pronounced 'la neenya' and Spanish for 'the girl child').

CLOUD SEEDING

One of the few deliberate attempts to change the weather has been the seeding of clouds with chemicals to induce rain. Other attempts, such as the dispersal of fog at airfields by burning oil to raise the temperature have been even more localised, though this latter operation was a quite common procedure in the Second World War. Cloud seeding became popular in the 1950s and 1960s in dry regions of the Earth for crop irrigation.

An aircraft would take off with a cargo of silver iodide or of dry ice (solid carbon dioxide). The pilot searched for a suitable large cumulus cloud over the crop-growing area and released the chemicals into the cloud top. The introduction of the chemicals acted like a catalyst and induced the supercooled water droplets in the cloud to turn to ice. Ice crystals would then grow quickly and start falling. Once started, the normal cloud

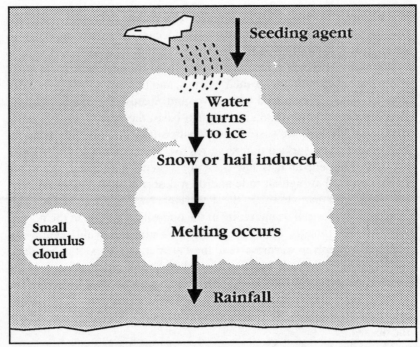

An aircraft seeds a large cumulus cloud (perhaps with silver iodide) to try to induce rainfall.

process took over (hence the expression 'seeding') and produced a shower which would fall as rain at the Earth's surface and thus benefit the crops growing in this marginal, perhaps semi-desert area. Roughly speaking, the seeding turned a cumulus cloud into a cumulonimbus.

So much for the theory, but reality was somewhat less rosy. Cloud seeding could only be carried out when suitable large cumulus clouds were present; the chemicals were expensive; the shower might not fall quite where it was needed. Further studies of the effectiveness of such programmes in Australia, Israel and the USA opened up the argument even further. Showery rain is, by its very nature, patchy in occurrence and it was difficult to prove that any extra rainfall had been induced, even when compared with similar but unseeded areas.

During the Vietnam War, the seeding technique was used by the USA to try to increase the rainfall along the Ho Chi Minh Trail by which the Vietcong were supplied and reinforced. The two rainy seasons in which this systematic attempt was made were wetter than average but still within the normal year-to-year variations, so the evidence of effectiveness was inconclusive. Hurricane seeding to try to reduce the strength of the system before landfall is a similar idea and has now been discarded.

Reference must also be made to related techniques which have attempted to forestall heavy hail by firing chemical-laden rockets or artillery shells. Here, the intention was to trigger the cloud into precipitating before it was naturally ready to do so, with the result that rain or small hail fell rather than large, damaging hailstones. The Soviet Union has tried this method quite widely but without convincing evidence of success.

MAJOR SCHEMES

During this century there have been several serious suggestions about the use of ice, water and land resources. One scheme was to tow an iceberg from the Antarctic to the Arabian Gulf where it would provide a much-needed source of fresh water. Such icebergs are of almost pure water, being formed from accumulated snow. (Even the smaller pieces of ice which form from the freezing of sea-water leave most of the salt behind in the freezing process.) Apart from needing several nuclear-powered tugs to handle it, the iceberg would leave a plume of cold water behind along its route and would have a pronounced effect on the area of the Gulf where it was grounded and used.

Another suggestion designed to lengthen the growing season in the northern Soviet Union was to spread soot on the snow surface in the spring. This would allow it to absorb more of the Sun's heat instead of reflecting it, and thus melting would be more rapid. Crops could be planted earlier to enjoy an extended growing season.

As with most of these major ideas, there would be knock-on effects. If the temperature were higher, then the pressure patterns and the winds would change. Jet streams would be slightly diverted. Increased rainfall would affect some areas whilst others would miss out. If a neighbouring country had a poor harvest they would undoubtedly blame the project, whether it was truly responsible or not. No one would be able to say what would have happened if the scheme had not been put into effect, because one abnormal year could be put down to chance. Even if it was repeated for several years running, it would be impossible to say if any systematic changes had resulted – after all, the climate might have changed anyway!

INLAND SEAS AND LAKES

Many of the world's middle- and low-latitude lakes are drying up, from Lake Chad to California. Much of this is a natural process which seems to have been going on for several thousand years. However, during this century, rivers have been dammed or heavily used for irrigation purposes and this has exacerbated the problem. The Aral Sea in Soviet Central

Asia is a prime example. Water from the Amu Darya and Syr Darya, which feed it, have been used to irrigate the cotton fields of Uzbekistan. However, evaporation from the inland sea continues, so there is a net loss of water. The level of the Aral sea has dropped 13 m (40 ft) in the last 20 years or so and former fishing ports are left totally dry, many miles from the receding shoreline. Huge areas of increasingly salty sand are exposed and air quality has decreased due to the combination of salt, dust, fertiliser and crop sprays, resulting in an increase in infant mortality.

One suggested solution has been to divert some of the water of major northward-flowing Asian rivers southwards to supplement the Aral Sea. Unfortunately this would deprive the Arctic Ocean of part of its supply of fresh water, and the balance between fresh and salty water is important for ice formation – fresh water is less dense and tends to lie on top of saline sea-water. Soviet scientists argued long and hard over the possible impacts of this scheme, which is now shelved. Cotton production has been reduced and efforts made to clean up local industry. It might be thought that a reduced Aral Sea would mean less evaporation and therefore less rainfall in this 'weather-kitchen' region of Central Asia, but of course the irrigated crops will also 'push' water into the air to a greater extent than the semi-desert land surface would have done in their absence. More water vapour will evaporate from a thousand square kilometres of irrigated crops than from a hundred square kilometres of lake. On the other hand, if the lake should dry up *and* the irrigations ceases, both sources of atmospheric moisture would be cut off and this could mean a reduction in rainfall.

Elsewhere in the Soviet Union, the level of the Caspian Sea had been falling, but has now stabilised. Further east, Lake Baikal is over 1500 m (5000 ft) deep, contains almost a fifth of the fresh-water on the Earth and is relatively unspoilt. Its importance and value are now recognised.

California and other parts of western USA face the same kind of water-resource problems, though fortunately with higher rainfall on the nearby mountains and smaller distances involved. Demand for water per head of population is very high in California, and people who have enjoyed a seemingly limitless supply find it difficult to react to reductions.

By and large, artificial lakes in the desert, such as Lake Nasser, which was created by the Aswan Dam in Upper Egypt, have little effect on the local climate, and it is much larger areas of changing land use which are the significant meteorological factors.

THE WATER CYCLE AND THE RAIN-FORESTS

If we could analyse the column of atmosphere above our head, we would find that it contains enough water to make 25 mm (1 inch) of rain, which is typically about 12 days' rainfall. It follows that a constant supply of water vapour must be replacing that lost from the air in rainfall, and this leads us to re-examine the water cycle of the atmosphere. Water vapour evaporates from the oceans and moist land surfaces, and on some subsequent occasion condenses into cloud droplets. Rain may then fall on the land areas of the world, but rivers and ground water eventually take the water back to the ocean, thus completing the cycle. Although 70% of the Earth is ocean, where evaporation continues almost unabated, there is also an important source of atmospheric moisture onshore. Apart from the obvious evaporation of dew and puddles, plants 'breathe out' moisture which they have mainly taken in through their roots. This transpiration is a very effective mechanism, and a square kilometre of moist, 'steamy', tropical rain-forest can push more water vapour into the atmosphere than a square kilometre of ocean. (It has, with its many leaves, a larger total surface area.) This moisture will be somebody else's rainfall.

RAIN-FOREST DESTRUCTION

When large areas of forest are felled in the Amazon Basin, in Southeast Asia or Central America, the cleared land is less effective at converting ground water into atmospheric water vapour. After rainstorms, the run-off is rapid and the limited vegetation is shallower rooted and less tall. Thus land clearance can induce a feedback mechanism whereby less rain falls either in that vicinity or elsewhere. It may well be that other factors such as large areas of warmer-than-average or cooler-than-average sea surface temperatures are more important in bringing drought to marginal semi-desert areas of the world, but a reduction in transpiration is likely to be detrimental. Rain-forest destruction can therefore contribute to desertification elsewhere, as well as causing local soil erosion.

Even more important than the water cycle is the effect upon the carbon dioxide content of the air. Trees remove carbon dioxide from the air, whereas burning them increases the atmospheric content. Therefore burning the forests is a double blow to the greenhouse effect.

In a meteorological sense, this trend of forest clearance could be quite quickly reversed if the political will were present. The tropical rain-forest areas can regenerate growth very quickly. That this regeneration will not bring a return to the original diversity of plant and animal life is important, though outside the meteorological argument.

CFCs AND THE OZONE HOLE

CFCs are chlorofluorocarbons, chemical compounds which are used in air conditioners and refrigerators as a coolant, in foam packaging, spray cans (decreasingly now) and as solvents for cleaning electrical components.

They can be released into the atmosphere when a refrigerator is broken up, when a can of hairspray is used or when packaging is crushed among other refuse. Also, some escapes to the atmosphere during the manufacture of these and other products. The amounts of gas produced are small but they have a long life in the atmosphere, probably about a century, and they react with ozone high above the Earth's surface. They are responsible for a 'hole' in the ozone layer above the Antarctic, though the expressions 'weak area' or 'thin patch' would be more appropriate. Some other chlorine-based compounds do the same sort of damage. (Ozone produced at street level is poisonous but high in the atmosphere it is a vital natural constituent of the air.)

The first indications of decreasing ozone came from measurements made by British Antarctic Survey scientists working at Halley Bay. Other readings made in the northern hemisphere have suggested a very slight decrease here too.

So why is the ozone layer important? Situated in the stratosphere some 10 to 60 km (6 to 36 miles) up from the Earth's surface, it is mainly above the altitude where high-flying aircraft travel. The atmosphere here is very thin with a pressure less than one-tenth of that at the Earth's surface. The radiation from the Sun arrives here and reacts with the molecules of oxygen (O_2). Some of these split up and the free atoms combine with oxygen molecules to form ozone (O_3). But it is not just a production process, for the ozone molecules too will split and revert to oxygen, so there is a constant process of formation and decay in the ozone layer. CFCs interfere with this process. The importance of ozone is that it intercepts a significant proportion of the ultra-violet radiation arriving from the Sun. Ultra-violet constitutes only a tiny proportion of the Sun's incoming energy but it is potentially harmful to humans, causing an increased risk of cataracts and skin cancer. The distribution of ozone in the stratosphere has not been fully documented. It varies with time of day, with the season of the year and in different latitude bands. In the Antarctic, it has a two-year cycle with the ozone hole worse in alternate years.

Scientists have a lot of ground to cover before full explanations are available and the possible consequences for crops, for humans and for the atmosphere can be analysed. Environmental groups have successfully pressed for a ban on CFCs. The USA led the way in this respect with legislation in the 1970s, then in 1987 an international meeting was held in Montreal at which considerable progress was made towards implementing a wider reduction in CFC use. Now a total ban is in sight, though unfortunately production will continue for a time, and then further escape into the air will follow unless refrigerator disposal, etc., is properly organised. The CFCs will continue their damage for many years, perhaps for a century.

CITY POLLUTION

The urban heat island is quite noticeable, as we have seen, but it is air pollution which really creates concern in our cities. This is a problem which came to public notice with the smogs in London and elsewhere in the winters of the 1940s and particularly in December 1952, caused mainly by coal burning in private homes and in power stations. Not for nothing was Edinburgh known as 'Auld Reekie' (i.e. 'Old Smokey'). The smog problem was thought to have been solved by smokeless zones and by the removal of power stations to the countryside (where pollutants still contribute to acid rain on a continental basis and the greenhouse effect on a worldwide basis, but not to such immediate damage). Now the question of air quality has returned, this time largely thanks to the motor vehicle.

Lead levels can be reduced by using unleaded petrol; poisonous carbon monoxide can be turned into carbon dioxide by catalytic converters. Most of these converters and other technological fixes make the engine just a fraction less efficient and so we actually end up with increased carbon dioxide, thereby contributing a slightly larger amount to the greenhouse effect. And even after the converters have done their work, hydrocarbons and minute particles of soot are emitted into the air. I am not suggesting that unleaded petrol and catalytic converters are pointless, merely that they do not prevent all harmful emissions. More and more technology is one way to help clean up our cities, but burning less petrol is another.

It is difficult for the casual observer, walking out into the street, to tell whether the atmosphere is clean or not. Serious pollution in a city can sometimes be smelt, and people prone to asthma or other respiratory problems may actually feel ill. Usually though, in the absence of measuring equipment, it is visibility which gives the clue to how polluted the air has become. Poor visibility can result either from water droplets in the air (fog) or from high levels of pollution (smoke or haze) but it is usually caused by the *combination* of moisture and tiny particles.

Minute specks of pollutant (nuclei) attract moisture even when the air is not all that damp. Salt is a good example of a natural hygroscopic (i.e. water-attracting) substance, but many of the chemicals that come out of chimneys can do the same. A tiny water droplet will grow around the pollution particle like a dew droplet on a spider's web. Millions of minute polluted water droplets, individually invisible or very close to it, will affect the visibility as we look down a city street or across an urbanised landscape. However, on very hot days, the relative humidity will be low and the air may be much dirtier than it looks.

Much of the improvement achieved in our industrial cities in the 1960s and 1970s is now being reversed by vehicle emissions. The wider global trend has, of course, always been downwards, but we were so pleased at the improvement in our cities that we failed to appreciate the slow world-wide changes.

Drier, sunny cities do not suffer from the wet smogs of middle and high latitudes, but the air pollution is there too, in what are sometimes called 'photochemical smogs'.

Vehicle exhaust fumes are a major source of concern in Los Angeles, Tokyo, Santiago (Chile) and Athens, to name just four. Nor is it just the more affluent countries which are affected – for Cairo, Jakarta and Bangkok suffer too. The moisture content of the air is too low in these hotter climates for visibility to be cut down to a few yards as it was in the London smogs, but vehicle exhaust gases react with the energy supplied by sunlight to form a photochemical smog which is similarly unhealthy, and which incidentally includes ozone! The term 'ground level ozone' distinguishes the unwanted (and poisonous) presence of this gas in our streets from the useful protective ozone layer high in the stratosphere.

The key meteorological factor in the development of all these pollution episodes is calm conditions often linked with an inversion or warm layer just above. Strong winds will blow the exhaust away and dilute it by mixture with clean air from aloft, so on breezy days the air will be clean. For people living in and commuting to cities, perhaps Tokyo's answer of face masks will eventually catch on, although the introduction of integrated transport systems using electrical vehicles would be better, or people could even walk.

ACID RAIN

City pollution is a local problem; acid rain is a continent-wide problem; the greenhouse effect is a world-wide problem. Acid rain was one of the first environmental issues to set government against government, and was responsible some years ago for Britain being dubbed 'the dirty man of Europe'.

Pollution within London in the 1940s was localised and it was largely eliminated by reducing coal-burning in and close to the city. The changeover to taller chimneys on power stations and factories (the 'high-stack policy') and shift to the location of power stations in the countryside largely saved British cities from smogs. As far as Europe is concerned though, the sulphur dioxide and nitrogen oxides are still coming their way.

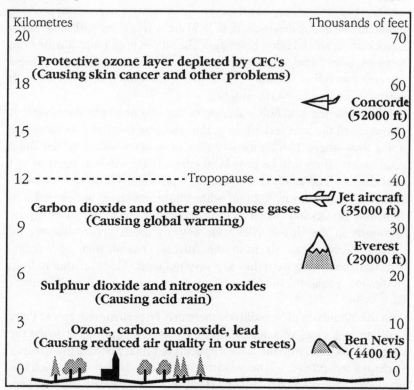

Kilometres / Thousands of feet

20 / 70

Protective ozone layer depleted by CFC's
(Causing skin cancer and other problems)

18 / 60

Concorde (52000 ft)

15 / 50

12 ------------------ Tropopause ---------------- 40

Jet aircraft (35000 ft)

Carbon dioxide and other greenhouse gases
(Causing global warming)

9 / 30

Everest (29000 ft)

6 / 20

Sulphur dioxide and nitrogen oxides
(Causing acid rain)

3 / 10

Ozone, carbon monoxide, lead
(Causing reduced air quality in our streets)

Ben Nevis (4400 ft)

0 / 0

Some of the environmental problems caused by emissions of trace gases and other pollutants.

We call this acid rain, though some of the pollution which drifts along with the wind and is deposited when it is not actually raining.

Many of the pollutants which are wafted away from chimneys and vehicle exhausts by the wind are removed from the atmosphere over the next thousand miles, and various technical terms are used to describe the removal process. At the simplest level, there is 'wet deposition', when rain plays a part, and 'dry deposition' when the pollutants literally fall out of the sky or are intercepted by plants, trees and buildings.

The experts subdivide the true acid rain cases of wet depositions into 'rain-out', when the acidic particles form nuclei for raindrops within the cloud, and 'wash-out' when the pollution particles are floating along below the cloud and are 'zapped' by big raindrops which fall from above. Either way, you get acid rain. Clean rain, which absorbs some gases and is therefore slightly acid, has an acidity measurement (a pH value) of about 5.6. Much of the rain in Europe and northeastern USA has a value around 4.3, which is markedly acid (pH 7 is neutral) – little wonder, then, that limestone statues rot away. The insidious dry deposition also plays a powerful role in this destruction, so 'acid air' works along with acid rain to attack cathedrals and other buildings. The output of sulphur dioxide from factories, power stations, cars and so on can be visualised by picturing a wheelbarrow full of sulphur. This is the typical output in a year for each person in Europe or North America.

Dry deposition is mainly a feature of the area nearer to the source. It continues all the time, relentlessly, though some weather conditions are worse than others. During the day-time in summer with sunshine and a good breeze, there will be little local effect. Light winds at night or just after dawn will generally create more of a problem. Those who study the effluent plumes identify 'lofting', when all the emissions are carried well aloft, and 'fumigation', when an inversion traps them in the lowest layers. Obviously in the British Isles with westerly winds predominating, we usually receive clean air from the Atlantic. Examination of visibility statistics shows that easterlies are very polluted. Much of this is from continental emissions but some of it is from our own pollutants coming back again.

In the mountains of Scandinavia there may be perhaps only two or three really serious cases of acidification in a year. One may occur when the winter snows melt, with the locked up acids of winter flooding the streams. Perhaps a second case will occur with a southwesterly airstream which had previously stagnated over Britain. However, southerly and southeasterly winds from central Europe are also likely to be sucked in just ahead of a rain-bearing front and wash-out is then prodigious, as the air is almost emptied of its pollutants. There are also natural sources of sulphur compounds, such as algal blooms caused by the multiplication of plankton in the oceans.

Trees are undoubtedly dying in some areas of the Alps, and elsewhere in Europe. At first, it was thought to be a straightforward effect of acid rain, then insects were thought to be attacking trees weakened by pollution. Later ideas put some of the blame on ozone caused by air pollution. The further scientists delve into the problem, the more complex and wide-ranging it becomes.

Acid in lakes and rivers is, however, not just from rain. Changing land-use means that coniferous forests are more widespread in some upland areas. Clean rain seeping through such areas may produce acid run-off. Also the link between acidification and the death of fish is not straightforward. The acid rain unlocks aluminium in the soil and rock, and it is this which affects the fish. Adding lime to the lakes counteracts the acidity and provides a short-term solution. Once again the message is that one problem cannot be analysed on its own. Air quality, tree health, insect activity, river-flow, chemical changes in the soil and reaction in fish are all related. Meteorology is just one of the sciences involved in studying ecology.

PRINCIPLE OF THE GREENHOUSE EFFECT

Carbon dioxide has, as we have noted, always been present in the atmosphere. (It may have played a role in past climatic changes by natural variations in its concentration – for example increasing when carbon-rich rocks are weathered or decreasing in the air when dead sea-creatures accumulate on the sea-floor, thereby removing carbon for millions of years until the rocks which they form are once again exposed.)

Since we have had carbon dioxide in the air for billions of years, the greenhouse effect is already at work. The greenhouse gases in our atmosphere already keep the Earth 33 Celsius (about 60 F) warmer than we would otherwise be. When scientists talk about greenhouse warming, what they are really suggesting is that the 33 C might become for example 35 C. We are not starting a new phenomenon, but 'turning up the wick' on an existing process.

For those interested in the exact mechanism, it lies in molecular physics. Just as a light-bulb gives out a different form of energy from a warm radiator, so the Sun (external surface 6000 C) gives out a different form of heat from the Earth. The molecules of carbon dioxide allow through the Sun's radiation, which is at a wavelength of 0.3 to 2.0 micrometres, and they intercept the Earth's radiation which is at wavelengths around 10 to 15 micrometres. Some of the heat from the Earth which is intercepted is then re-radiated upwards but the overall effect is to slow down the rate of cooling. We can imagine that after a long winter night, the dawn temperature would be a little less cold than it would otherwise have been. (In reality we are also losing heat by radiation in the day-time but, during the morning at least more heat is coming in from the Sun than going out so we don't notice it.)

Remember too, that we are not talking solely about carbon dioxide, other man-made gases contribute. Carbon dioxide is aided and abetted by CFCs, methane, nitrous oxide and others, which all contribute to the predicted warming; and here we must add in another surprise – water vapour is also a greenhouse gas, and as such it will give an extra twist to whatever damage the other greenhouse gases cause.

A warmer atmosphere will induce more evaporation and thus more water vapour, so this has to be allowed for in computer forecasts of climate. It is another example of a positive feedback effect. There will also be other feedbacks, some adding to the warming and some slowing it down. No doubt there will be some which have not yet been taken into account.

Another surprise is that the principle of the greenhouse warming was suggested as long ago as 1827 by the mathematician Fourier and developed through the last century by John Tyndall and Svante Arrhenius.

Whilst the name itself does at least suggest the extra warmth inside a greenhouse, perhaps the best analogy is that doubling the carbon dioxide would be like throwing an extra blanket around the Earth. Moreover it is a blanket which will be difficult to throw off once it is in place.

CARBON DIOXIDE SOURCES

Almost everything we burn in quantity contains some carbon. Much of this carbon ends up as the gas carbon dioxide.

In our power stations it is coal, oil and natural gas which are the culprits, just as they are with sulphur dioxide emissions. Factories use power too, and also include chemical and burning processes. Even on the farm vegetation includes carbon and some of this ends up as carbon dioxide when stubble is burnt. Cars burn petrol and the main end products are water vapour and carbon dioxide. None of the current bits of bolt-on technology get rid of the CO_2. Thus our sources are plentiful and have an obvious link with population size and level of prosperity. The more prosperous or 'developed' a country is, the more power, petrol and raw material it uses.

An industrialised country of 50 million people will produce roughly ten times as much carbon dioxide as an industrialised country with 5 million people. France, with 70% of its electricity produced by nuclear stations, is a slight exception. Nuclear power stations do not produce any significant carbon dioxide emissions. As far as the greenhouse effect is concerned, nuclear power is clean (other arguments against it of course exist). Ordinary fossil-fuel power stations are being fitted with equipment to reduce other gases like sulphur dioxide, in order to reduce acid rain. This flue gas desulphurisation makes the power station slightly less efficient, so more coal, oil or gas must be burnt; the result is slightly more carbon dioxide. It would be just feasible to fit further equipment to remove the carbon dioxide, but this would dramatically reduce efficiency and we would end up with other waste products. Opponents of this move say that because the operating efficiency would be almost halved, we would have to build a new power station alongside every existing power station. Also, we would have to find places to dump the waste materials. Whatever exaggerations are involved in the calculations, the idea that more technology can

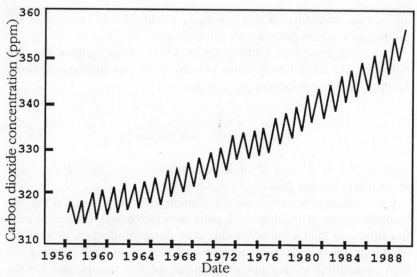

The carbon dioxide content of the air has risen from about 280 parts per million in pre-industrial times to around 350 ppm now. The amount in the air varies during a year because the trees of the northern hemisphere take up carbon dioxide during their growing season, but the general trend is clearly upwards.

solve the problems seems dubious. The attraction of producing less power but using it more efficiently is overwhelming.

WHERE IN THE WORLD . . . ?

A recent report by the World Resources Institute for the United Nations gave a league table showing which countries were contributing most to greenhouse gas emissions. The highest 12 producers were USA followed by USSR, Brazil, China, India, Japan, West Germany, UK, Indonesia, France, Italy and Canada. It showed that the USA was producing 20% of world emissions, the UK 2.7% and Canada 2.0%.

However, this could be a misleading list for it obscures the really interesting question of how much per person? A new league table based on per capita omissions gives a totally different picture. The highest 12 per capita producers were (again in descending order) Canada, Ivory Coast, Brazil, USA, Australia, East Germany, Saudi Arabia, Netherlands, UK, West Germany, USSR and Colombia. They ranged from 4.5 tonnes per person at the top of this list in Canada, through 2.7 tonnes in the UK, down to 2.2. tonnes in Colombia. On this per capita list China (population 1.1 billion) was 24th and India (population 700 million) was 25th with 0.34 and 0.28 tonnes respectively. Contrast these low values in Asia with an average consumer in the developed world who is responsible for producing 3 tonnes per year of carbon dioxide.

The population of the Earth is expected to rise from 5 billion now to 8 billion by AD 2030. Extrapolating present trends, we shall also be using far more fuel and resources per person.

CARBON DIOXIDE 'SINKS'

Carbon dioxide sources are well understood, but we should also think about where the gas goes.

If we measure the carbon dioxide content of the air in a city street, the readings will go up and down with every car which passes. If we measure it in a rural area then it will vary from day to day depending on whether the wind trajectory has taken the air across a nearby town. Only by going to a high mountain in an unpolluted region can we get a true picture. On the quiescent volcano of Mauna Loa in Hawaii, measurements have been made for many years uncontaminated by local industry (or by volcanic gases!) The readings show a fairly steady year-by-year upward trend in the carbon dioxide content of our atmosphere, accelerating rather than slowing in recent decades. There are minor fluctuation each year, notably a drop during the northern hemisphere summer when trees and other vegetation 'breathe in' more carbon dioxide during the growing season.

When calculations are made of the amount of CO_2 being emitted into the air and the rise shown by the Hawaiian measurements, we find that there is a shortfall. Only about half of the CO_2 emitted stays in the atmosphere. There are three billion tonnes per year which go missing and we do not yet know whether that missing carbon ends up in the oceans or is absorbed by trees.

At one time it was assumed that the oceans were absorbing nearly all the missing CO_2, but then that was thrown into doubt. Certainly some enters the ocean, helps the formulation of tiny sea creatures and finally falls to the ocean floor.

But perhaps it is the trees which are removing a significant proportion of it from the air and it remains temporarily 'locked up' in the vegetation. But how long can trees carry on absorbing carbon? When a tree dies naturally, the carbon is gradually released back into the air as it decays. If the tree succumbs to a chain-saw attack and is then burnt, the carbon is released immediately.

As far as the greenhouse threat is concerned it will be good news if it is conclusively proved that the oceans are removing the missing carbon dioxide, because they can (probably?) carry on doing so for millions of years. If it turns out that the trees are playing an important role, then that will be very bad news, for there must be a limit to the amount they can take up.

It will be obvious that we have a very complex balance between absorption and release of carbon dioxide. What is certain though is that coal, oil and gas are fresh sources which we have unlocked. Whatever cushioning effect the oceans and trees are having, there is still a net increase of about three billion tonnes of carbon dioxide each year.

Evidence from Greenland ice cores shows us that at the end of the last ice age the warming was accompanied by an increase of carbon dioxide and a decrease of methyl sulphonic acid – a gas produced by plankton in the oceans. One conclusion is that the multiplication of plankton plays an important role in controlling the greenhouse effect. Now that we are interfering with the atmosphere in an unnatural way, we need to know what effects there will be upon the plankton. We may be relying upon them to stabilise our climate!

GREENHOUSE FEEDBACK MECHANISMS

We have seen that a slight warming of the atmosphere will mean more evaporation from the oceans and so the air will carry more moisture. As water vapour is also a greenhouse gas, more water vapour means a more pronounced greenhouse effect – this is the most obvious positive feedback which carbon dioxide will set going.

Further positive feedback occurs if the sea-ice starts to retreat earlier each spring in the Arctic: less ice means less reflection of the Sun's heat and therefore more heat to be absorbed by the sea.

The role of clouds is again difficult to quantify, but more evaporation does not *necessarily* mean more clouds because a warmer atmosphere can hold more moisture without being saturated. Clouds are therefore one of the big unknown factors. They may cause a negative feedback which slows down the warming, or they might be part of another positive feedback loop.

When the climate changes, the ocean currents inevitably change, so there are bound to be more responses here. We really do not know yet what these will be.

BIOSPHERE 2

Most of the research about future climate will take place using computers, but there is still a place for traditional scientific observation and measurement. Biosphere 2 is a real, live experiment whereby eight people will be sealed inside a 3.5 acre (about 1.5 hectare) glass dome, in Arizona, USA, starting in autumn 1990. Barring medical emergencies, the volunteers will remain in the dome for 2 years, growing their own food, and thereby conducting a mammoth experiment which embraces many disciplines.

The structure is some 180 m (600 ft) long divided internally into residential, farming and wilderness zones. The last-named is by far the largest and part of its function is to help remove from the internal atmosphere the carbon dioxide produced in the residential and farming zones. Amongst other innovations is a scheme for pumping polluted air into the soil where micro-organisms 'scrub' it clean. As Mark Nelson, one of the Biosphere 2 scientists, has commented, 'all those years we have been pumping our dirt into the air and we should have been pumping our air into the dirt'.

The enclosed environment is cut off from Biosphere 1 (which is the remainder of the Earth) and intended to be self-sustaining and self-regulating. Inevitably, comparisons are made with Jim Lovelock's Gaia concept of the Earth. It is hoped that important new discoveries will be made about the relationship between human life, plant life and the atmosphere, some of which may be highly commercial.

OTHER GREENHOUSE GASES

Carbon dioxide is, in tiny amounts, natural to our atmosphere, but is on the increase. It is the classic greenhouse gas but not the only one.

Methane is another gas present in tiny proportions, but the amount in the atmosphere appears to be increasing quite quickly. Its natural sources are rotting vegetation and the digestive systems of large ruminant animals. We have added to the natural output from swamps and peat-bogs by flooding huge areas for the cultivation of rice, and have also vastly increased the number and individual size of cattle. To put it bluntly, when cattle belch or fart, considerable quantities of methane are released – the product of bacterial action in their stomachs.

Nitrous oxide is yet another greenhouse gas, always present naturally as a very minor constituent of the air, which is increased by burning fossil fuels like petrol and by the use of nitrogen-rich fertilisers.

CFCs are not natural and have recently come to prominence because some of them destroy the ozone layer. However, they too are greenhouse gases. Worse still, as we switch away from using CFC 11 and CFC 12 to other CFCs which are non-damaging as far as the ozone layer is concerned, we may in fact be changing to gases which are *worse* for the greenhouse effect. This is another example of a technological fix to one problem causing trouble elsewhere.

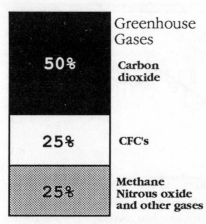

Greenhouse
Gases

**Carbon
dioxide**

CFC's

**Methane
Nitrous oxide
and other gases**

A rough idea of how different gases contribute to the greenhouse effect. There is some doubt about the exact contributions but carbon dioxide and CFCs are certainly important.

Ozone occurs naturally high in the atmosphere in the layer known as the stratosphere, where it is suffering depletion due to CFCs. However, in the traffic-polluted air at lower levels it is on the increase, and in our troposphere it acts like a greenhouse gas.

So we end up with quite a list: carbon dioxide CFCs, methane, nitrous oxide, ozone and other trace gases. Carbon dioxide is about half of the story, and it is convenient when we run computer simulations to talk about an effective 'doubling of carbon dioxide', when what we really mean is doubling the strength of the cocktail. Finally, but very important, the calculations must add in water vapour, which increases as we get warmer and which is itself a greenhouse gas.

THE OBSERVED WARMING

During the first 90 years of this century, world-wide temperatures have risen about 0.5 Celsius (0.9 Fahrenheit). The rise has not been steady, for the northern hemisphere experienced a slight dip in the 1960s and 1970s, but the 1980s were the warmest decade so far. It must be emphasised that those are world-wide values, averaged over land and sea in every latitude and longitude. Any attempt to relate the world values to temperatures in a tiny area of the Earth's land-surface, such as the British Isles, would probably result in confusion. No doubt there are some corners of the globe which have cooled. The warmest year of all was 1988 followed by 1989, 1987, 1983, 1981, 1980 and 1944 in that order.

One of the reasons why the 1980s produced such high values was the well-marked El Niño events in the Pacific. Whether they should be looked on as a special case and the temperature values for the 1980s therefore regarded as anomalous is very questionable. After all it is conceivable that

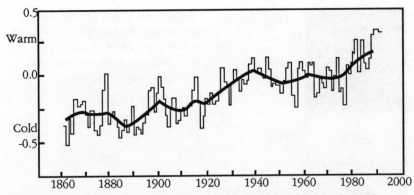

The global temperatures have generally risen during the last 100 years, but with considerable year to year fluctuation. The 1980s have been especially warm but 1944 for example was also a warm year. The solid line represents a smoothed graph of temperature changes. (Source: the Climate Research Unit at the University of East Anglia.)

El Niño could be partially a product of global greenhouse warming rather than a completely separate cyclical event.

There are perhaps two key questions. Are the quoted values of global warming real rather than being caused by systematic instrumental errors? Have we caused the warming by emitting greenhouse gases? The answers to each question are 'probably yes' or 'almost certainly yes' depending upon who you ask.

LAND AND SEA TEMPERATURES

First of all, the higher temperatures of the late twentieth century, and especially of the last decade, need to be examined carefully. The temperatures are calculated by averaging thousands of readings from land and sea. The land values are generally read by a human being from a mercury-in-glass thermometer housed in a louvred screen. Maximum and minimum temperatures are used to estimate the 'average' temperature rather than the values every minute or every hour. What could cause a systematic bias apart from genuine rising temperatures? Perhaps the exact timing of the observations has become earlier each day because the observer knows that all the other readings (of pressure, wind, etc.) must be completed, then typed on the teleprinter and sent to the local collecting centre. However, making the observation ten minutes earlier should not lead to a systematic recording of higher temperatures. Generally speaking the maximum and minimum values will not be occurring exactly when the reading is taken. Perhaps the instruments have themselves changed? For example, the expansion of the glass itself might alter with some change in the manufacturing process. Perhaps the neighbouring towns have grown and we are measuring the localised urban heat islands. Perhaps the site is on an airfield with more warm tarmac and hot aircraft exhausts. Possibly the screen is not painted so glaringly white nor washed so regularly – the darker, dirtier screen would be warmer and thus result in slightly higher temperatures inside. It is known that screen designs have changed, especially before the middle of this century. Nevertheless, scientists have cross-checked observations at different locations and rejected suspect sites including ones where urban warming is evident before drawing conclusions. However, having taken all these complexities into account, it still seems that land temperatures have risen.

Sixty years ago most sea temperatures were measured by dropping a canvas bucket into the sea, hauling it on to the deck and then sticking a thermometer in the water. On cold windy days the water in the bucket could cool before the thermometer was read. During and since the Second World War there has been an increasing tendency to report the temperature as measured by a thermistor at the water intake. The depth below the surface of this water intake will vary with the size and type of ship. In rough weather this would not matter because the top 10 m (30 ft) of water will be thoroughly mixed and all at the same temperature. In very calm weather, however, it could perhaps have an effect.

Since the 1970s many of the recorded sea temperatures have come from satellites. The infra-red instruments which they carry measure the emitted radiance from the sea surface and that is converted to a temperature. In a flat calm this is likely to be different from that measured by a ship, and moisture and haze in the intervening air can also bias the measurements: the problem can be avoided by using ships' data as a calibration check. Meteorologists have taken great care to analyse and correct all these and other possible biases. Whilst it is possible that some other sources of bias have been overlooked, it seems unlikely that a major world-wide error exists in the data. In other words, sea temperatures do seem to have genuinely risen.

IS THE WARMING CAUSED BY HUMAN ACTIVITY?

The cooler period of the Little Ice Age has not been properly explained despite the possible link with the lack of sunspots, and nor therefore has the warming which occurred as temperatures recovered in the nineteenth century.

If the temperatures of Europe vary from one century to the next, then so could those of the whole globe. Some of the climate changes of the past have been on a scale of one decade to the next. There is no certainty that the present warming is a result of human activity, but for the first time we have a logical link between cause (the greenhouse theory) and effect (the observed warming). Further guidance comes from computer models of the effect of increasing carbon dioxide. The observed warming is consistent with what the models say it should be.

Proof in such matters never arrives suddenly. It comes gradually in small packets of accumulating evidence. Occasionally, perhaps, there is some negative evidence. If the greenhouse fears are valid, the evidence will gradually swell until it eventually becomes overwhelming. Some would say that this point has already been reached. For individual scientists, the dilemma is whether to lay their opinions on the line when they are 60% sure or to wait until they are 99% sure. The dilemma is exacerbated by the knowledge that the *observed* warming lags many years behind the *committed* warming. If the warm decade of the 1980s was caused by the emissions of the 1950s and 1960s (because of the lag in the system) then further warming would still occur even if we stopped the emissions today.

GLOBAL CLIMATE MODELS

Global climate models, known as GCMs, are the method by which scientists predict future warming. They consist of a huge computer program which contains most of the aspects of the current Earth's weather systems, but the option of one or two changes to imitate an atmosphere with more carbon dioxide. Typical calculations use 600 to 650 ppm (parts per million) of CO_2, i.e. double the levels observed in the 1950s and 1960s. They are essentially the same as the day-to-day forecast models but allowed to run for years rather than just for days. (Not real years, simulated years!) The depressions and anticyclones which they predict are individually spurious but we assume that the averages which they give are realistic. GCMs are very expensive in terms of computer time, since you have to simulate at least two years' worth of the 'new' climate in order for them to settle down at the new equilibrium temperature. A few attempts have also been made to run 'transient models' which imitate the gradual transition to higher CO_2 values,

The two biggest uncertainties are how the oceans respond and whether the coarse grid-scale of the models can give a realistic forecast. Despite those questions, most GCMs are in reasonable agreement that an effective doubling of CO_2 will warm the Earth by between 3 and 5 Celsius (5 to 9 F).

THE FUTURE

Any forecast of the future, whether economic, political or meteorological, is subject to errors. Given the paucity of hard facts perhaps the best way to illustrate the possibilities (and to cover most of the eventualities!) is to provide three different scenarios: the optimistic, the pessimistic and some sort of middle-of-the-road view. To some extent these three scenarios are a mish-mash of conflicting opinions but hopefully they still throw some light on the subject. I must emphasise that these are personal suggestions and in no way represent any 'official' viewpoint.

AN OPTIMISTIC VIEW

The observed warming is largely the result of normal random variations of climate. Just as we have mild winters and cold winters in Britain, the Earth has warm decades and cold decades. Since we do not fully understand what caused the climate changes in historic or prehistoric times, we are not in a position to put a cause and effect label on the current slight warming. Further work needs to be done on the Milankovitch calculations and their effect on climate.

However, if a little of the warming does result from the increase in greenhouse gases then it may be no bad thing. At least it is in the 'right' direction for the majority of the Earth's surface and it may even be counteracting what would otherwise have been a cooling period, to judge by ice core sequences.

If we do find firmer evidence of human-induced warming during the next 20 years then we have the technology to react.

A PESSIMISTIC VIEW

Over the last decade or so we have seen a rapid sustained rise in temperature. The greenhouse cause is reasonably well understood. Further, we are still emitting greenhouse gases and, given the lag of the system, we are therefore committed to rising temperatures over the next 30 years. Even worse, since world-wide political moves are currently minimal, we shall continue to emit gases throughout the 1990s, which will extend the period of committed warming to at least AD 2030. Whenever we stop emitting these gases, we still have some decades of warming in the pipeline after that.

It may be that the oceans have been acting as a delaying mechanism for the past 50 years and that things are further down the road than we suspect. By now the trees may be nearing their limit for carbon dioxide absorption, and we do not know how the oceans are going to react to changing winds and temperatures. When the ocean currents do change, it may be with a sudden jump.

The consequences of warming will include rising sea levels which will threaten developed areas (Netherlands, Florida, Venice, Leningrad and eastern England), which can just about cope by building barriers and sea walls, and also less-developed countries (Bangladesh, Maldives and other coral islands), which cannot cope. Almost all parts of the Earth will get warmer, but it will be the huge changes in rainfall patterns which will be damaging. The changes will be so rapid that vegetation belts, such as the great coniferous forest of Eurasia, will not be able to keep pace with the northward-moving zones of weather. Fungal diseases and plagues of insects will be able to move in and proliferate, attacking the weakened plant-life.

Some areas which are dry now will experience heavy monsoon rains and floods. Hurricanes will become more common and more violent. Some areas which have barely sufficient rain now, such as the fringes of the Sahara, will become total desert. Moreover, these changes will not take place in a gradual way, but perhaps in sudden jumps as the Earth's atmosphere switches to new and unforecast modes. A slight trend towards wetter weather in one particular area could be followed by a sudden shift to very dry weather as a new circulation pattern of the world's winds becomes established.

In this pessimistic view of major and perhaps abrupt changes, there will be winners and losers. We need international agreements to limit the greenhouse effect *before* the scientists with their global prediction models know who will be the winners and who will be the losers. If we wait until the predictions are fairly widely agreed, then international dissent will be inevitable.

Unfortunately, as politicians are usually in power for only 5 to 10 years or so, they tend to concentrate on the short-term results of their actions. The economic and social effects of a sudden cut-back in fuel consumption are immediate, whereas the longer-term greenhouse effects will not come for a decade or two. To a politician, the incentive of a place in the history books may be too far away to be attractive. Politicians can always hide behind the scientific uncertainties by saying that more research is needed. Worse still, the world population (currently 5 billion) is increasing more quickly than ever. Since all the gas emissions can ultimately be looked upon as 'per capita' emissions, the influence of population growth on the greenhouse effect is obvious.

For a significant reduction in greenhouse gas emissions to be achieved, there must be incentives. These would have to include incentives for ordinary individuals not to use their cars, for companies to conduct their business in a fuel-efficient manner and for nations to reduce their greenhouse gas output. To devise such incentive schemes will prove to be impossible. That is the pessimistic viewpoint expressed by some.

SOME MIDDLE-OF-THE-ROAD FORECASTS

We do not know when the effective carbon dioxide content of the atmosphere will have reached double its pre-industrial levels, but AD 2030 seems a reasonable estimate. This does not strictly mean double the CO_2, but a large increase of CO_2 with the remainder of the effect made up by other gases like CFCs, methane and nitrous oxide. More precisely speaking, it is 'the equivalent of doubling the carbon dioxide'.

The various models give a variety of estimates for the warming that will occur as a result, but 3.5 C (6.3 F) is a typical result. This does not mean that it will be 3.5 C warmer as early as 2030, because this is an 'equilibrium' forecast. In other words, it is the value at which the Earth's temperature would settle down if the effective CO_2 content remained at the doubled level and no more. Because of the lag in the oceans, the real temperature rise will be slower. The warming of 3.5 C is therefore the committed warming which will be in the pipeline by 2030.

The actual rise in temperature by 2030 will be perhaps 2 C (3.6 F), but with more to come whatever cut-backs are happening around that time.

I should point out that '2 C warmer' is rather meaningless, if we do not answer the obvious question – warmer than what? The answer is 'warmer than it was before the substantial warming commenced', and in practice we can consider this as the 1960s.

To those who think that this is a trivial increase, we should examine what a 3.5 C rise means. A hot day may be 7 C above average; a hot week may be 5 C above average (being composed of perhaps some really hot days and some days which are only slightly above average). An exceptionally warm month will only be 3.5 C above average. Under the new greenhouse regime *every* month would be expected to be that warm. Some months would be as much as 7 C above our current values whilst an exceptionally cold month would be like an average month now.

The 'normal' level of temperature would have shifted, but variability would still occur, though perhaps slightly more or less than at present.

If we draw a line down a map of western Europe through Scotland, England and France, some of the changes are illustrated. The annual average temperature in Dundee was 8.5 C (47.3 F) for the period 1931–60 (and very similar in the 1960s and 1970s): a 1 C (1.8 F) warming would make its climate roughly similar to York; 2 C (3.6 F) would make it as warm as Oxford; 3 C (5.4 F) would bring it to the level of Poitiers in Central France; and 4 C (7.2 F) would make Dundee like Bordeaux. Of course there would still be some differences. The day lengths would not change and the Sun would still reach the same altitude in the sky. Nevertheless, the analogies are powerful. The average temperature difference between Southern England and the major wine growing region of southwestern France is about 2 C.

CHANGES IN THE POLAR REGIONS

The weather in the polar regions varies more from year to year than in the tropical rain-forests, for example. It is difficult to see if there are already any definite trends, though some Antarctic scientists and submariners measuring ice thickness in the Arctic have suggested that there are. Part of the trouble stems from the short period of good-quality records and the large changes that have always occurred from year to year and from decade to decade.

Greenhouse scientists suggest that the warming effects should show up first in the Arctic and it is in the interiors of the northern continents where the temperature rises will be most marked, e.g. Siberia and Canada.

CHANGES IN TEMPERATE LATITUDES

One key question is whether the track of temperate latitude depressions will be displaced towards the Poles, and whether such depressions will be weaker or more powerful, During the ice age, the depression track was almost certainly further south. On a warmer Earth it would therefore possibly be further north. One could argue that the Arctic will warm up more than the tropics and the temperature contrast on which depressions depend for their strength will therefore be reduced. Even if the lows do get a fraction weaker they could still carry just as much moisture. At least one computer prediction for the British Isles suggests that we will get warmer in both winter and summer, and that winter rainfall will be increased, especially over the mountains of the north. The Scottish Highlands already have ample rain. What the UK as a whole would then need is better water resource management. If temperatures rise by an average of 2 Celsius and rainfall remained fixed at its present level, our landscape would become much drier because there would be more evaporation. We will need more rain just to stand still. However, a logical conclusion of a significant warming is that when it does rain in the summertime, the *rate* of rainfall will be higher because of the greater moisture capacity of the warmer atmosphere. In other words, our summer thunderstorms could become slightly more tropical in character with flash floods an increasing threat. This is particularly relevant to those considering drainage in our concrete and tarmac city environments. We in Britain could end up with both a shortage of rainfall for crops and an increase in incidents of flash flooding.

As yet, there is no agreement about the rainfall changes either here or in the continental interiors. Computer results differ widely. Central Asia and the American Midwest are not suffering systematic reductions in rainfall despite the 1988 dry summer and dustbowl fears in the United States. Ironically, that summer alerted people to the greenhouse danger.

CHANGES IN THE TROPICS

The temperature changes in the tropical regions will probably be less than the world average. Warmer air will be able to hold more moisture so rain when it does fall will be even heavier. Even so, some areas will lose out.

Logically, tropical cyclones (i.e. hurricanes, typhoons, etc.) should become a more important feature of the weather. There is at present a sea temperature threshold of 27 C (81 F) necessary for hurricanes to form. If typical tropical sea temperatures rise to nearly 30 C (86 F), then such tropical cyclones will become far more common, unless other features cause the threshold temperature to rise.

Perhaps though, the threshold is much less precise and the important thing is the difference between the warm, moist air near the surface and the cooler air aloft. Then if the whole atmosphere warms up the vertical temperature differences would not change much, so hurricanes might not become more common. What does seem logical though is that these tropical cyclones will carry more moisture, which means that more latent heat will be released and they will therefore become more violent. It is silly to try to prove a theory on the basis of a couple of examples, but Hurricane Gilbert in 1988 and Hurricane Hugo in 1989 were more powerful than usual.

Hurricanes and typhoons become really important when they hit land. If they carry more moisture then the rainfall they produce in areas such as Mexico, Florida, India, China, Mozambique and Queensland (Australia) will be increased, but much of it will be lost as flood water.

THE PREDICTED RISE IN SEA LEVEL

When the climate gets warmer, the sea level rises for two reasons. First of all, some parts of the ice caps will melt, primarily in Greenland and

Antarctica. Secondly, the ocean water expands as the temperature rises (like mercury in a thermometer). Surprisingly, it is this second factor which is expected to play the bigger part in raising the average level of the World's oceans in the next half century or so.

A fairly typical prediction is the rate of about 1 cm (0.4 inches) per year from AD 2000 to 2030, thus achieving a rise of 30 cm (12 inches) above the present level by AD 2030. This assumes that the current rate of rise is very small, and that the process does not get properly underway until about the turn of the century.

Again, this change may not sound significant, but it will mean more events like the coastal flooding at Towyn in early 1990, more occasions when we have to close the Thames barrier and, as the century goes on, an increasing threat of disaster if a storm surge happens to coincide with a natural high tide on the east coast of England. Elsewhere in the world, two of the key questions are whether coral reefs can grow quickly enough to keep pace with the rising level of the ocean, and whether the developed countries will step in to help Bangladesh and other nations at risk.

OTHER SOURCES OF POWER

The quantity of fossil fuel burnt by any nation depends upon the population size and the fossil fuel consumption per capita. One way to reduce consumption is to burn fuel more efficiently and to increase insulation in buildings. Alternatives include switching away from fossil fuels to nuclear power or the nuclear fusion which may be developed in the next century. Geothermal heat is a realistic alternative in Iceland and perhaps with improved technology in many countries. Experiments are under way in Cornwall.

Hydroelectric power is already in use in Scotland, Wales and to a very limited extent in southwest England. One of the troubles with dams everywhere in the world is that they trap the sediment flowing downstream, and the river flow below the dam is therefore permanently altered.

WIND, WAVE AND TIDAL POWER

The British Isles are very well placed for wind power, particularly the west and north which catch the brunt of the westerlies as depressions track northeastwards. In Orkney the wind is already harnessed to generate electricity and in the Carmarthen area of Wales a further experimental system is to be built. California already has its wind farms with scores of towers carrying a three-bladed 'windmill'. Winter provides our strongest winds and that is when energy demand is highest, but it is the long duration of fresh to strong winds rather than a short-lived gale which is required. On the negative side, these wind farms could be described as unsightly.

We are also well placed for wave power, with the Atlantic swell often reaching our western coasts from depressions in the centre of the Atlantic even when the local winds are calm.

We also have a much higher tidal range than most parts of the World. France has a working tidal barrage on the River Rance on her northern coast. Negative aspects here include the alteration to mudflats where wading birds feed.

As with many suggestions it is the hard economics which ultimately determine success or failure. More power must be generated by such projects than was used in their manufacture, installation and servicing. Good research and then mass production may be the key to reducing costs.

SOLAR POWER

This is a source of natural energy for which the British Isles are not so well placed. The sunniest areas of the eastern Sahara have 4000 hours of sunshine a year; the Costa del Sol and Costa Blanca have 3000 hours, as do many of the Mediterranean coasts. Our sunshine totals vary from 1000 hours on the Scottish mountains to 1450 hours per year (about 4 hours per day) in the English Midlands and up to 1800 hours along the south coast. Also, much of the sunshine, especially in the north, is low-angle. However, it is not quite as black a prospect as one might imagine. Solar panels still receive heat when the weather is cloudy. If the cloud is thin or patchy and the weather is bright, then this 'diffuse radiation' from the Sun which successfully gets through the clouds is quite significant. Often it can be more than half of that on a cloudless day. On the other hand, the greatest solar power comes in summer when it is least needed. More power-sharing (in the electrical sense) would enable sunny countries to export solar-generated electricity to the winter regions of the world. Super-conducting cables will make world-wide electricity exchange feasible. The world's weather variations will always allow some natural power generation somewhere on Earth.

Again, the efficiency of solar panels is a vital part of the equation. The perfect solar panel absorbs all the energy falling upon it as it tracks the Sun across the sky. If you install a fixed solar panel then it should point south, or perhaps just a fraction east of south if you are in an inland location where the afternoons are more cloudy than the mornings. The angle at which it should be pointed towards the Sun varies with the season, but will in practice probably depend on the slope of your roof. In London the Sun reaches 62° above the horizon in late June, but only 15° above in midwinter, and these are the noon values.

The wisdom of having rapidly accelerating petrol-driven cars with a single occupant has already come into question. Solar-powered cars are already under development.

INSULATION

Insulation is not a glamorous subject like solar power, but it is effective. Poorly lagged hot-water tanks and pipes are blatant sources of wasted heat. The heat loss through the walls of a house depends on many factors but notably the temperature difference between indoors and outdoors, the thickness of the walls and the conductivity of the materials.

Insulation reduces the conduction of heat outwards. It could be argued that the greenhouse effect will make insulation less necessary. Two points here: insulation works now and substantial warming is probably some way off. Secondly, even if winter was effectively shortened by two months, we would still need heating for five months in the year. A typical temperature rise in Britain during April is 3.5 C (about 6 F) in the month. If we do eventually warm the climate uniformly by that enormous amount then we will turn our heating off a month earlier and a further month will be gained in the autumn. Once again this scenario may seem attractive to a parochial Briton, but it would surely be at the expense of some other very negative changes. Let us hope that international agreements forestall these predictions.

INCENTIVES FOR REDUCING EMISSIONS

Incentives must act at three levels – for the individual, for business, and for nations. Let us look at these one at a time.

Individuals are starting to talk about their greenhouse fears but they still have their central heating set up high and they drive half a mile to the shops rather than walk. One possibility would be to quadruple the price of petrol and heating fuels, but this would cause inflation and, surprisingly, the resulting cut-backs might be largely temporary. However, the signs are that individuals are prepared to accept a certain amount of restriction providing that 'everyone else does the same'.

Businesses are proclaiming how green they are, especially those with a very public image which announce their environmental awareness on their packaging. (It is difficult to know whether they are telling the truth.) Incentives or penalties are needed for companies, which presumably will have to be financial since that is what business is all about. Scientists must be involved in the watchdog process.

Nations now have leaders who are aware of the threat of climate change but national incentives are difficult to devise. On the principle of 'the polluter pays' perhaps every nation should pay a levy on every ton of fuel used (whether locally produced or imported) into an international fund. This fund could be used to help the developing countries.

GLOSSARY

Adiabatic process One in which no heat enters or leaves the system, for example in the theoretical study of a rising 'bubble' of warm air.

Advection Horizontal movement of air, for example bringing colder air to the British Isles ('cold advection').

Albedo The amount of light reflected by a surface, usually expressed as a percentage. Fresh snow has an albedo of 80 per cent.

Airmass A body of air in which the horizontal changes in temperature and humidity are relatively slight. The two main types are 'Polar' and 'Tropical' indicating the origin of the air.

Anabatic Wind A local wind which blows up a slope heated by sunshine.

Anemometer Instrument for measuring wind speed.

Aneroid Barometer A 'without liquid' barometer – basically a partially evacuated metallic capsule surrounding a spring.

Anticyclone A region of high pressure. The words 'high' and 'anticyclone' are interchangeable.

Backing The changing of the wind in a counter-clockwise direction.

Bar Unit of pressure approximately equal to that of the atmosphere, divided into millibars, the usual units.

Barograph	A recording barometer – an aneroid capsule, the expansion and contraction of which produces a trace on a chart wound around a revolving drum.
Barometer	Instrument for measuring pressure. The original invention of Torricelli consisted of a long tube full of mercury.
Boundary layer	The lowest part of the atmosphere which is directly affected by the Earth's surface, usually regarded as being 2000-3000 feet deep. The word 'boundary' is also used in modelling in a different sense to indicate the geographical edge to a numerical model (as in 'the western boundary').
Buys Ballot's Law	If you stand with your back to the wind in the northern hemisphere, then low pressure is to your left.
Condensation	The process of formation of a liquid from its vapour. In the atmosphere the cooling of air leads to condensation of water from water vapour.
Convection	The process of vertical motion created by buoyancy due to warming of air in the atmosphere; convection can, of course, occur in any fluid. The expression 'convective cloud' usually means cumulus or cumulonimbus.
Coriolis effect	Because of the rotation of the earth, air moving from one place to another appears to an observer standing on the earth to be deflected. The deflection is to the right in the northern hemisphere and is to the left in the southern hemisphere.
Cyclone	An area of low pressure. In middle or high latitudes usually referred to as a 'low' or 'depression'.

Dew point	The temperature to which air must be cooled for condensation to occur.
Diurnal effects	Those which usually occur daily.
Doldrums	Region of light winds near the Equator.
Drizzle	Liquid precipitation in the form of small drops, falling from low, layered cloud.
Evaporation	The process by which water is changed into water vapour.
Fog	Small water droplets in suspension in the air at ground level, effectively a very low level cloud, *Hill fog* is low cloud enveloping hills. The cloud may be formed by the forced uplift as the air flows over the hill or may just be very low level cloud which happens to be over high ground. *Radiation fog* forms overland on a clear night with light winds.
	Sea fog forms over the sea when air blows from a warm area of water towards a colder one. Sea fog is a particular case of what the textbooks refer to as *Advection fog* when air blows from a relatively warm area towards a cold one, say with lying snow or a frozen ground.
Föhn effect	The mechanism responsible for the warm dry wind which occurs to the leeward side of mountains or hills.
Front	The boundary between two airmasses of different type. A front usually lies in a trough of low pressure and is marked by discontinuities in wind direction and velocity, humidity, temperature, weather and visibility. Precisely how marked will be the discontinuity varies greatly from one front to another. A *cold front* is one whose movement is such that colder air is replacing a warmer airmass. A *warm front* is one where warmer air is replacing cold. An

occluded front or 'occlusion' is one where the cold front has caught up with the warm for the two fronts effectively to merge.

Geostrophic scale

A scale relating the spacing of isobars to the wind speed.

High

A region of high pressure. May be referred to as an anticyclone. A *blocking high* is one which is stationary and sufficiently large as to prevent the normal west to east movement of lows. An *intensifying high* is one in which the central pressure is rising and the system probably increasing in size. A *declining high* is one where the central pressure is decreasing. May be known as weakening or, if the decrease in pressure is rapid, as collapsing. A *subtropical high* is one of the highs which compose the quasi-permanent belt of high pressure of the subtropics (this is the part of the surface of the earth between the tropics and latitude 40 degrees).

Horse Latitudes

Region of light winds in the subtropical high pressure zone (where horses on sailing ships were said to be eaten or thrown overboard).

Hurricane

The name given to those tropical cyclones which occur in the West Indies and the Gulf of Mexico. Sometimes used more widely for other tropical cyclones. See also 'typhoon'.

Inversion

A shallow layer where it gets warmer with altitude.

Isobar

A line joining points with equal pressure (on a weather chart).

Jet stream

A strong narrow current of air at high levels in the atmosphere.

Katabatic wind

A wind which blows down a slope which is cooling at night time.

Lapse rate	The decrease of temperature with height.
Lenticularis	Adjective used to describe cloud having a lens shape and usually associated with standing waves.
Local winds	The behaviour of winds which can be attributed to local, often topographical, effects rather than the large-scale pressure pattern. Sea breezes, anabatics, katabatics and winds around headlands are examples of local effects which might either create winds in their own right or modify to varying extents the (large-scale) pressure gradient wind.
Low	An area of low pressure. Also known as a 'depression' (and in the tropics as a 'cyclone'). A *complex low* is one with two or more identifiable centres. A *deepening low*, one where the central pressure is decreasing. May be referred to as intensifying. A *filling low* is one where the central pressure is increasing.
Mesoscale phenomena	These are smaller than 'synoptic scale' features like depressions and ridges but larger than 'microscale features'. Mesoscale phenomena may be split into large mesoscale (say 10 to 100 km across) and small mesoscale (from 10 km in size down to 1 km or less).
Monsoon	A seasonal wind. The Asian monsoon is the principal example.
Psychrometer	Instrument for measuring the dew-point and hence the humidity, by first measuring the air temperature and the wet bulb temperature.
Rain	Precipitation consisting of drops of water falling from layer cloud. See also 'drizzle' and 'showers'.

Ridge	A pressure pattern of curved isobars convex towards low pressure, often an extension of a high. The area of relatively high pressure between successive lows.
Showers	Liquid or solid precipitation from convective cloud. Frequently intense and sudden in character, a shower can stop and start abruptly while rain may persist for many hours.
Sleet	Rain and snow falling simultaneously. Also commonly used to describe snow which melts as it lands.
Stratosphere	The second major layer of the atmosphere, extending from about 12 km to 50 km, in which the temperature usually increases with height. The upper limit is the 'stratopause'.
Synoptic chart	A chart for a fixed time, e.g. midday, which is used to locate highs, lows and fronts, etc., which are 'synoptic features'.
Temperate latitudes	Broadly speaking that part of the Earth lying between the polar regions and the subtropical highs.
Trade winds	Winds which persist for much of the time between the subtropical highs and the equator. They are north-easterly in the northern hemisphere and south-easterly in the southern.
Transpiration	The process by which water in plants is transferred as water vapour to the atmosphere.
Triple point	On a weather chart, the point where the cold front, warm front and occluded front meet.
Troposphere	The lowest major layer of the atmosphere, extending from the ground to roughly 12 km,

in which the temperature generally decreases with height. All our clouds and precipitation are produced in the troposphere. Its upper limit is the 'tropopause' above which is the stratosphere.

Trough

A pressure pattern of curved isobars which are convex towards the higher pressures. A front will usually lie along a trough. A trough, however, need not be associated with a front.

Typhoon

The name given to tropical cyclones in the northern Pacific area.

Veering

The changing of the wind in a clockwise direction.

Warm sector

The area behind the warm front and ahead of the cold.

BELFAST PUBLIC LIBRARIES

APPENDICES

APPENDIX I

Temperature Conversion Tables

FAHRENHEIT TO CELSIUS

F	C	F	C
100	37.8	50	10.0
99	37.2	49	9.4
98	36.7	48	8.9
97	36.1	47	8.3
96	35.6	46	7.8
95	35.0	45	7.2
94	34.4	44	6.7
93	33.9	43	6.1
92	33.3	42	5.6
91	32.8	41	5.0
90	32.2	40	4.4
89	31.7	39	3.9
88	31.1	38	3.3
87	30.6	37	2.8
86	30.0	36	2.2
85	29.4	35	1.7
84	28.9	34	1.1
83	28.3	33	0.6
82	27.8	32	0.0
81	27.2	31	−0.5
80	26.7	30	−1.1
79	26.1	29	−1.7
78	25.6	28	−2.2
77	25.0	27	−2.8
76	24.4	26	−3.3
75	23.9	25	−3.9
74	23.3	24	−4.4
73	22.8	23	−5.0
72	22.2	22	−5.6
71	21.7	21	−6.1
70	21.1	20	−6.7
69	20.6	19	−7.2
68	20.0	18	−7.8
67	19.4	17	−8.3
66	18.9	16	−8.9
65	18.3	15	−9.4
64	17.8	14	−10.0
63	17.2	13	−10.6
62	16.7	12	−11.1
61	16.1	11	−11.7
60	15.6	10	−12.2
59	15.0	9	−12.8
58	14.4	8	−13.3
57	13.9	7	−13.9
56	13.3	6	−14.4
55	12.8	5	−15.0
54	12.2	4	−15.6
53	11.7	3	−16.1
52	11.1	2	−16.7
51	10.6	1	−17.2

CELSIUS TO FAHRENHEIT

C	F	C	F
50	122.0	0	32.0
49	120.2	− 1	30.2
48	118.4	− 2	28.4
47	116.6	− 3	26.6
46	114.8	− 4	24.8
45	113.0	− 5	23.0
44	111.2	− 6	21.2
43	109.4	− 7	19.4
42	107.6	− 8	17.6
41	105.8	− 9	15.8
40	104.0	−10	14.0
39	102.2	−11	12.2
38	100.4	−12	10.4
37	98.6	−13	8.6
36	96.8	−14	6.8
35	95.0	−15	5.0
34	93.2	−16	3.2
33	91.4	−17	1.4
32	89.6	−18	−0.4
31	87.8	−19	−2.2
30	86.0	−20	−4.0
29	84.2	−21	−5.8
28	82.4	−22	−7.6
27	80.6	−23	−9.4
26	78.8	−24	−11.2
25	77.0	−25	−13.0
24	75.2	−26	−14.8
23	73.4	−27	−16.6
22	71.6	−28	−18.4
21	69.8	−29	−20.2
20	68.0	−30	−22.0
19	66.2	−31	−23.8
18	64.4	−32	−25.6
17	62.6	−33	−27.4
16	60.8	−34	−29.2
15	59.0	−35	−31.0
14	57.2	−36	−32.8
13	55.4	−37	−34.6
12	53.6	−38	−36.4
11	51.8	−39	−38.2
10	50.0	−40	−40.0
9	48.2	−41	−41.8
8	46.4	−42	−43.6
7	44.6	−43	−45.4
6	42.8	−44	−47.2
5	41.0	−45	−49.0
4	39.2	−46	−50.8
3	37.4	−47	−52.6
2	35.6	−48	−54.4
1	33.8	−49	−56.2

APPENDIX II

Atmospheric Pressure Conversion Table

Millibars	inches	millibars	inches	millibars	inches
960	28.35	990	29.23	1020	30.12
961	28.38	991	29.26	1021	30.15
962	28.41	992	29.29	1022	30.18
963	28.44	993	29.32	1023	30.21
964	28.47	994	29.35	1024	30.24
965	28.50	995	29.38	1025	30.27
966	28.53	996	29.41	1026	30.30
967	28.56	997	29.44	1027	30.33
968	28.59	998	29.47	1028	30.36
969	28.61	999	29.50	1029	30.39
970	28.64	1000	29.53	1030	30.42
971	28.67	1001	29.56	1031	30.45
972	28.70	1002	29.59	1032	30.47
973	28.73	1003	29.62	1033	30.50
974	28.76	1004	29.65	1034	30.53
975	28.79	1005	29.68	1035	30.56
976	28.82	1006	29.71	1036	30.59
977	28.85	1007	29.74	1037	30.62
978	28.88	1008	29.77	1038	30.65
979	28.91	1009	29.80	1039	30.68
980	28.94	1010	29.83	1040	30.71
981	28.97	1011	29.85	1041	30.74
982	29.00	1012	29.88	1042	30.77
983	29.03	1013	29.91	1043	30.80
984	29.06	1014	29.94	1044	30.83
985	29.09	1015	29.97	1045	30.86
986	29.12	1016	30.00	1046	30.89
987	29.15	1017	30.03	1047	30.92
988	29.18	1018	30.06	1048	30.95
989	29.21	1019	30.09	1049	30.98

Hours of daylight by latitude

The table shows the period between the rising and setting of the sun. It does not include the period of twilight before and after sunrise and sunset. On the equator twilight lasts about twenty minutes. At 30°N and S twilight lasts about half an hour before and after sunrise and sunset. At 50°N and S this period increases to about forty minutes, and at 65°N and S in midsummer twilight lasts all night.

The term 'twilight' used here refers to 'civil twilight' which is the period during which the sun is not more more than 6° below the horizon. Under clear skies and with good atmospheric conditions normal outdoor activities should be possible during the period of civil twilight. If the length of twilight is doubled and added to figures for day length given in the table below, it will give a good idea of the length of adequate daylight for each latitude. For the southern hemisphere use the column of 'southern months'.

LENGTH OF DAY IN VARIOUS LATITUDES (in hours and minutes on the 15th of each month)

Month	Equator	10°	20°	30°	40°	50°	60°	70°	80°	Pole	'Southern months'
J	12.07	11.35	11.02	10.24	9.37	8.30	6.38	0.00	0.00	0.00	J
F	12.07	11.49	11.21	11.10	10.42	10.07	9.11	7.20	0.00	0.00	A
M	12.07	12.04	12.00	11.57	11.53	11.48	11.41	11.28	10.52	0.00	S
A	12.07	12.21	12.36	12.53	13.14	13.44	14.31	16.06	24.00	24.00	O
M	12.07	12.34	13.04	13.38	14.22	15.22	17.04	22.13	24.00	24.00	N
J	12.07	12.42	13.20	14.04	15.00	16.21	18.49	24.00	24.00	24.00	D
J	12.07	12.40	13.16	13.56	14.49	15.38	17.31	24.00	24.00	24.00	J
A	12.07	12.28	12.50	13.16	13.48	14.33	15.46	18.26	24.00	24.00	F
S	12.07	12.12	12.17	12.23	12.31	12.42	13.00	13.34	15.16	24.00	M
O	12.07	11.55	11.42	11.28	11.10	10.47	10.11	9.03	5.10	0.00	A
N	12.07	11.40	11.12	10.40	10.01	9.06	7.37	3.06	0.00	0.00	M
D	12.07	11.32	10.56	10.14	9.20	8.05	5.54	0.00	0.00	0.00	J

Conversion Factors

Length   1 inch = 2.540 centimetres or 25.40 millimetres

1 foot = 0.3048 metres

1 yard = 0.9144 metres

1 nautical mile = 6080 feet or 1.15 statute miles

1 statute mile = 5280 feet

1 degree of latitude = 69.057 statute miles
= 59.969 nautical miles
= 111.137 kilometres

1 metre = 3.28084 feet
= 39.3701 inches

1 kilometre = 3280.84 feet
= 0.62137 statute miles
= 0.5396 nautical miles

Speed   1 mph = 0.8684 knots
= 1.467 feet per second
= 0.4470 metres per second
= 1.609 kilometres per hour

1 knot = 1.152 mph
= 1.689 feet per second
= 0.5148 metres per second
= 1.853 kilometres per hour
= 101.3 feet per minute

1 metre per second = 3.6 kilometres per hour
= 1.94254 knots
= 2.23694 mph
= 3.28084 feet per second

1 kilometre per hour = 0.277778 metres per second
= 0.539593 knots
= 0.621371 mph
= 0.911344 feet per second

Pressure   1 bar = 1000 millibars

1 millibar = 1000 dynes per square centimetre
= 0.750 millimetres of mercury
= 0.02953 inches of mercury

1 standard atmosphere = 1013.25 millibars
= 1.03323 kilogrammes per square centimetre
= 760 millimetres of mercury
= 29.9213 inches of mercury
= 14.6960 pounds per square inch

Mass   1 pound avoirdupois = 453.59 grams

1 kilogram = 1000 grams
= 35.274 ounces
= 2.204623 pounds

British Climate Data

Kew in West London is representative of much of lowland England. St Mary's demonstrates the mild southwest and Tynemouth the cold springs of the eastern coasts. Blaenau Ffestiniog at 750 feet (229m) is an example of our western uplands and is the only station here at any significant altitude. Stirling is in central Scotland. Lerwick in Shetland and Dublin on the relatively sheltered east coast of Ireland.

	J	F	M	A	M	J	J	A	S	O	N	D	Year
Kew, London													
Average Max. C	6	7	10	13	17	20	22	21	19	14	10	7	14
Average Min. C	2	2	3	5	8	12	13	13	11	8	5	3	7
Rainfall mm	54	40	37	37	46	45	57	59	49	57	64	48	593
Sunshine hours	46	64	113	160	199	213	198	188	142	98	53	40	1514
St. Mary's, Scilly													
Average Max. C	9	9	11	12	14	17	19	19	17	15	12	10	14
Average Min. C	6	6	7	7	9	12	13	14	13	11	9	7	9
Rainfall mm	91	71	69	46	56	49	61	64	67	80	96	94	844
Sunshine hours	62	81	130	192	235	228	207	208	155	121	76	57	1752
Tynemouth													
Average Max. C	6	6	8	10	12	16	18	18	16	13	9	7	12
Average Min. C	2	2	3	5	7	10	12	12	11	8	5	4	7
Rainfall mm	62	45	39	38	48	47	64	74	55	61	64	53	650
Sunshine hours	42	65	98	152	179	178	169	146	124	91	51	35	1330
Blaenau Ffestiniog													
Average Max. C	6	6	8	11	14	17	17	17	17	13	9	7	12
Average Min. C	1	1	3	4	7	10	11	11	10	8	5	2	6
Rainfall mm	252	155	129	144	133	130	206	210	223	261	214	285	2342
Sunshine hours	44	59	84	97	155	157	114	100	99	73	37	45	1064
Stirling													
Average Max. C	6	7	9	12	15	18	19	19	16	12	9	7	13
Average Min. C	0	1	2	4	6	9	11	11	9	6	3	2	5
Rainfall mm	101	66	57	56	64	61	87	81	92	103	91	104	963
Sunshine hours	32	65	98	131	159	168	134	130	107	72	50	30	1176
Lerwick													
Average Max. C	5	5	6	8	11	13	14	14	13	10	8	6	9
Average Min. C	1	1	2	3	5	7	10	10	8	6	4	3	5
Rainfall mm	109	87	69	68	52	55	72	71	87	104	111	118	1003
Sunshine hours	25	51	90	132	165	158	125	117	105	67	33	14	1082
Dublin													
Average Max. C	8	8	10	13	15	18	20	19	17	14	10	8	13
Average Min. C	1	2	3	4	6	9	11	11	9	6	4	3	6
Rainfall mm	67	55	51	45	60	57	70	74	72	70	67	74	762
Sunshine hours	59	71	104	151	193	180	148	152	118	98	63	49	1386

World Climate Data

Spitsbergen represents the polar regions; Berlin a rather continental example of temperate latitudes; Rome and Malta have Mediterranean climates; Cairo is near the northern fringe of the Sahara whilst Khartoum is in the 'Sahel' at its southern fringe with a short rainy season. Mombasa is close to the Equator with a double rainfall peak.

	J	F	M	A	M	J	J	A	S	O	N	D	Year
Spitsbergen (78N)													
Average Max. C	−7	−7	−9	−5	−1	4	7	6	3	−1	−3	−5	−1
Average Min. C	−13	−14	−15	−12	−5	1	4	3	0	−5	−8	−10	−6
Rainfall mm	26	25	24	15	20	19	25	40	36	39	37	31	337
Sunshine hours	0	3	77	229	254	165	154	133	74	13	0	0	1102
Berlin (52N)													
Average Max. C	2	3	8	13	19	22	24	23	20	13	7	3	13
Average Min. C	−3	−3	0	4	8	12	14	13	10	5	2	−1	5
Rainfall mm	46	40	33	42	49	65	73	69	48	49	46	43	603
Sunshine hours	48	62	143	175	233	244	238	223	180	111	47	34	1738
Rome (42N)													
Average Max. C	11	13	15	19	23	28	30	30	26	21	16	13	21
Average Min. C	5	5	7	10	13	17	20	19	17	13	9	6	12
Rainfall mm	71	62	57	51	46	37	15	21	63	99	129	93	744
Sunshine hours	131	124	179	212	263	275	334	307	243	189	123	111	2491
Malta (36N)													
Average Max. C	14	15	16	18	22	26	29	29	27	24	20	16	21
Average Min. C	10	10	11	13	16	19	22	23	22	19	16	12	16
Rainfall mm	90	60	39	15	12	2	0	8	29	63	91	110	519
Sunshine hours	170	177	225	264	305	344	386	354	283	232	172	154	3066
Cairo (30N)													
Average Max. C	19	21	24	28	32	35	35	35	33	30	26	21	28
Average Min. C	9	9	11	14	17	20	22	22	20	18	14	10	16
Rainfall mm	4	4	3	1	2	1	0	0	1	1	3	7	25
Sunshine hours	213	234	269	291	324	357	363	351	311	292	248	198	3451
Khartoum (16N)													
Average Max. C	31	33	37	40	42	41	38	36	38	39	35	32	37
Average Min. C	16	17	20	23	26	27	26	25	25	25	21	17	22
Rainfall mm	0	0	0	1	7	5	56	80	28	2	0	0	179
Sunshine hours	329	313	323	325	322	302	268	267	287	319	324	328	3707
Mombasa (04S)													
Average Max. C	32	32	33	31	29	29	28	28	29	30	31	32	30
Average Min. C	23	24	24	24	23	21	21	21	21	22	23	24	23
Rainfall mm	17	10	30	108	149	54	34	47	46	62	66	32	655
Sunshine hours	254	255	282	231	201	231	211	248	255	273	276	270	2987

INDEX